THE PENNINE DALES

The area which Dr Raistrick describes in *The Pennine Dales* – the northern part of the 'Pennine Chain' between the Aire Gap and the river Tyne – contains some of the most spectacular scenery in England. He roughly defines it by a rectangle that joins Carlisle and Newcastle in the north with Lancaster and Harrogate in the south. The valleys of Eden and Lune form its western edge, and the Great North Road lies a few miles beyond its eastern boundary. It embraces not only lush valleys like Wharfedale and Wensleydale but also a wild moorland plateau and the rugged summits of Ingleborough, Whernside, Penyghent, and Crossfell.

In this book – the first detailed and comprehensive survey of the Pennine Dales – Dr Raistrick outlines the history of the region from Mesolithic man to the present day. He describes its geology and climate; the growth of villages, towns and markets; the development of mining, textiles and agriculture; and the effects of the Industrial Revolution and the coming of the railways.

But the book presents as well the detail of a richly varied region – of Bronze Age huts and Norman castles; of the Pennine Way and Fountains Abbey; and of natural features like Cauldron Snout, Gordale Scar and High Cup Nick – and mirrors a powerfully independent people, for it was here that non-conformity and congregational choirs, Mechanics Institutes and brass bands took root.

Much of the Pennine Dales is now National Park or Nature Reserve, yet the need for planning and control is urgent if it is to be protected from the enormously rising volume of traffic. Tourism, of course, is a major industry, and at the end of his book the author suggests the most attractive routes for walking and driving.

Dr Raistrick's book is the product of deep knowledge and love of a part of the country where he has lived all his life. Throughout, he brings into relief, more clearly than ever before, the special characteristics as well as the remarkable unity of one of the most beautiful and exciting regions of England.

ARTHUR RAISTRICK was born and bred in Yorkshire. He was educated at Bradford Grammar School and Leeds University, where he took his degree of MSc and PhD. Since 1945 he has been Extra-Mural Tutor at the Universities of Leeds and Durham, and has been a lecturer for the WEA since 1922. He has written several books on various aspects of the history and life of the North Country and has been a regular contributor to many learned journals. He is actively concerned with the Yorkshire Dales National Park and the Standing Committee on National Parks.

ARTHUR RAISTRICK

The Pennine Dales

ARROW BOOKS

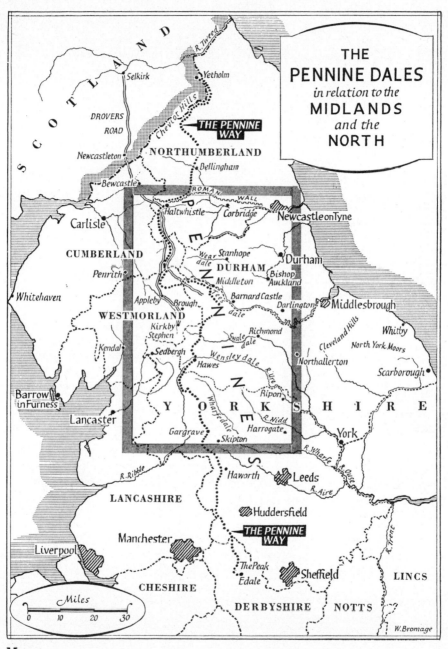

THE
PENNINE DALES
in relation to the
MIDLANDS
and the
NORTH

Map 1

ARROW BOOKS LTD

3 Fitzroy Square, London W1

AN IMPRINT OF THE HUTCHINSON GROUP

London Melbourne Sydney Auckland
Wellington Johannesburg Cape Town
and agencies throughout the world

First Published by
Eyre & Spottiswoode (Publishers) *Ltd 1968*
Arrow edition 1972

Made and Printed in Great Britain
by Flarepath Printers, St. Albans, Herts.
and bound by William Brendon, Tiptree, Essex

ISBN 0 09 906400 6

The Pennine Dales

Contents

	Acknowledgements	*page* 13
	Introduction	15
1	Physical description	21
2	Physical background: *geology – topography – climate – natural history*	34
3	Prehistory	52
4	Settlements and early history	69
5	The rural landscape	85
6	The growth of towns and markets	101
7	The recent past: 1750–1900	118
8	The recent past: 1900–1960	133
9	Vernacular architecture	147
10	Monastic architecture – castles – art	164
11	Literature and Music	181
12	The Pennine Way	198
	Conclusion	214
	Bibliographical notes	218
	Index	227

The Pennine Dales

Illustrations

Between pages 40 and 41   1 Sedbergh and the Howgill Fells
   2 *a* Conistone Pasture
      b A Widdale farm group
   3 *a* Teesdale, Langdon Beck
      b Prudhoe Castle, Tyne Valley
   4 Wharfedale – Barras (hill farm)

48 and 49   5 Malham Cove
   6 Malham West Field
   7 Ingleborough, seen across Ribblesdale
   8 *a* Mortham Tower, at the junction of
      Greta and Tees
      b Nappa Hall, Wensleydale

64 and 65   9 Malham West field – lynchets
  10 *a* Castle Bolton – milk donkey
      b Upper Wensleydale – old dales knitter
  11 Blanchland, Northumberland
  12 Thorpe West field, Wharfedale – lynchets

80 and 81 13 Ingleborough – the summit pyramid
  14 Whitley Castle, South Tyne valley – Roman fort
96 and 97 15 Littondale
  16 *a* Bentham, West Yorks – Cattle Mart
      b Leyburn Market
      c Pennine Way Pioneers

Between pages *112 and 113* 17 Gordale valley

18 *a* Tan Hill

b Kilnsey – sheep sale

19 *a* Muker, Swaledale

b Semer Water–Upper Wensleydale, North Yorks

20 Penyghent

128 and 129 21 Reeth, Swaledale

22 Upper Weardale, Ireshopeburn and Wearhead

23 High Close, Grassington – Romano-British 'Celtic' fields

24 *a* Swaledale – bringing in a sick sheep

b Escomb Church

144 and 145 25 Ramsgill, Nidderdale

26 *a* Wensleydale – dalesman with 'budget' back can

b Stainmore – Tan Hill and Mickle Fell

160 and 161 27 *a* Wensleydale – milk collection

b Gunnerside Gill, Swaledale

28 Blue Scar, Littondale – limestone pavements

176 and 177 29 Appleby Castle and town

30 *a* Winterburn – Friar Head

b Burnsall Grammar School

Between pages 176 and 177 31 *a* Field limekiln
                                   b Limekiln
                             32 Ingleborough – from the south-west
            192 and 193   33 High Force, Teesdale
                             34 Littondale
                             35 Richmond Castle
                             36 *a* Kisdon Falls – on the Swale, near Keld
                                   b Pennine Way – Ten End

            216 and 217   37 Eggleston Abbey
                             38 Buttertubs
                             39 *a* Buttertubs Pass – between Wensleydale and
                                        Swaledale
                                   b Tan Hill – sheep sales
                             40 Enclosure walling of 1792

MAPS

1 The Pennine Dales in relation to
the Midlands and North *frontispiece*
2 The Pennine Dales 16–17
3 Administrative divisions of the
Pennine Dales area 22
4 Caves, waterfalls, rock features and scars 38
5 Distribution of Anglian, Danish,
and Norse place names 73
6 Market roads 106
7 Castles, earthworks, Roman camps,
monastic sites 168
8 Pennine Way and motor routes 200

DIAGRAMS

1 Alston Block 24
2 Askrigg Block 27
3 Northumbrian Fault Block 41
4 Small Iron Age farm settlement 62
5 Intakes and enclosures 115
6 'Crucked' barn 152
7 Two 'hall houses' 156

The Pennine Dales

Acknowledgements

Acknowledgements and thanks for permission to reproduce photographs are due to Bertram Unne for plates 1, 2b, 3a, 5, 7, 8a, 8b, 10a, 10b, 16a, 16b, 18a, 18b, 19a, 19b, 20, 21, 24a, 25, 26a, 27a, 30a, 33, 36a, 39a, and 39b, as well as for the picture that appears on the end-papers; to University of Cambridge, Committee for Aerial Photography for plates 9, 11, 14, 32, and 34; to Ministry of Defence, Crown Copyright for plates 12, 22, 23, and 29; to Aerofilms and Aero Pictorial Ltd for plates 3b, 17, 28, 35, and 37; to C. Crosthwaite for plates 6, 27b, and 38; to Tom Stephenson for plates 16c, 26b and 36b; to G. V. Berry for plate 13; to C. H. Wood Ltd for plate 15; and to the National Monuments Record for plate 24b. Maps 1 and 2 were drawn by W. Bromage.

Introduction

During the 1920s summer parties from a guest house near Alston used to make their way to a group of mine buildings, a few hundred feet below the summit of Cross Fell. From this 'base camp' they would go to the summit to watch sunset and sunrise, an experience, if the weather was good, never to be forgotten. In the evening light the western edge of the long ridge, of which Cross Fell is the highest part, seems to plunge down at a fearful rate into the Vale of Eden more than two thousand feet below, while far across the Vale the Lake District mountains stand in glorious silhouette against the sunset sky. To the north, still more lightly sketched in, are the outlines of the Solway Firth, on rare occasions glowing like burnished gold under the last rays of the sun, with behind it the hills of Galloway dominated by Criffel. To the east, a wide extent of dusky moorlands steadily declines in broad ridges between shadow-filled valleys, until both are lost in the distance. The detail of this eastward land of the Pennine Dales must wait for the sunrise for better definition, and then glimpses of gleaming rivers and many flood-lit summits are seen stretching to the horizon. Towards the north and north-east the land falls away more rapidly, with shorter and deeper-cut valleys leading into the through valley of the Tyne which links Cumberland with the east coast. Across the Tyne the Cheviots and their attendant moors and mountains are dimly seen.

One might be standing on the upturned edge of a gently inclined highland plateau into which the many valleys have been deeply scored but have remained as the less important feature, our deepest impression being of a heathery or grassy moorland reaching almost to the horizon. This land of the Tyne, Wear, and Tees is the northern part of the Pennines, broken from the rest by the broad pass of Stainmore.

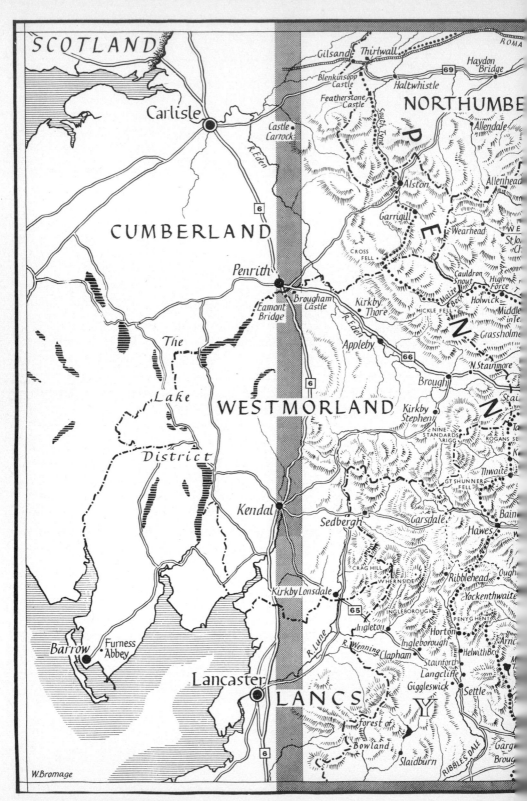

Map 2 *The Pennine Dales*

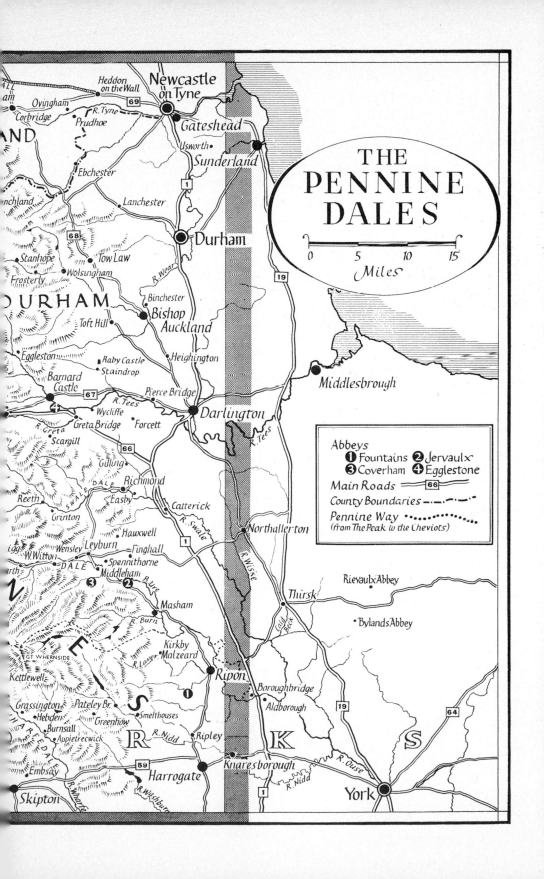

The Pennines have been known to generations as the 'Pennine Chain', 'the backbone of England', but it is only within this century that the name has been accepted to be a clever literary forgery. An Englishman, Charles Bertram (1723–65), was employed in Copenhagen as a teacher of the English language in the Naval College. To occupy his time he began to write a history of Roman Britain, but as he found the original material for some parts of the story very scanty he began to fill it in from his imagination. After years of hard work he produced a document of remarkable character and some genius which was published in the guise of a transcription of an early manuscript discovered by himself. He credited the work to Richard of Cirencester, a monk of Westminster Abbey, living in the fourteenth century. It was greeted as an outstanding discovery.[1]

For this chronicle Bertram invented many Roman-sounding names. One of these, for the long range of mountains in the north for which there was no proper name, was *Alpes Penina*. Defoe had referred to them as the English Andes, but Bertram's pseudo-discovery gave them a name which was at once accepted.

The Pennines form a piece of high country stretching from the Tyne valley in the north to the Trent valley in the south, a distance of about 140 miles. The northern part of the 'chain' is generally about thirty miles wide and much of it more than two thousand feet above sea level. The southern half is generally about twenty-five miles across and, while it is largely above a thousand feet, it only rarely reaches two thousand feet.

The market town of Skipton in Craven, on the river Aire, is very nearly the exact centre of the 'Chain', seventy miles from the Tyne and sixty-six from Ashbourne in Derbyshire at the southern end. The river Aire has given its name to the 'Aire Gap', a valley which makes a low pass right through the Pennines, not rising anywhere above four hundred feet above sea level. This pass divides the Pennines into two equal portions which, though having much in common, still show some differences in their geological and physical character.

The area with which this book is concerned (see opposite title page and pages 16 and 17) is the northern part of the 'Pennine Chain' lying between the Aire Gap and the Tyne. The area is roughly defined by a rectangle that joins Carlisle and Newcastle with Lancaster and Harrogate; the valleys of Eden and Lune form its western edge, and the Great North Road (A1) lies a few miles east of its eastern boundary. As well as the wild moorlands of the fells, it includes some of the most spectacular mountain scenery in England.

THE REGIONS OF BRITAIN

The Pennine Dales

I

Physical description

Travellers who have made the journey by railway from Leeds to Carlisle – along the old Midland Railway line through Skipton, Settle, and Appleby – must, after leaving Skipton, have been more and more impressed by the surrounding scenery. From Skipton to Settle on the north side of the line, high hills quickly draw nearer, and around Settle they become precipitous and patterned by limestone scars and crags divided by vivid green pastures. For a few miles north of Settle the line plunges through many deep cuttings and short tunnels, or runs on embankments until, at Helwith Bridge, it emerges into the open ground of upper Ribblesdale. Here and for several miles the way is flanked by the two mountain masses of Penyghent on the east and Ingleborough on the west. The gradient known as the 'big hump' is climbed to Ribblehead and the long tunnels begin after the first of the great viaducts – Batty Moss, known as the Ribblehead Viaduct. This is near the watershed between the Ribble and the Ure drainages, and it strides above Batty Moss, 165 ft high at its highest part, and 440 yards long.

At the north end of this viaduct the train enters Blea Moor Tunnel, 2,629 yards long, and reaches there a rail level of 1,151 ft OD.* The line emerges high on the side of steep fells, with a breath-taking view over the head of Dentdale across to the mass of Whernside. Two more impressive viaducts cross gorge-like torrent courses, and then the train roars through Dent station, the highest on the line (at 1,145 ft OD), with a massive range of snow fences along the fell side above it. The Rise Hill Tunnel, of 1,213 yards, carries the line into the head of Garsdale, which then emerges, after tunnel and viaduct, tunnel and viaduct, into the magnificent

---

* O D means 'above Ordnance Datum', the level from which all heights on maps are measured; this is the mean sea level at a fixed point on the English coast.

Map 3 *Administrative divisions of the Pennine Dales area*

through valley of Mallerstang and so to the head of Eden dale across the watershed of England. The Ais Gill signal box in Mallerstang is at the highest point of the line, 1,169 ft OD, and near by the line crosses the infant river Eden on the Ais Gill viaduct. When we escape from the narrow pass of Mallerstang, with its confining fells rising to over two thousand feet above sea level, the long run down the Vale of Eden through Kirkby Stephen and Appleby to Carlisle is still a route of high scenic quality. From many viaducts and embankments there are lovely views of the river, and on the west the panorama of the Lake District mountains balances the long Cross Fell escarpment of the North Pennines on the east.[2]

In taking the direct line up Ribblesdale we have left to the west of us a region of splendid mountain country. The mass of Ingleborough (Plates 13 and 32) is the finest of the Yorkshire mountains, and beyond it Whernside (not to be confused with Great Whernside – not quite so high – in Wharfedale) and the Leck, Barbon, and Middleton Fells stretch away to the valley of the Lune. Dentdale and Garsdale run down to the Rawthey valley across which to the west the Howgill Fells stand alone within their girdle of three valleys. On the east is the Rawthey, the west side has the Lune with its splendid gorges below Tebay, and on the north the head waters of the Lune run down Ravenstonedale. These fells stand in a beauty which is unique in our area. They are of slate not limestone, and their geological relationship is with the Lake District fells around Windermere. Their masses are rounded and their turf velvety; deep gullies make shadowy folds on their sides, and their slopes are entirely unbroken by terrace or large rock outcrops (Plate 1). Whenever they are seen from the limestone country they appear as a smooth polished gem, their colour is high and they form a self-contained picture lovely enough to make one catch one's breath, complete and perfect. They are unenclosed, free of all walling, with no human mark on them beyond a rare green track seen from a distance only as the faintest of green hair lines drawn round the fell shoulder.[3]

On the west side of Mallerstang and north of Garsdale there are two fells, Baugh Fell and Wild Boar Fell, with Grisedale and Uldale between them. They are massive and lonely fells but rewarding to the walker. The summit of Wild Boar Fell is like a table-top, with the wide plateau of the Wild Boar Fell Grits of Millstone Grit age, a mile in length from north-east to south-west and with precipices along its eastern face called the Black Bed, Yoadcomb, and High White Scars. Baugh Fell is a little more rounded and lacks the precipitous edge, but its top is formed by about 500 ft of Millstone Grit which supports peaty mosses and small tarns.

In nearly all its features and history the northern mass of the Pennines between Stainmore and Tyne has a unity which makes the geologist's name for it, 'Alston Block', particularly apt. From Cross Fell (2,930 ft OD), near the western edge,

23

the drainage radiates to the Tees, Wear, and South Tyne, all of which have their head waters within a few miles. There is a clear mountain skeleton or framework to this 'block' also focusing on Cross Fell – with the long ridge of the Cross Fell

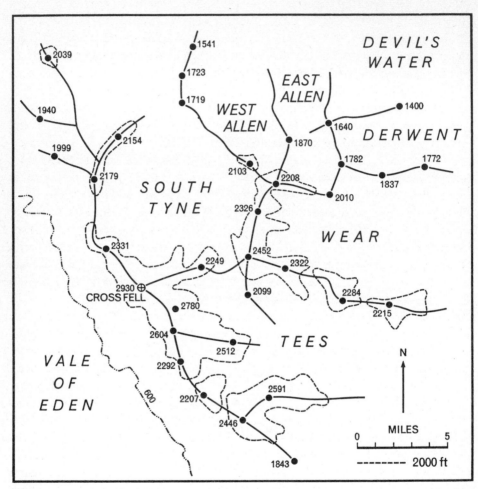

Diagram I   *The Alston Block, with drainage basins and watersheds; heights of summits above sea level; 600 ft and 2,000 ft contours.*

range nearly north-west to south-east, and two ridges (perhaps a little complicated by minor spurs) trending to north-east and south-east – like a primitive outline of the letter K. Between the branches of the 'K' the rivers South Tyne, West and East Allen, Devils Water and Derwent, occupy the north-eastern sector, the Wear

24

the central, and the Tees the southern part. Tees and Wear have long major valleys comparable with the Yorkshire Dales, but the northern rivers are shorter and steeper, with valleys much more intimate, and with juvenile gorges and many features of lesser scale character than are found in most of the larger dales.[4]

The westward face of the Cross Fell edge has many short mountain torrents which plunge down gorge-like valleys until they reach the floor of the Vale of Eden, when they become lowland streams tributary to the Eden river. Only the river Gelt and the Croglin Water rise on the upper spurs and run for two or three miles to the north-west before turning west down the scarp. These are both in the north-west part of the range.

North of Stainmore the country slopes from west to east. This barren likeness must be clothed with texture and colour, given detail, converted to a living landscape within which Nature's creatures, plants and animals and humans, can find a home. If we were to walk from the north-west corner for three or four days along the upland ridges – within which are enfolded the valley heads of Tyne, Derwent, Wear, and Tees – we would encounter some of the wildest moorlands in England. As we cross from peak to peak – or rather summit to summit, for none of the summits is sharp – the journey is like a passage from one giant stepping-stone to another rising above a sea of heather moors and mosses.

The three arms of the 'K' mountain skeleton are all about fifteen miles long, their general level declining steadily from the Cross Fell node. Their length is studded by high points like the knobs on some prehistoric monster's backbone. On the three ridges and their spurs there are over twenty summits reaching above two thousand feet and the same number above fifteen hundred feet – it is big country (Diag. 1).

This northern mass of fells drops quickly from Mickle Fell, 2,591 ft OD, into the Stainmore Pass, an undulating eight-miles-wide patch of bleak country, generally about 1,200 to 1,500 ft OD. Hidden within this waste there are four tributaries of the river Tees – the Lune, Balder, Deepdale Beck, and Greta. The greater part of Stainmore is unpopulated except for sheep and grouse, and settlement is limited to a few farms in Lunedale and Balderdale, never sufficient to form a hamlet (Plate 18a).

The largest settlement is the village of Bowes on the Roman road near the east end of the pass, where the Romans had a fort and the Normans built a castle. The greater part of Stainmore forms the outmoors of villages in Teesdale, Mickleton Moor, Hunderthwaite Moor, Cotherstone Moor, and, from the west, Bowes Moor. The upper part of the Greta drainage is Stainmore Forest, with Lune

Forest to the north. Stainmore is crossed by the Roman road, now A67, one of the busiest of the Pennine crossings, and one which, in winter, is subject to extremely heavy snowfall and drifting. The road from Brough to Middleton is of less importance. From north to south a great drove road of the seventeenth and eighteenth centuries crosses all the dales in turn, being almost entirely a grass-grown track. Apart from these, tracks are few and far between and the chief features are the recently constructed reservoirs in Lunedale and Balderdale.

The country between Stainmore and Airedale is known as the Askrigg Block, Askrigg being near the centre. The western edge is less obvious than the Cross Fell edge, but from Brough it runs south-west for twenty-four miles to Kirkby Lonsdale by Nine Standards Rigg, 2,144 ft OD, and seven other summits over two thousand feet, thus repeating the northern pattern. Between Stainmore and Wensleydale the high moorlands south of Tan Hill have four summits over two thousand feet, and wide heather-clad moors declining steadily to about a thousand feet near Richmond (Diag. 2).

The mass of fells south of the upper waters of the Ure forms Craven,[5] with its well-known cluster of high peaks, Whernside, Ingleborough, Penyghent and Fountains Fell, and five others all above two thousand feet. The head waters of the Wharfe, Ribble, and Wenning lie among these fells. On the north-east flank of Great Whernside the river Nidd runs through a short dale between the lower parts of the Ure and Wharfe valleys. The western part of these fells leads on to the Howgills, a regular triangular mass radiating from its central point in the Calf, 2,220 ft, and separated from the Askrigg Block by the narrow Rawthey valley.

In Craven the pattern of heathery or grassy moorland is changed, for it is limestone which makes this area famous. The surface of the Great Scar Limestone, and of many of the limestones which occur in the strata above this, are devoid of soil and form extensive pavements carved by rain into fantastic patterns. It is a country dominated by limestone scars and pavements, with underground streams, caves, and potholes, and limestone cliffs and gorges of great size (Plates 5 and 38).

In the area west of Skipton and north of the Kirkby Lonsdale road as far west as Barbondale, and north of this line as far as Swaledale, there are limestone features which attract visitors. Near the village of Malham in Craven, at the head of Airedale, is the Cove, about half a mile north of the village, an amphitheatre of naked limestone crag, 240 ft high, vertical and even in some places overhanging (Plate 5). From its foot a stream emerges which makes Malham Beck, later to join with other streams and become the river Aire. A mile to the east of Malham the long line of scars is broken by a deep narrow rift where a path disappears between slightly

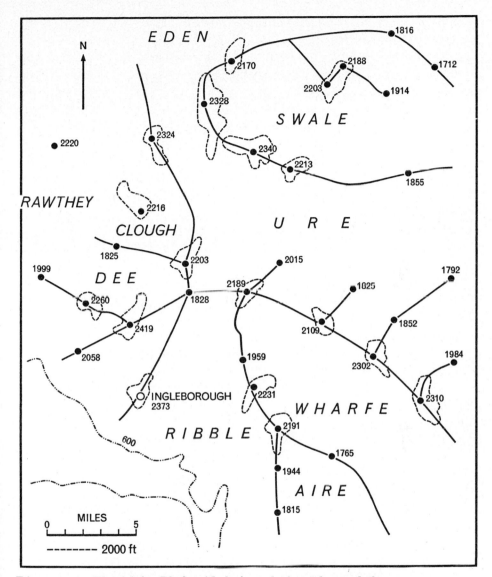

Diagram 2 *The Askrigg Block, with drainage basins and watersheds;*
heights of summits above sea level; 600 ft and 2,000 ft contours.

overhanging cliffs 300 ft high into a gorge closed by a stream descending in two high waterfalls from a hole high up in the limestone mass. It is possible to climb up alongside the lower fall, or through it when the stream is not too full, and then to get out of Gordale by the scree shoot which comes down to the foot of the upper fall. The Gordale valley above the upper fall is typical of many in the limestone area, a deep, narrow slit, walled in by almost continuous cliffs or 'scars' of limestone, often difficult or nearly impossible to climb (Plate 17). Both the Cove and Gordale Scar are cut into the long feature made right across country by the mid-Craven Fault, of which Attermire Scars and Giggleswick Scar are also a part. Above the Cove there is a valley with high limestone scars, called the Dry Valley, because the stream which made it now flows by an underground course.

Giggleswick Scar, the long line of cliffs on the north side of the main Kirkby Lonsdale road over both sides of Buckhaw Brow, west of Settle, is a part of the Craven Fault. Ingleborough stands on a triangular platform of limestone which is bounded by the Craven Fault on the south, and Ribblesdale and Chapeldale to east and west, these coming together at Ribblehead. Streams run off the upper slopes of the mountain, but soon disappear underground when they reach the limestone, penetrating deep into its mass by potholes which may eventually reach depths of three or four hundred feet. The final depth to which the streams could descend is determined by the floor of older slates on which the limestone lies at the unconformity. The waters travel through the limestone by enlarged joints and fissures and caverns are frequently worn along their course. They emerge at last at the junction of the limestone and slates. Sometimes, as at Clapham Cave and at White Scar Cave near Ingleton, the stream exit channel is big enough to be followed through a whole system of caves. There is a fine tourist cave at Stump Cross on Greenhow Hill, 4¾ miles from Pateley Bridge in Nidderdale and 5¼ miles from Grassington in Wharfedale. Here the stream has gone deeper and the show cave is in parts of the abandoned upper levels, with chambers and passages which contain some very fine formations.

The potholes are generally a succession of deep vertical shafts. For their exploration appropriate tackle, including rope ladders, and considerable skill, are needed – though the mouths of some of the better known, such as Gaping Gill and Alum Pot on Ingleborough, and Hunt and Hull Pots on Penyghent, are regularly visited.

In Wharfedale Kilnsey Crag is a famous limestone scar, and the whole upper dale is walled by continuous scars. In Swaledale limestone features are scarce except around the head, where Kisdon Hill and the gorge of the Swale by Kisdon are spectacular, and the near-by Swinnergill valley, tributary to the Swale near the mouth of Kisdon, has a lower portion which is an extremely narrow gorge between high limestone cliffs. The waterfalls in some of the lateral valleys such as East Gill are very fine. Wensleydale has great lengths of limestone scars along its flanks, but as these are mainly formed in the thinner limestones of the Yoredale Series they are much more delicate than the massive features in Craven. The falls both in the main river valley and in most of the side valleys are the special glory of the Wensleydale (Yoredale) limestones.

In Dentdale and Garsdale, the limestone character is again best seen in the tributary streams or in short sections of the river course. Such deep-cut gorges as that of Flintergill at Dent, and many of the becks which come into the Rawthey above Sedbergh, are very exciting, while the river Clough in its lower part cuts rock pools, gorges, and rapids through the limestone at Garsdale Foot. In the north end of Mallerstang, there is again some good limestone scenery on the Warcop Fell area. Along the Cross Fell edge the valleys dropping down to the west frequently have limestone features, and in the Tees, at Cronkley Scar and Falcon Clints, the limestone is again prominent. In all these northern areas, however, the limestone features are subordinate to the general topography, not dominant as in the Craven area.

The north Pennines are better known by their numerous 'dales' than by their fells. Like the fells, the dales have an approximate symmetry about Stainmore; Weardale and Teesdale north of the pass and Swaledale and Wensleydale south of it all run from the western fells to the east. Each has many tributary 'dales', shorter, varied in character, but all worthy of exploration. The northern part of the Alston Block has its shorter dales of the South Tyne, the Allendales, Devils Water, and Derwent, north of the Wear and running north or north-east. The Askrigg Block has, south of Wensleydale, the valleys of the Nidd, Wharfe, Ribble, and upper Aire running south-east or south. The main difference between the two blocks is in the short dales of the south-westerly corner, Garsdale, Dentdale, and the Rawthey valley, and the through valley of Mallerstang at the head of Wensleydale.

The most impressive approach to a view of one of the dales is to come upon it from the high moors – what the dalesfolk call, so expressively, from off the 'tops'. One has spent the day, perhaps, up in this world of heather, with grouse or curlew providing a commentary to one's every moment, and with wide views of moorland cut by faint runnels and gullies, many of which are, in fact, the gaps of the dale lip seen in foreshortened perspective. The high ground begins to decline and one may come to the edge of the heather and peat and enter a world of benty grass and occasional stream heads. Then comes the moment when one looks 'over the edge' – the convexity of the hill has reached the point where one can look back up the gentler slope of moorland, or forward down what often appears to be an almost precipitous slope into the valley. We are near the dale head, and see below us the great bowl where upland streams run together to form the dale's river. Rough pasture drops in terraces broken by fronts of rock outcrop, the pasture improving as it gets down to the 'moor wall', below which lies the network of old and winding intake walls enclosing the pastures that generations of men now forgotten have won from the moor.

At the moor edge there will be one or two gathering folds where sheep are collected, counted, sorted out, and separated. Lower, and near the stream junctions, a bigger maze of folds may be discerned, and the structure of a 'dipping place' or 'wash fold', where in years past, lively scenes of sheep dipping have taken place. Dipping was a time of turmoil with an underlying discipline. Sheep, men, boys, and dogs milling around, constantly on the move, were none the less performing efficiently a necessary part of the farmer's and the shepherd's work; boys were learning and dogs were carrying themselves with an importance and dignity which would often make them shrug off the attempted attentions of a visitor.

If instead of scrambling down the hill we turn along the edge we soon find the spot from which we can look, it may be for miles, down the upper dale, with its increasing width of bottom lands, its occasional farms becoming more frequent, and perhaps its hamlet or village which marks the dale head (Endpaper Plate). There we stand, suspended between the organized and social life of the hamlet and farm, and the wild outdoors of the 'tops' shared with the grouse and curlew, the occasional fox, and the ever-present sheep. This edge between dale and fell offers the most exciting views, the other side of the dale lying in front, seen at such an angle that it appears as an air-photo, such that a six-inch map presents the dalesman with a familiar picture of his country.

As the dales widen so the moors appear to retreat, a greater area of enclosed pasture intervening between the old enclosures of the valley farms with their meadows and the moorland 'tops'. Most of these intermediate pastures have been the subject of enclosure by agreement or by Act of Parliament in the late eighteenth or early nineteenth centuries, and the great areas into which they are now divided are the 'allotments'. The moors are generally common or stinted pastures on which the farmers have rights of sheep grazing, peat, and bracken or bedding with, occasionally, other rights. Nearly two-thirds of all the common land of England occurs in the northern counties and over these commons 'the people are allowed by custom if not by right, to wander more or less freely, subject only to certain restrictions in the interests of forestry and water-undertakings', and, one might add, of grouse rearing and shooting.[6]

The valleys in their mid-course carry good farmland, mainly used by dairy herds, plantations, wooded riversides, and many attractive villages. As they open out in the lower part of their course, there are castles and abbeys, and larger villages or even small market towns, often located round a castle. Richmond, with its castle, and with Easby Abbey only a mile away, is the market for Swaledale. In Teesdale there is Barnard Castle and its town. Castles are numerous and varied, some still lived in as Featherstone, Raby, and others, or ruined like Richmond, Middleham, or Bolton. Abbeys occupy lovely positions which attract and delight many visitors – Blanchland on the Derwent, Eggleston in Teesdale, Easby in Swaledale, Jervaulx and Coverham in Wensleydale, Fountains on the Skell, tributary of the Ure, and Bolton Priory on the Wharfe are some of the larger and better known monastic settlements.

The dales are also known and visited for many features of natural beauty – the river falls on the Ure at Aysgarth, or those on the Swale at Keld and Kisdon; High Force and Cauldron Snout on the Tees, and Thornton Force and all the falls in the Ingleton Glens. There are the high falls of Hardraw Scar on a tributary of the Ure, and the isolated and majestic fall of Cautley Spout in the Howgills. The wooded gorges of the Tees below Middleton and Barnard Castle and of the Greta and Tees near Rokeby were remembered by Macaulay's exile when far away he wrote that he

Heard on Lavernia, Scargill's whispering trees
And pined by Arno for my lovlier Tees

Limestone offers many wonderful features. The high precipices of Kilnsey Crag, Gordale, and Malham Cove are perhaps the best known in the southern area, but Cronkley Scar on Tees, and the gorges of the Allen near Staward Pele, or the Sneep on the Derwent, would have many defendants for pride of place among the beauty spots of the north. The area of the Yorkshire Dales south of Stainmore forms the Yorkshire Dales National Park, and the whole length of the higher moorlands from south to north is traversed by the Pennine Way, one of the finest walks in Britain. This book will attempt to illuminate some of the great wealth of interest of every kind which the area has to offer, in the fields of natural history, history ancient and modern, architecture, etc., and in the life of its people.

The dalesfolk do not conform to any single type, but some characteristics are often stronger in some areas than in others. In the western fell country there is a sufficient admixture of original Norse stock to leave us with tall, 'lish' men, tireless on the fells, slow of speech and shy of easy conversation. Skilled with sheep and completely self-reliant they are quiet, friendly, and very observant people. Not many people wander on the fells without their knowledge, and very few visitors can approach their knowledge and understanding of nature. In the dales there is some Danish farming blood, and this, with the isolation of the small dales communities, has created a character which dalesmen soon recognize. The true-born dalesman has a keen sense of humour, but it is not easily displayed. It is often rather grim, like the moors and the weather around him, and it is always cautious and given to understatement. 'It's noan so bad', or 'it could have been worse' are the phrases of high praise, and an inquiry after a dalesman's health, met with 'nobbut (only) middlin' may mean real illness, while 'noan so bad' in this context really means 'splendid'. A subject is approached slowly – a discussion of the weather, a remark or two about the sheep, a few words about health, with plenty of time for thought between each sentence leading to 'Well, ah'll be goin' now', and the vital matter, the sole reason for meeting slipped in as though it were an after-thought; that is the only seemly way of a conversation between true dalesmen. Easy speech and facile thoughts are the brand of the 'off-comed' non-dalesbred.

In Swaledale and the Alston Moor area, mines and their problems often take the place of sheep, though since the decay of the mining industry much of the talk of mines is reminiscent and nostalgic. The weather remains the constant topic, and is the backbone of every greeting, emphasizing that in these upland areas life has always been subject to the stress of wild weather and has always been difficult and marginal.

The true dales character is being overlaid now with a veneer dictated by the increasing number of town visitors. The motor-car has broken down the remoteness and isolation. The townsman's fetish of 'ham & egg & cake' tea in the country, and the 'cereal, bacon & egg, toast and marmalade' breakfast, have brought about a uniformity of visitors' diet such that from John o' Groat's to Lands End the visitor can correctly forecast his menu and need fear no departure from it. In the back kitchen the true dales ideas of food and feeding persist but are a private matter for the family and its true friends. The true ramblers still seeking the tops on foot know the unpretentious farm and cottage where food is local and substantial, eggs are always in the plural, cheese is local, real and naked, and good pasty and spice-cake are infinitely better than the more polite shop 'cake' sometimes still in its paper cup.

Underneath all this, however, the true dales stock continues, shy and unrevealing but carrying forward a way of life that demands vigour and courage against fell country and weather, and compassion and understanding for sheep and stock, combined with a willingness to live without ambition and artificiality. To be born in the dales and of dales stock is to share this rich life, but the visitor, no matter how much a stranger, will still be able to appreciate dales hospitality and to enjoy the character that accompanies it. Condescension and 'superiority' are sure means of missing all that is best in the dales.

2

Physical background:
*geology – topography –
climate – natural history*

From the Tyne to the Trent throughout the whole length of the Pennines there is an underlying unity of rock and structure which no local variations or special features can completely obscure. There is almost infinite variety of detail held firmly within the broad lines of a dominant overall pattern. The scenery has throughout the subtle relationships, development, modulation, and perpetual return to the dominant theme and key that is the joy of a symphony. The source of this unity is the geology: the rocks and the geological events which have shaped and modified them, their physical properties, the way they lie, and the effects of weather and life upon them. The Aire Gap, of course, divides the Pennines into two almost equal portions, north and south, and this book is concerned only with the northern portion; none the less, much of what is said of the north Pennines will be true also, with only the differences of local colour and detail, of some part of the south.[1]

The Pennines are carved almost entirely from rocks which belong within the geologist's Carboniferous system. These rocks are the accumulated deposits of ancient seas, coastal swamps, and river deltas of some 250 to 330 million years ago. They were formed in an age when fish were the dominant backboned animal, when amphibia were still a young, evolving group and the most advanced child of evolution, when forests and a land flora were new, and when hardly any of the plants and animals we now know had evolved. Almost all the fossil remains of creatures and plants from the Pennine rocks are those of forms now completely extinct. The outlines of the geography of the world were then entirely different; sea and land occupied very different areas from those now represented in our

34

continents and oceans, and the oceans themselves covered much more of the earth's surface than they do now.

Although the Pennines are made almost entirely of Carboniferous rocks there are a few places where a foundation of older and very different rocks can be seen. On the south-western flank of Craven the rivers have, in places, cut down through the Carboniferous strata, and for some part the valley floors are cut into slates and other older rocks. Near Malham Tarn a small area of green slates is exposed; Ribblesdale, from Horton down to Stainforth, reveals slates which have for generations been the basis of a quarrying industry. The tributaries of the Wenning, running off the Ingleborough and Whernside fells, have a part of their course in similar and also in much older rocks well seen in Crummackdale and near Ingleton. On the west side of Craven Barbondale runs along a line which separates the limestones of Craven on the east from older slaty rocks on the west, and the valleys of the Rawthey and Lune are cut in the slaty rocks of the Howgill Fells.

North of Stainmore smaller and fewer areas of the older rocks are seen. Between High Force and Cauldron Snout in Teesdale a small area of slate is marked by the ruins of the 'Pencil Mill', where for much of the last century slate pencils were made from a suitable bed within this slate. Other patches of older rocks are to be found in a few of the gills on the face of the Cross Fell edge, where many of the rocks can be seen to resemble some of those forming the Lake District to the west.

To understand the Carboniferous rocks we need at least an outline picture of this foundation on which they were deposited.[2] In far distant ages of the earth's history, probably before any recognizable forms of life had evolved, the rocks which are called pre-Cambrian were formed in primitive oceans, compressed and folded up into continents and mountains, then worn down to a great plain – processes which spread over scores and even hundreds of millions of years. Earth movements took some of these plains beneath the sea, probably about 500 million years ago, and more rocks (sediments) were deposited, only to follow the same cycle of compression, folding into mountain ranges, wearing down to an uneven plain, and then submersion into a new ocean basin. The sediments deposited in this new sea about 330 million years ago were the first of the Carboniferous group. They lay across the folded and eroded edges of the older rocks to make what the geologist calls an unconformity. This unconformity is now seen in classic exposures at many places in Craven. At Thornton Force at the head of Twistleton Glen, Ingleton, the Kingsdale Beck plunges off the Carboniferous limestone on to the upturned edges of pre-Cambrian slates, and the limestones are seen resting on the slates in a clear line which a hand can span with thumb and little finger touching worlds more than 300 million years apart. No one with imagination can be

35

insensitive to this experience. While the Ingleton Glens reveal the pre-Cambrian, other and later rocks are seen in Ribblesdale and other areas.

The best-known exposure of the unconformity is that at the old Arco Wood Quarry near Helwith Bridge in Ribblesdale (SD 800701).* Here there is a splendid section of the Horton Flags (of Silurian age) standing almost on end and sheared off, with the massive beds of limestone lying in horizontal layers across the upturned edges. This is one of the several old slate quarries no longer worked, so the section, because of its size and quality, has been listed as a geological site of national importance, to be preserved.

The floor on which the Carboniferous strata now rests is in fact an ancient worn-down land surface with the relict stumps of mountain ranges of the preceding Devonian period forming hills and valleys. At the beginning of Carboniferous time there was an irregular topography, with a mountainous continent to the north and a newly submerged sea floor over the north of England, in which there were several troughs of deeper water separated by shallows. Much of the sediment brought into this sea was carried by rivers from the northern continents and dropped to fill the northern troughs, leaving clearer sea farther south, over what is now Craven. We see the result of this in the massive pure limestones, many hundreds of feet thick, which form the Great Scar limestone of Craven, which is the same age as part of the masses of shale, sandstone, and thin limestones in the lower Carboniferous of the Alston Block.[3]

The Yoredale Series which follows above the Great Scar limestone was deposited in shallower seas, almost lagoons, and is much more uniform over the north Pennines, though still with thicker limestones to the south and more shale (mud) and sandstone (sands) to the north. The Yoredale Series was named by Phillips, the first geologist to make a study of all Yorkshire, and in his classic book *The Geology of Yorkshire* (1836) he says, when choosing a standard section of the rocks which follow above the Great Scar (or Mountain) limestone: 'The upper end of Wensleydale is therefore adopted. The total thickness of the upper limestone series is about one thousand feet . . . constituting what I call the Yoredale series.' There is a 'rhythmic succession' in these beds, shale followed by sandstone, then the sandstone followed by limestone, then shale, sandstone, limestone, again and again. Each limestone weathers out into a long scar usually with a vertical front, and the shales weather away easily and leave the top of the limestone like the tread of a stair. The sandstones are often concealed under the scree from the limestone and form the lower part of the rise, less steep than the vertical limestone.

* National Grid Numbers.

Particularly in Wharfedale and Wensleydale, the heart of the true Yoredale country, the limestone scars run for miles along the valley sides and are the most striking feature of the scenery. Some of the limestones may be a few score feet thick, and the effect is that the valley sides mount in a series of scars and gentle slopes, like the treads of a gigantic staircase (Plates 15 and 28). Farther north the limestones are thinner and less obvious, but none the less the shape of the ground is there, and throughout the north Pennines a person climbing the fellside has the experience of surmounting a steep, almost vertical rise, crossing a gentler slope, only to find another rise, and another and another after that.

This 'rhythm' is responsible for the great abundance of waterfalls. Every side-stream leaps over each limestone in turn, and there is no part of England with anything to compare with the number of falls and with the beauty of these tributary streams. Some of the falls over the thicker limestones are high – like Hardraw Scar, 80 ft, Mill Gill Force and Parker Gill Force near Askrigg, and Ashgill Force near Garrigill – while others come down in a series of steps, bed by bed. Every fall has its own particular character and beauty.[4]

Some of the Yoredale sandstones are very flaggy, and these have contributed a most important feature of the traditional dales building from the seventeenth century onward: the stone-slate (locally called 'grey slate') roofs. Near Hardraw, but higher in the series than the Hardraw limestone, the flags under the Middle limestone have been worked for centuries both by large quarries along the outcrop and by very extensive underground mining. These flags have been quarried at very many other places in the dales. The Hardraw and Coverdale flags are the best quality, thin and smooth and in large sizes, and were carried long distances for the more important buildings, while others, thicker and coarser, were used near where they occurred for cottages and farm buildings. For one who knows the dales buildings well enough many of the roofing slates can be recognized for the place of their origin, each having a little of a local peculiarity about it. From Wharfedale to the South Tyne beds of flags occur which vary from massive paving flags to the finer qualities of roofing slate, and they have been quarried for generations, but because of their weight have seldom been exported out of the Pennine valleys. On the west some beds of the true slates which underlie the Carboniferous limestone, particularly those of Ribblesdale and Ingleton, were quarried, and many houses in the Wenning, Lune, and Rawthey valleys have roofs of these thinner green and blue-green slates.

Above the Yoredale series the rocks are the coarser sandstones and shales of the Millstone Grit, the remnants of sandbanks and mudflats of an enormous delta from rivers coming from the northern continent. The series is thickest in south

37

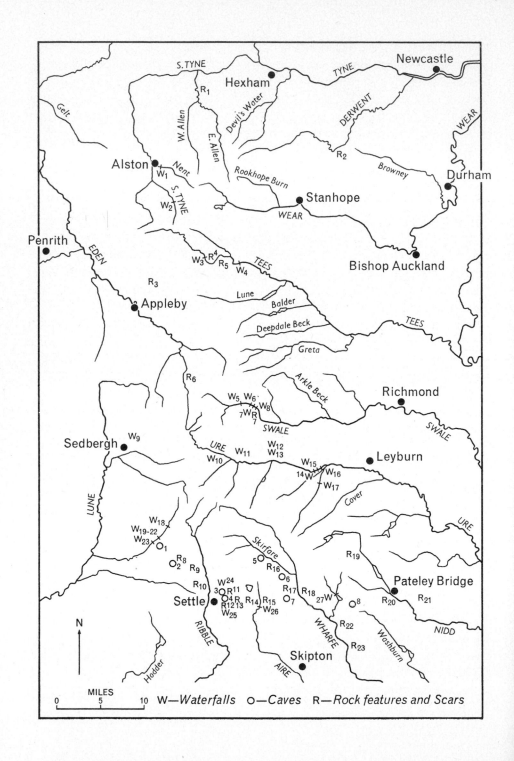

MILES

W—*Waterfalls* O—*Caves* R—*Rock features and Scars*

Map 4 *Waterfalls, caves, rock features and scars*

Waterfalls w

1 Nent Force
2 Ashgill Force
3 Cauldron Snout
4 High Force
5 Wain Wath Force
6 Catrake Force
7 East Gill Force
8 Kisdon Force
9 Cautley Spout
10 Mossdale Foss
11 Hardrow Force
12 Whitfield Force
13 Mill Gill Force
14 Aysgarth Falls, upper
15 Aysgarth Falls, middle
16 Aysgarth Falls, lower
17 Burton Foss
18 Weathercote
19–22 Ingleton Falls
23 Thornton Force
24 Catrigg Foss
25 Scaleber Foss
26 Janet's Foss
27 Blea Beck Fall

Caves o

1 White Scar Cave
2 Clapham Cave
3 Victoria Cave
4 Attermire Cave
5 Skoska Cave
6 Doukybottom Cave
7 Calf Hole Cave
8 Stump Cross Cave

Rock features and scars R

1 Staward Peel
2 the Sneep
3 High Cup Nick
4 Falcon Clints
5 Cronkley Scar
6 Stenkrith Gorge
7 Kisdon Gorge
8 Trow Gill
9 Moughton Nab
10 Giggleswick Scar
11 Langcliff Scar
12 Attermire Scar
13 Benscar
14 Malham Cove
15 Gordale Scar
16 Arnberg Scar
17 Kilnsey Crag
18 Dib Scar
19 How Stean
20 Guys Cliff
21 Brimham Rocks
22 Trollers Gill
23 the Strid

Yorkshire, where it may be as much as five thousand feet or more, but northward it is thinner, and around the Tyne valley may be reduced to a few hundred feet at most. These grits are the rocks which form most of the hill summits and the ridges between the dales. On Ingleborough, Penyghent, and the peaks of Craven, the lowest bed of the Millstone Grit forms a resistant cap, weathering as a flat plain above the abrupt edge of the highest limestone. In Wild Boar Fell the grit is three or four hundred feet thick and makes its own barrier of crags. In the Alston Block again it caps Cross Fell and all the summits.

In the upper Yoredales and in the base of the Millstone Grit there are thin coal seams, so that we have the apparent anomaly of coal pits (mostly eighteenth and early nineteenth century) near the summits of the fells. The true Coal Measures of the greater coalfields are later than the Millstone Grit and lie along the east flank of the Pennines, where, because of the steady dip, the Millstone Grit disappears beneath them.

The present disposition of the rocks and the form of the country is very much the product of subsequent geological events. The structure which dominates and almost defines our area is a group of large-scale dislocations along which the rocks have been fractured in 'faults', where a vertical displacement of the two sides of the fracture has taken place. The boundary faults of the north Pennines are very large, but though they are complex structures they can be seen to run for scores of miles and in most of their length to form such prominent features as the thirty-mile-long wall of the Cross Fell edge. In the dales a complex of smaller faults in certain areas has led to the formation of the various mineral fields.

The boundary faults can be pictured as a reversed figure 3 – the straight top stroke would lie along the south flank of the Tyne valley, represented by a fault, known as the 'Stubblick Dyke', running from a few miles east of Hexham to near Castle Carrock. Through Castle Carrock a fault running north to south turns to the south-east to Brough under Stainmore, and with all its branches is known as the Pennine Faults. From Brough south-west towards Kirkby Lonsdale the Dent Fault makes a striking feature, then meets the west end of the Craven Faults. These start as the Barbon Fault, swinging to the south-east and then east, through Ingleton and Settle, by Malham and across Wharfedale and beyond Pateley Bridge in Nidderdale (Diag. 3). Where the Pennine and Dent faults meet there is an area of fantastically disturbed rocks, which can be seen in the area around Augill Beck, to be thrust up into a position where their layers are standing vertical or are twisted into all sorts of attitudes. A downfold, or syncline, runs eastward from Brough, forming Stainmore.

The faults on the west are very big, the Pennine faults having the strata on the

1. Sedberg and the Howgill Fells. The north-west corner of the Yorkshire Dales (W.R.) National Park.

2a. *Conistone Pasture – typical limestone pasture on the terrace of the Great Scar limestone.*

2b. *A Widdale farm group. Small meadows round the farms and hill pasture above. A few dairy or breeding cattle and large flocks of sheep are kept at such farms.*

3a. *Langdon Beck, Teesdale.*
Typical one- and two-storey houses of the country north of Stainmore.

3b. *Prudhoe Castle, Tyne Valley.*

4. *Barras = 'Bargh-hus' = hill farm. A Norse foundation sheep farm on the fell edge above Wharfedale. A typical dales 'long house' (house on right and 'shippon' on left under one roof).*

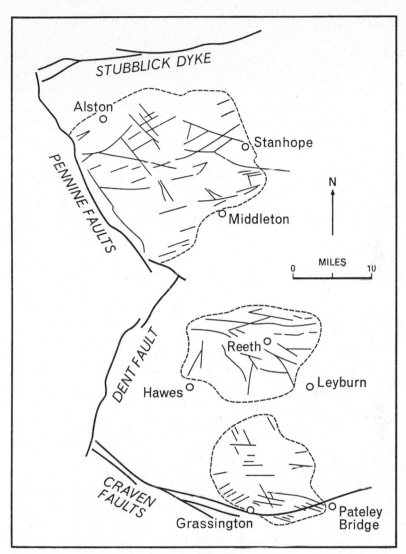

Diagram 3 *The Northumbrian Fault Block;*
boundary faults and mineral fields.

east side lifted up some few thousand feet above the same rocks which now actually lie under the floor of the Vale of Eden on the west side. Along the Stubblick Dyke this great uplift in the west decreases steadily to the east, as do the Craven Faults to the south, so that a simplified picture would be that of a desk lid hinged north and south on the east of the Pennines, and its free edge on the west, thirty miles away, lifted up nearly a mile. Thus geologically the whole country has a tilt to the east. Other later movements have converted the two parts north and south of the Stainmore syncline into slight domes, with their centres near Cross Fell and Ingleborough.

This uplift and doming is responsible for the charm of the dales, their very individual character and constantly varied detail. The massive Great Scar Limestone, the top of which is at about 1,200 ft OD around Ingleborough, steadily declines to east and north-east, to appear only in the valley bottom in Wensleydale at the Aysgarth Falls, far below the floor of Swaledale. By this slope Ribblesdale and upper Airedale (Malham Moor) enjoy scenery dominated by the Great Scar limestone; Wharfedale and Wensleydale have the best of the Yoredales, but Swalesdale is essentially a Millstone Grit valley, with only the upper part of the Yoredales making the lower valley slopes. The rivers start high up in the base of the Millstone Grit, and in their steep upper course quickly cut down into the lower strata, then, as their course flattens out to a lesser slope than that of the strata, the lower valley cuts through later and later rock. In all dimensions the vertical succession, the curvature of the dome, the shape of the river valley, secure that no two valleys nor any two parts of a single valley are alike.

In the Alston Block the streams are more radial to the dome, and the courses of the northern streams are shorter and steeper than those of the Tees and Wear. The general picture given for the southern block still applies, except that the Great Scar limestone is represented by strata of a Yoredale type, so that massive limestone scenery on the scale of that of Craven is not to be found. The northern block, however, has an additional geological feature which is not present in the south – the Great Whin Sill.

The end of the Carboniferous period, after the formation of the Coal Measures, was a time of great earth stresses which resulted in mountain building. The Hercynian movements (named from the Hertz mountains) were responsible for much of the uplift of the faults which we have discussed and for the main elevation of the Pennine Chain. During these movements a vast quantity of molten rock magma was squeezed into the strata through many fractures reaching up from great depth. The magma forced apart some of the beds of the Yoredale series and spread as an enormous sheet, underlying all the Alston Block and much of

Northumberland and east Durham. This sheet solidified as the Whin Sill, a blue-black crystalline rock called quartz-dolerite, in a layer which in places may be as much as 240 ft thick, but which is generally between 80 ft and 100 ft thick.[5]

The Whin Sill is very hard and resistant to weathering and stands out as bold crags. It has a partial columnar jointing, rather like that of the Giants Causeway, so that it makes perfectly vertical crags. The southern edge makes the magnificent falls of the Tees at High Force (Plate 33), and again at the long cascades of Cauldron Snout. In High Cup Nick, on the west flank of the Cross Fell edge, it forms the magnificent horseshoe of vertical crags which makes this valley unique. The most spectacular and best-known features are farther north in Northumberland: the noble crags used as a foundation for a great length of the Roman Wall, the crags on which are perched Dunstanborough and Bamborough Castles, and the whole of the Farne Islands. Near Middleton in Teesdale, at Holwick, and near High Force and at several places in Weardale and in Northumberland, the Whin Sill is the basis of large-scale quarrying for road metal, and this is in fact a major industry in the northern dales.

During the formation of the Alston and Askrigg domes a geometrical pattern of small fractures, ENE, NNE and WNW, was created. These, which were small faults, were infilled by minerals, some of high economic value – ores of lead, zinc, and iron, and some called the 'gangue minerals' like quartz, calcite, fluor spar, and barite, which carried the others in solution or accompanied them and which make the bulk of the vein filling. There are three principal areas of veins forming the mineral fields: Alston Moor – in which we include Weardale and Teesdale – Swaledale and Wensleydale, and Grassington and Greenhow. These fields have all had mining as a principal industry for some centuries, and the development and final decline of mining, though differing in detail in each field, has had the same overall effect and influence on the lives of the dales people.[6]

A very long period, to be measured in many scores of millions of years, followed the mineralization, during which the Pennines stood as an island in surrounding seas. Gradually subsidence recurred and the Pennines were submerged by the Cretaceous sea,* in which the Chalk seen now at Flamborough, the Downs, and much of the south-east, was formed right across the country, though now entirely eroded off the Pennines. The giant reptiles, dinosaurs, and the earliest birds, and even the first ancestors of the mammals evolved during what the geologist calls the Mesozoic period.† After the Cretaceous period of quiet, the Tertiary‡ followed,

* Approximately 70 to 80 million years ago.
† Extended from approximately 250 to 70 million years ago.
‡ Followed from about 70 to 1 million years ago.

43

during which there was a vast amount of earth movement, when the Alps, the Himalayas, Andes, and many other of our largest (because newest and least worn down) mountains were raised. In this country we had only the outer ripples of this movement, enough to fold up the strata in the Weald and south of the country and to lift the Pennines again into a range of mountains, probably still with a smooth cover of chalk. In the north-west the vast volcanoes of Mull, Ardnamurchan, Arran, Skye, and, farther away, the volcanoes which built up Iceland and other areas, were active. It was down the smooth dome of chalk strata over the Pennines that streams and rivers began to run, and by the time they had cut their courses right through the chalk they had been fixed with little reference to the different kinds of rock beneath. There have been few changes of any major significance in these courses in subsequent times.

It was during the few million years of the later Tertiary that the young rivers cut their valleys, increased their size towards maturity, and, along with all the other agents of weathering, carved out the scenery very much as we see it now. Close study of the Tertiary fossils shows that towards the end of the period the climate became steadily colder as the last great geological event of our story approached. This was the Great Ice Age of the Pleistocene period. In this last period snow accumulated on the mountains of north-west Europe until it formed glaciers, and these increased and coalesced into a vast ice sheet covering Scandinavia, with a subsidiary centre over Scotland. The fringes of this sheet reached south into France and east as far as the Ural mountains; to the west it reached the Atlantic across Scotland and included most of Ireland and England. In this country the cover of ice was thickest over Scotland, but in the north of England the thickest part was over the Lake District, completely covering the highest mountains around Scawfell. The surface declined radially from this centre, and across the Vale of Eden just failed to cover Cross Fell. Southward again it declined and in Yorkshire some of the mountains – Ingleborough, Penyghent, Buckden Pike and a few others – just had their summits clear above the ice while farther south most of the high moorlands of Yorkshire and Derbyshire were clear of ice though covered by snowfields.[7]

The chief effect of the ice cover was the smoothing off of the topography by the grinding of the moving ice, so that a vast accumulation of weathered rock and scree was removed, hill summits were rounded and valleys were slightly deepened and changed from a V-section to a U shape such as is seen to perfection in Littondale. The rock debris was carried by the ice to lower ground and as the ice melted it was dropped in various forms. The lower ground is generally covered by a sheet of 'boulder clay', a stiff clay which includes pebbles and boulders of many kinds

44

of rocks brought from the higher ground. This clay is sometimes only a few feet thick and is the source of much of our soil, but in places it may be tens of feet or even a hundred feet or more thick. It has in many places provided an excellent brick clay and is worked in the lower valleys for this purpose. In certain areas the rock debris is dropped and moulded into oval hillocks, 'drumlins', which are crowded together over large areas. In the Vale of Eden there are hundreds, and large areas of drumlins occur near Ribblehead and between Settle and Skipton. Drumlin country presents great difficulties for road and rail construction, demanding large numbers of cuttings and embankments if a fairly direct line is to be made.

Across all the valleys the melting glaciers deposited crescentic mounds of debris as 'terminal moraines' and these have left a major feature of the dales scenery. Behind these bars, often thirty or forty feet high and up to a mile wide, stretching completely from side to side of the valley, lakes were impounded, so that at the end of the Ice Age and until comparatively recent times the dales were indeed a lake district. There may be as many as six of these barriers up the length of a single valley, each holding up a lake which was two or three miles long. These lakes gradually filled up with gravels and silts brought in by the streams, and were partly drained by the river cutting down a deeper channel through the moraine, but most of them remained a watery swamp until the late medieval period and were a great factor in the settlement of the dales. The ends of the moraines provided good well-drained gravel sites on which many of our villages are located. The former lake areas are now wide stretches of alluvium, many of them subject to occasional flooding; they make good meadowland but because of the depth of water-logged silt they are avoided by roads and buildings, and nearly all roads cross the valleys over the moraines. On the fells there are many small tarns of glacial origin, filling hollows in the boulder clay or impounded by a moraine. Malham Tarn is still a lake, although it is being reduced by the infilling at the inlet stream and by the growth of Tarn Moss. It rests on one of the areas of Silurian slates revealed under the limestone, near the north Craven Fault which is only a few hundred yards away, and its waters are upheld by a moraine like a small dam. Semer Water is also glacial in origin, and the short course of the river Bain which connects it to the Ure is cut through glacial debris for much of its length.

By far the most important effects of the Ice Age have been those on the soils and climate, on which the plant and animal life has been and still is so dependent. In general the soils of the upland regions tend to be derived from the underlying rocks which during the Ice Age were swept bare of any rock debris, so that in areas of similar geology these soils show a remarkable unity over a large area. The

45

lowlands were in general covered by glacial drift and alluvium and show much greater variety. From the geological simple structure it has followed that there are only three broad groups of upland soils on the north Pennines – in Craven the Great Scar Limestone provides a very thin limy soil; in the moorland areas of the Yoredales the soil is more mixed, while in the high fells of the Millstone Grit there is a sandy, acid soil. These different soils, combined with the upland weather and conditions of rainfall and temperature, support their own pattern of vegetation.

Limestone is soluble in rainwater charged with carbon dioxide, and most of its weathering is by solution. Only a very small residue of insoluble material is left, often including a high proportion of iron salts. Soil is thin and in some places entirely absent, leaving the great expanses of limestone pavement which are such a feature of the Ingleborough and Malham areas. Wide extents of limestone 'pavements', with the joints weathered out in deep clefts or 'grikes' separating the 'clints', surround Ingleborough and make the platform from which the steep upper peak of Yoredale strata rises. Broad Scars on Malham Moor and Scar Close, Ingleborough, are splendid areas of clints where every stage in their development can be clearly seen (Plates 13, 17 and 28).

The high content of lime keeps a limestone soil light and crumbly, and this, together with the free drainage provided by the joints, keeps the limestone soil comparatively dry, even in periods of heavy rainfall. It is because of this that there is such a concentration of prehistoric sites to be seen on the limestone terraces; the areas were sought out for their dryness, and there has been almost no accumulation of soil to bury the structures built upon them.

The Millstone Grit carries a soil which is a complete contrast with that of the limestone. The coarse sandstones and the abundant shales together form a soil that is sandy, porous, and of a low fertility on the grits, and a heavy clay on the shales. Most of the Pennine summits are covered by a cap of grit which forms a sandy soil entirely deficient in calcium, so that organic matter can accumulate and drainage becomes impeded, the soil becomes wet and acid or 'sour', and usually has a thick cover of peat (Plate 26b). The clays derived from the shales are rarely found on the summits but are formed on the hill slopes, creep downwards, and form belts of heavy soil along the lower hill flank, a soil which can support thick woodland.

The Yoredales, with the limestones, shales, and sandstones, offer the most variation. The limestone terraces and scars form belts of limestone pasture (Plate 2a) while the shales and sandstones make a following zone of wetter, sourer soil, so that on a Yoredale hillside these soils follow one another in alternate strips. On the lower slopes the shale belt is often clothed with woodland, and where shales and sandstones become thicker towards the north the valleys are often well wooded, as in the lower South Tynedale, the valley of the Derwent, and many of the tributary streams of the Wear. The narrow tree belts followed by limestone scar and a terrace of good pasture are seen to perfection in Wensleydale and to a less degree in upper Wharfedale.

The soils derived from the glacial drift are varied, with clay, sand, and gravel in different proportions, but they are only found in patches on the higher ground and are mainly the soils of the valleys and the plains. They are thick and capable of deep cultivation and improvement so that almost everywhere they are covered now with an agricultural vegetation of fine meadow, and in the lower dales and in areas of less rainfall with arable crops. In the dales they generally provide the basis for the dairy farming fodder crops.

Except in the south-west the higher fells are covered with heather and peat moor which shows variations mainly related to altitude and wetness. Three plants are dominant on the moors – heather (*calluna*), bilberry (*vaccinum*), and cotton grass (*eriophorum*) – responding to different conditions and each forming a definite type of moor. Heather flourishes best on gritstone moors up to about 2,000 ft above sea level, in situations where for some part of the year the ground is fairly dry. The gritstone areas on the eastward slopes of the Pennines carry the finest heather moors, generally flanking the mid course of all the valleys.[8]

Above 2,000 ft the bilberry flourishes better than the heather, except where the ground is boggy. In the bogs, particularly on thick, poorly-drained peat, the cotton grass takes over, and its 'cotton-like' seed tuft whitens the whole moor in a manner comparable with the wonderful purple spread of the heather flower. In the dales an old name for the cotton grass flower is 'bog-baby-warning' and this name, learned in early childhood, is a lifelong reminder of the dangers of the ground on which it grows so well. If drainage is impeded sufficiently to hold stagnant water, then *sphagnum* moss will form vivid green and very dangerous patches of deep bog.

The peat of the high moorlands has a long history and preserves in itself a story which otherwise would not be known. Peat consists of plant material which has been preserved in anaerobic – that is, air-free – conditions, easiest found in a very wet bog. In time such vegetation is changed to a mass of humic material in which many plant structures are preserved, and in which, in particular, pollen and seeds blown from near-by woodland remain in remarkably fresh condition. The germ plasm of the pollen grains of course has gone, but the cases appear fresh and are perfectly recognizable. They can be got out of the peat by dissolving away the other humic materials, and can then be determined under the microscope. Tree pollens are abundant and it is at once clear that different layers of peat, from the oldest and deepest up to the newest, contain the pollen of a definite succession of trees, the proportions of which change in a constant order. The picture which the tree pollen preserves is that of a steady return of trees after the scouring of the Ice Age, in a definite order, and of the development of a forest cover far more complete than today. Modern research has made it possible to date these changes in the forests and to learn something about the climates they enjoyed.[9]

Peat from many parts of the Pennines has been examined in this way and the results confirm a general picture. In the later part of the glacial period a thin peat containing Arctic plants was formed on Cross Fell, and similar peats have been recognized in the Malham Tarn Moss and the silts which fill the Linton Mires glacial lake. The plant remains show that there was a cold climate with some cover of juniper scrub and crowberry heath on the hills, with a little pine and birch here and there. About 8300 B.C. the climate began to be progressively warmer and drier, and hazel formed thin woodlands which before 6000 B.C. had been invaded by pine. It was in these hazel-birch-pine thin forests and in the glacial lakes that Mesolithic man hunted and fished. The plants in the Malham Tarn peat suggest that the summers may have been a little warmer than at present, though winters were very cold and dry. After 6000 B.C. a wetter but warmer climate caused the pine woods to decline, and their place was taken by alder woods with some oak, hazel, and elm in drier parts. On the open ground the rock rose (*helianthemum*) flourished as it does today. Increased rainfall helped the formation of sphagnum bogs and peat. The wet period began to fall off about 3000 B.C. and the later Neolithic and Bronze Age people had a warm, dry period during which the forest cover of oak, alder, lime, and ash, with birch, spread over the fells to over 2,000 ft OD. The climate during the Bronze Age was better than that of today, and man could occupy many sites which now would be almost untenably cold and wet.

About 500 B.C. there was a rapid deterioration and the climate became much wetter and colder – the tree cover died off the higher fells and bogs and a peat cover quickly extended, leaving few desirable areas except the better-drained limestone terraces. This poor climate lasted through the Roman occupation, but the sixth to the ninth centuries A.D. were very dry, and it was in this period of much better conditions that the Anglo–Danish woodland clearances were made in the lower lands of the valleys and plains.

The cold, wet climatic periods were mainly responsible for extensive peat growth and for the eventual spread of 'blanket peat' over nearly all the fells above about 1,000 ft OD. The growth of the peat killed off much of the high forest which

5. *Malham Cove. A limestone cliff 250 feet high, with Malham Beck emerging at the base.*

... by ... from ... and the High Barns, Malham West Field.
A fine example of eighteenth-century stone walling following enclosure by agreement.

7 (below). *Ingleborough, seen across Ribblesdale from the limestone scars above Langcliffe.*

8a. *Mortham Tower near the junction of Greta and Tees.*
A pele tower with Elizabethan extensions.

8b. *Nappa Hall, Wensleydale. A pele tower house with hall and kitchen wing added in the sixteenth century. View across Wensleydale to Addlebrough.*

could not survive these poor conditions, and unregulated sheep grazing has completed the destruction even in the sheltered valley heads where otherwise there might have been useful woods. The climate at present is very closely related to the topography, with a great contrast to be found between the exposed fell tops and a deep, sheltered and south-facing valley head, although only a mile or two may separate them.

Rainfall is closely related to the altitude and is affected by the steady rise of the land surface from the east coast to the high summit ridges of the western edge of the Pennines. The prevailing wet winds are the south-westerlies, which give a precipitation of more than 60 inches a year over most of the Cross Fell range, parts of the Cross Fell edge receiving 70 inches, with 78 inches on Cross Fell itself. This heavy rainfall diminishes to the east, so that at Stanhope and Middleton-in-Teesdale and in the Tyne valley as far west as Haltwhistle it only averages 35 inches a year. In the Askrigg Block there is a similar pattern separated by a belt of lower rainfall across the Stainmore depression, where it rises only to a little over 50 inches near the Westmorland border. Baugh Fell and Risehill, the high ridge between Wensleydale and Wharfedale, and the Whernside–Ingleborough–Penyghent group, however, have over 80 inches a year, with the highest fall around Ribblehead. The 60-inch rainfall area extends eastward from this to Barden Fell and the moors around Greenhow and Nidderdale, with a belt of between 40 and 60 inches in the Wharfe valley and the low ground across upper Airedale to Settle.[10]

Combined with this high rainfall there is a considerable period of snow cover, which on the highest fells around Cross Fell may be between 100 and 140 days a year. The temperatures have an important bearing on the formation of peat and on the growing season for grass and other crops. The 'growing season' is taken as the period during which the daily mean temperature rises above 42° F, and the duration is reckoned between the first and last days with this temperature. At Moorhouse at the head of Teesdale, at 1,840 ft above sea level, the growing season is about 165 days, and on Dun Fell, 2,780 ft OD, only 128 days. Below about 700 ft OD, however, the valleys generally have more than 200 days from the beginning of April to the second week in November. These short growing seasons along with the heavy rainfall and frequent cloud cover make the grazing season on the higher fells a very short and poor one. The grass is late to grow, and in some places the earliest 'bite' is the young growth of the cotton grass, locally called 'moss crop'. In the higher sheep farms the meadows and home pastures have to be eaten late and opened early to get ewes in condition to bear and suckle their lambs, and the utmost advantage has to be taken of the short grazing season on the fells. As far as crops are concerned, there are few places above 1,000 ft OD where

49

oats can be ripened, and the making and winning of hay is difficult and chancy, the getting sometimes going on until far into September.

There is a broad zone at the lower edge of the heather moors which is best described as grass moor. This is clothed with grasses which vary very much with the relative wetness of the ground and its acidity. Where soils are highly leached and acid, the 'mat grass', *Nardus*, dominates with its very coarse rough clumps, but where some limestone is present and the acidity drops, then sheep's fescue, *Festuca ovina*, makes a much richer pasturage. Where flushes occur, that is seepages or springs of ground water making wettish patches, then *Molinia*, the purple moor-grass, is the dominant, and may have with it much of the rush, *Juncus*. The sweetest grasses are on the limestone terraces in the Yoredale limestone country, where a fine turf is made up basically of sheep's fescue and meadow grass and gives the vivid green colour to these stripes of hillside. In the valleys the meadows are often bent grass, *Agrostis*, improved with some rye-grass.

The wild flowers of the Pennines include many great rarities and there are in places some very special floras. In Teesdale and a few places in Craven there is a flora which may be a residual of the glacial period, which includes such arctic species as *Dryas octopetalla, Saxifraga oppositifolia*, and many others, with large areas of high fell moor filled with the cloudberry, *Rubus chamaemorus*, and with bear berry and others. In the lower valleys there are such floras as those of Wharfedale, with rare gentians, orchids, heleborines, etc., all of which are famous and carefully guarded. Only a very large volume could deal adequately with this aspect of the Pennines. In some places there are whole pastures of the mealy primrose, *Primula farinosa*, or of the globe flower, *Trollius europaeus*, and in others the various orchids make a brilliant mat of colour. The north Pennines offer a rich fare for the careful botanist, but the picker and collector of flowers and plants will find a very rough welcome and will be well watched.

The birds of the moorlands seem to be dominated by the artificially preserved grouse, but the sound that all fell walkers love is that of the curlew so abundant in this area, and on the lower slopes and fields of the valleys, the lapwing, or as we call it the pewit or tewit. On some of the tops the buzzard is to be seen, and on the moors of the Alston Block a few pairs of ravens and peregrine falcons still breed. Temperley has noted dunlins nesting on one or two remote mosses, and the merlin and golden plover both breed fairly widely.

From the deposits in caves and in the peats the bones of a wide range of animals have been obtained, including bear, wild boar, wild cattle, wolf, and deer, all of which are now extinct. The fox is probably the most evident by his raids on poultry and occasionally on lambs, but organized cub-hunts are now keeping this animal in check. Otter, badger, stoat, and weasel still inhabit the valleys, but apart from these most of the mammalian fauna is confined to mice, voles, and other smaller creatures, some of which are the prey of the larger birds, and some of which themselves prey on the grass roots and tussocks of the fells and on the seedlings in woods and plantations. The preservation of large areas of moorland as grouse moor, and of other parts as sheep walk, has greatly reduced the fauna during the last two centuries, and it is now no longer a common experience to catch a glimpse of either fox or badger, and the otter is far better known by his track than by his presence.

The twentieth century, however, has seen a great change in the prospects for keeping at least some of our fauna and flora by the formation of the Nature Conservancy. The threat to the countryside inherent in much of the development before the First World War had led in 1912 to the forming of the Society for the Promotion of Nature Reserves, and in 1926 the Council for the Preservation of Rural England widened the movement towards preservation. The Second World War made the problem very clear and in an early phase of it, in 1941, a conference on Nature Preservation in post-war Britain outlined problems which became the special study of a Wild Life Conservation Committee set up as part of the Hobhouse Committee on National Parks. These many studies and the constant pressure of naturalists and others interested in the countryside found expression in 1949 in two ways. A royal charter established the Nature Conservancy, and the National Parks Act added provisions for the Conservancy which it had not been possible to define in the charter. The first duty laid upon the Conservancy was to establish Nature Reserves and to designate areas or Sites of Special Scientific Interest (S S S I). On the larger Nature Reserves, many controlled experiments were to be carried through, aimed at a better understanding and preservation of natural environments and the study of afforestation and grazing in relation to wild areas.

There are many Nature Reserves, but in this book a description will be given of two contrasted ones within our area, Malham Tarn in Yorkshire, and the Moorhouse Reserve in Teesdale. With their help the loss of wild life and rare species has been prevented and a great body of experience gathered in the regeneration of moorland and control of many varieties of environment.

3

Prehistory

The great Ice Age was not a period with a monotonously unchanging arctic climate – there were times when the climate became warmer, the ice edge shrank back towards the centres in which the ice mainly accumulated, and large areas of country were left free of ice. These milder periods may have lasted some scores of thousands of years (the whole Pleistocene period within which the glaciations occurred lasted about a million years), long enough for some vegetation to creep back over the land and for animals to move into these areas from the south. The warmest of these so-called 'inter-glacial' periods may have had a climate a little warmer than ours today, while other periods had conditions more like those of the present-day tundras of Siberia. There is some very interesting evidence of all this in the north Pennines, derived from the 'cave earths', the debris filling some of the caves in the limestones, and from the river gravels.

Victoria Cave near Settle is the most famous of such localities. The cave, now excavated, is a large opening in the face of the high limestone cliff of Langcliffe Scar. There is a very large main chamber with a smaller chamber opening off from one side of it. When the cave was discovered on Queen Victoria's coronation day (hence the name) it was nearly filled with clay and rock debris. A sequence of different layers was found in the filling material, and these layers contained materials of very different ages. In the lowest layers of the clay and debris were found bones of animals we would now associate with much warmer countries – lion, hippopotamus, rhinoceros, hyaena, elephant – and these may even belong to the period before the Ice Age, though more likely they are the remains of animals roaming here during the warmest interglacial. Above a thickness of debris there was another layer which contained the bones of animals which flourished in a much colder climate – the woolly rhinoceros adapted for severe arctic conditions, cave bear, and others which may have inhabited the caves in the colder spell as the ice returned and again covered the whole country as far south as the Thames. There is still another different group of animal remains in material above another thickness of rock debris which accumulated during the later part of the glaciation. These bones are the remains of a more familiar northern group of animals, still known in northern latitudes – reindeer, arctic fox and hare, bison, brown bear, red deer, wolf, fox, and smaller mammals. It is this group of animals which still inhabited the area when the first men came northward on to the Pennines.

Round about eight thousand years ago men began to wander into this part of the country, hunting and fishing. They belonged to the end of the Old Stone Age (Palaeolithic) and preceded the New Stone Age (Neolithic), so it is logical to call them the Mesolithic or intermediate Stone Age folk. The first small groups of these people used bone and flint for most of their weapons and tools, and were great fishers. A tool of which very many specimens have been found, and which is always characteristic of their culture, is the harpoon, and one of these was found in Victoria Cave, along with some pebbles painted with ochre in primitive patterns. Other bone harpoons have been found in Attermire and Kinsey caves near Settle, and at Calf Hole Cave, Skyrethorns, only seven miles away (SD 964646), a tool like a chisel, made by setting part of a boar's tusk into a handle of reindeer horn, belongs to the same people. They fished in the many glacial tarns and lakes left by the Ice Age, and used the caves for shelter. They are spoken of as the Azilian people, taking their name from the caves at Mas d'Azil in France, where their remains were first studied.[1]

As the climate improved and the hills were clothed by hazel, pine, and birch woodland, another group of people, more hunters than fishers, came from the Continent, this time from the Belgian coastlands, and spread over most of the Pennines. They did not live here permanently but had camping places at lower levels on the warmer lowlands. One of their habitation sites has been excavated at Star Carr, 4¾ miles south of Scarborough, and here many tools of bone, harpoons, and some flint implements were found. On the Pennines the evidence of their wanderings is seen in the vast number of flint implements which are scattered widely over the higher ground above about 1,000 ft OD. The best-worked flints are mostly very small, well shaped, often less than an inch long, and because of this they were called, when first found, 'pygmy' flints. It must not be thought, however, that the people who made and used them were any less than normal height. Many of the flints are points which could have been used to tip light arrows, probably for use with a bow, and many are fine harpoon barbs; small

53

knives are also fairly common. Everything suggests that the people who used these flints were nomadic hunters and fishers, spreading over a selected area until the fish and game were becoming scarce. They would then, for many seasons, use another area, so that their remains are scattered in separated patches along the edge of the moorlands.[2] They were seasonal visitors, and in winter would retreat to their distant habitation sites. Their flints are found even as high as the upper slopes of Cross Fell and over all the north Pennines. At a few localities their flints are found along with the horn cores of wild cattle (*Bos taurus primigenius*, Boj., and *Bos taurus longifrons*, Owen.) which they may have hunted.

With a further improvement of the climate another group of people came into the area, the Neolithic. Besides flint these newcomers used polished hardstone for some of their tools, and they introduced what was in fact a revolution in the way of living. It was they who first made pottery, cultivated some of the wild grains, and domesticated animals for their use. On the Pennines they soon formed a peasant population which mingled with the remnants of the Mesolithic folk. This mingling changed the Mesolithic folk into a permanent part of the population of the area, and the mingling of the two stocks formed a very strong 'native' population capable of absorbing many later invaders, though in some cases accepting them as overlords.

Some of the Neolithic folk became traders; they quarried the fine-grained volcanic rock of the Langdale Pikes in the Lake District, roughed out axes from it and then traded these 'roughs' over much of the north of England. Either the people who bartered for them, or an intermediary 'middle man', finished the axe by grinding and polishing to a sharp edge and a very regular shape, and produced the axes or adzes with which some of the thinner woodland was cleared. Axes of flint were still used, and occasionally given a sharp edge by grinding, but they were gradually replaced by those of polished stone. The women dug in the cleared areas of woodland glades, and grew wild grasses and seeds, improving the stock empirically, and gradually achieving a primitive agriculture. The life of these communities must have been well based on a mixture of hunting, pastoral farming, and simple agriculture.

We can glean something of the conditions of their life from the material excavated in Elbolton Cave, Wharfedale (SD 009613), many years ago, and now to be seen in the Craven Museum, Skipton.[3] Among other deposits, both newer and older, there was an old level in the cave earths at which hearths with abundant charcoal occurred. These were towards the centre of the chamber, and around them were many fragments of coarse pottery, and the bones of domesticated animals, sheep, cattle, goats, and others such as otter and beaver. There were needles made of bone which were strong enough to sew skins, a few other tools of bone, and a bone whistle made from the canine tooth of a bear. The pottery was the remains of large cooking vessels, and of the kind called, from its type area, Peterborough ware. It is very thick, coarse, and hand-moulded, and was fired by placing a fire inside it. It was used, not on the fire, but by standing near the fire, and dropping into its contents smallish pebbles made red hot in the fire. These soon cracked with use and were rejected, and now are found in numbers as 'pot-boilers'. We can picture the women of the family who lived here, making pots, sewing skins for covering, and cooking meat and grain. They also probably made the bone tools. The whistle may have been for calling and controlling the dogs of which there is plenty of evidence. When the Neolithic folk had not got a handy cave for shelter, they may have used skin tents, sheltered within 'camps' or earthworks like the hill-top camps of the south. In the north, however, this kind of settlement is almost un-known.

Apart from the wide scatter of their axes, the commonest evidence of early man is the abundance of flint implements. They made beautiful arrow tips in the shape of a leaf or a diamond, often $1\frac{1}{2}$ or more inches long, very thin with flaking on both sides, and very sharp. They used scrapers for cleaning skins, knives, and crude spears. Their tools and implements are generally large and may even tend to be clumsy, except for the arrow points. There are not many Neolithic structures in the Pennine area, but towards the end of Neolithic time there were two develop-ments which were of importance and which have provided a few monuments. The dead were often buried in groups in burial mounds which enclosed several cham-bers and so are called chambered tombs, or, in some modifications, passage graves. In a long mound several chambers were built of stone which might be connected by a passage, and burials were made in each chamber. On the eastern foot of Penyghent, very near the road from Stainforth to Halton Gill, and 600 yards from Penyghent House to the south-west (SD 857733), lies the Giant's Grave. This is a large gravel mound in which some stones set on edge can still be seen at a few places. These are the remains of some of the burial chambers, but most of the larger stones have been dug out and carried away for gateposts and other farm uses. The mound is 54 ft by 50 ft and at the south end there is a small 'fore-court' giving the whole the appearance of a passage grave. This must have been an important burial site for the late Neolithic community of a large area.[4]

A more important type of monument is that which is called, for convenience, a 'henge', of which Stonehenge is a late and complex example. The henges were sacred enclosures, circular and varying in size up to huge ones of 1,500 ft or more in diameter. They have a circular flat area or platform, surrounded by a big ditch

55

with a bank outside it; the ditch is incomplete at one or more places, making a causeway across to the inner part. Excavation proves, as Stonehenge demonstrates, that the inner platform carried a circle of standing stones or of wooden posts, or more than one circle, forming a fairly open structure. It is thought that they were used for ceremonies of fertility rites or other sacred functions, and that possibly the ditch was made to define the sacred area, while the ordinary folk assembled to see the ceremonies could stand on the bank and so overlook the whole central area.

The henges are not very numerous and the biggest group in the country is near Ripon, where there are six within seven miles.[5] The henges were continued in use by the earliest Bronze Age people. There are two fine but small henges in the Pennine dales of which we are writing, one at Eamont Bridge near Penrith, and a few also in Derbyshire. At Grassington in Wharfedale there is a henge on the east side of the Yarnbury road, one mile north-north-west of Grassington (SE 015654). It is about 100 ft in diameter, crest to crest of the bank, and in the inner part about 70 ft in diameter. In Wensleydale there is another henge, $1\frac{1}{2}$ miles south-west of Aysgarth (SD 982873); this is slightly oval, the greatest diameter being 195 ft. They each have the usual bank with a ditch inside it, and one causeway. The date of these two monuments is probably within the two centuries 2000–1800 B.C.

About 1800 B.C. bands of warriors from the mouth of the Rhine came to this country and imposed themselves and their culture on the peasants. They brought a finer pottery, the custom of single burial in round barrows, and, a little later, the use of metal tools and weapons. Their chiefs and leaders had stone axes perforated for a shaft like a hammer, and judging from the size and weight of some of them these bigger ones must have been carried more for some ceremonial significance than for use. One feature associated with the opening of this new period, the Bronze Age, is the abundance of stone circles, particularly in the west and the highland part of Britain. These were introduced by another stream of related folk, who came from the Iberian coasts by Ireland and penetrated from the west coast. The general form of the circle is a bank of gravel on which are set a number of upright stones. Like the henges, the larger stone circles were probably places of some sacred or community significance. However, many of the barrows contain a circle of smaller stones, forming a 'kerb', and when the gravel of the barrow has disappeared the kerb may be left as a small 'circle', better distinguished as a 'burial circle', which is difficult to distinguish from an original free-standing monument. There is a fine example of a smaller circle near the bank of the Wharfe at Yockenthwaite (SD 900794): it is 25 ft in diameter, built with twenty stones set almost edge to edge, and to the north-west there are four more stones on a concentric circle. A small mound at the centre may indicate a burial. A much depleted circle at Bordley is marked on all the maps under its old and romantic name of 'Druid's Altar'; it has been robbed of all but three large stones which still stand prominently on the 50-ft-diameter bank. There are other stone circles on Grassington Moor, Hebden Moor, and at Fancarl, the latter easily reached from the road between Hebden and Greenhow, at its highest point on Fancarl, 200 yards north of the road and at SE 065632. The largest circle in the dales is that on Oxclose Pasture, under Nab End near Carperby in Wensleydale. It is not quite a true circle but is 92 ft by 78 ft, and had at least sixteen stones, of which nearly all are still there but fallen inward from the crest of the bank. There is another smaller circle not far away at Redmire, but this is not easy to find. Many stone circles have been destroyed, as their large stones make useful gateposts or throughs for dry walling. There was formerly a large stone circle near Eggleston in Teesdale and this was described a century ago as 'a uniform circle of rough stones, with an inward trench, and in the centre a cairn; much of the material has been taken away to mend the roads'. There are many true stone circles in the Vale of Eden and around the Lake District but none on the hills around Weardale and the northern dales. This emphasizes their Western origin, coming to the north of England by the Irish Sea coast and spreading across to the east by way of Stainmore and the Aire Gap.[6]

Besides the stone circles there are only a few burial mounds of the early Bronze Age to be seen on the ground, and the contents were generally more exciting than the low mounds which are now all that there remains to be seen. Near Scale House, Rilston, Yorkshire (SD 971568), a burial at the centre of such a mound was made in a split and hollowed length of an oak log. The body had been wrapped in a woollen cloak or shroud, and a few fragments of this (now in the Craven Museum, Skipton) prove to be a truly woven woollen cloth. In a barrow at Kirkhaugh, South Tyne, two miles north of Alston (NY 704494), there was a fine boat-shaped ear-ring of gold; in areas off the Pennines beautifully made jet necklaces and ornaments, with similar burials, fill out our picture of a strikingly dressed and wealthy aristocracy. At Seaty Hill, Malham (SD 907654), a burial of this age poses a puzzle. The top of a low hill has been shaped to a circular platform surrounded by a bank and ditch, and at the centre of the structure, cut into the material of the hill, there are two conical pits about 4 ft 6 in. deep. In one of them was seated a skeleton, his pit impinging on the other so that there was a space they had in common. The skeleton appeared to be staring through this space at a beautifully built cairn of limestone boulders in the other pit. Nothing was buried either with the skeleton or under the cairn. The two pits were covered by a low mound and that in turn by the very broad, flat mound. Such imposing burials are rare and the great mass of the population were the poor peasants mainly of Neolithic stock, living a hard life with few personal possessions, and not remembered by a marked burial place.[7]

Flint was still widely used to make barbed and tanged arrow points, scrapers, and knives, and some rather well-shaped spear-heads. Bronze was used increasingly for axes, hoes, and spears, but can never have been abundant among the peasants. In the later Bronze Age, itinerant bronze-smiths moved about the country, setting up their temporary foundry, melting up old bronze and new stock, and casting a few tools from moulds which they carried with them.

In 1859 a discovery was made at Heathery Burn Cave, Stanhope, County Durham, which threw some light on one of the wealthier families of the late Bronze Age. In a cave in the limestone (NY 989415) there was evidence of a fairly long occupation. The bones of several people, fragments of cooking pots, bones of beef, mutton, and game, axes, spears, and ornaments were there, along with a mould and tongs of use in making bronze axes. There was a fine bronze bucket, and a gold ring and bracelet. It seems almost certain that these could only belong to the family of an exiled person of wealth and importance, possibly a chief. Some of the articles were part of a four-wheeled, horse-drawn cart. It is likely that this family fled from some disturbance, it may even be from the invasion by early Iron Age warriors, and found a refuge in what was then an unoccupied piece of country. The chief, his followers, and his bronze founder seem to have perished in a great flood which scattered their remains and their goods in the gravels which covered the cave floor.[8]

After about 1000 B.C. the climate became wetter and cooler and settled farms began to be made, of which a few can still be seen. Perhaps the clearest is at Dewbottoms on the eastern side of Cowside Beck, on the footpath, Monks' Road, from Arncliffe to Middle House on Malham Moor (SD 912692). Five small fields, adjoining one another, are marked out by boundary walls of heavy gravel and turf banks, with many large stones on them. These are probably the foundations for a fence or palisade of light timber. Built in among these banks, and part of them, there are four circular huts and two rectangular ones. One circular hut, larger than the others, may have been the house of the head man of the family group. Near by among the limestone scars there are several rough, strong enclosures which could serve as sheep and cattle pounds, and all around is a wide area of limestone pasture. Throughout the limestone area of Craven there are great numbers of small, irregular fields with a single hut foundation in or near them, which may be of late

Bronze Age extending into the Iron Age. Farther north, beyond Wensleydale, these settlements are very rare, and it seems that the thinner limestones of the northern parts did not provide attractive country.

From these remains and the material to be seen in the various museums, a picture emerges of a Bronze Age community of peasant farmers, dominantly pastoral, but with enough cultivated plots to provide some form of bread and oatmeal porridge. Axes of bronze were rather precious tools and flint and stone were still the materials in common use. A few aristocratic leaders wore woollen clothing, had gold and jet ornaments, and practised elaborate burial ceremonies. They probably included a priesthood who were responsible for conducting fertility rites and setting the seasons. The Durham Pennines were very thinly populated in this period, the limestone soils of Craven and south Westmorland being the main area of settlement.

One of the few ancient legends of the Pennines has its origin in an area in which an Iron Age community continued to occupy a site on which Bronze Age people had lived. This was on the side of Semer Water in Wensleydale. During the centuries the water level had risen, due to the silting up of the outflow from the lake, and in 1937 it was decided to lower the level and to recover a strip of land round the margins. Later, at one place in the recovered area, a timber structure was found which had clearly been a small platform set on piles in the edge of the lake. Bones of red deer, and rings and fragments of iron proved it to have been an Iron Age habitation. Near the site a fine bronze spear-head and some barbed and tanged arrow points of flint proved that Bronze Age folk had lived there as well. Since then some Neolithic flint arrow points and a grain rubber have been picked up on the site, making its story one of nearly continuous occupation for a thousand years or more. We do not know when this, and possibly other pile dwellings which may be discovered, were abandoned due to the rising of the level of the lake, but legend suggests a catastrophic flood which may have been caused by a cloudburst, or, more likely, a landslide which blocked the exit of the lake. Whatever the original legend it was Christianized, and in the outlines of its present form may have been told by the monastic communities as a moral tale of warning.

At the time of the mid-winter solstice, says the story, the Druid priests of the native town which stood then where Semer Water now is, were holding their heathen ceremonies, the weather then being tempestuous. An angel disguised as an old and poor traveller came through the storm to tell them of the Christian message. His words were rejected as blasphemy against the heathen gods, and he was hounded out of the town. Travelling on in sorrow he came to a shepherd's hut where in compassion he was given shelter, food and a bed. The shepherd and his wife were moved by his stories of Christianity and were converted. In the morning, standing near the hovel on the fell side, and overlooking the whole of the town which had rejected him, the old visitor stretched out his arms and uttered his condemnation. 'Oh city, thou art fair to look upon, but thou art the habitation of hard, unfeeling and uncharitable men', and much more in the same manner. He concluded with the rhyme still known to all and taught to every child in the dale:

> Semerwater rise; Semerwater sink:
> And swallow all the town, save this lile house
> Where they gave me meat and drink.

As they watched there was a rushing of waters and the hollow was filled, drowning for ever the town which had rejected the angel's message. The lack of Christian compassion in the doom pronounced by the angel seems to have troubled no one. On still evenings people rowing about the lake believe that they can catch glimpses of towers and roofs deep in the water, and on rare occasions they can hear faintly the tolling of the bells in the drowned city. The anomalies, such as the lack of compassion and the tolling of bells in a heathen city, support this as a very ancient story embodied in the dim and timeless folk memory. The occasion was probably the abandonment of the pile dwellings, sometime during the Iron Age. The Christian tradition could have been added after the Roman Christianization of the north.

The simple peasant life, with the small hoe-cultivated plots of ground and dwellings which Strabo described as 'small huts that are merely temporary structures', was the normal life on the Pennines until the arrival of Continental immigrants bringing the La Tène cultures with them. This new group of people reached the coast in the east and south about the third century B.C., and by the latter part of the first century B.C. a few of them had reached the Pennines at a few points. They were Celtic in language and culture, skilled users of horse-drawn chariots and artistic workers in metal. They were a military caste and carried iron swords in elaborate sheaths. Swords of this kind and age have been found at Flasby near Skipton (now in the Craven Museum, Skipton), at Clotherholme near Ripon, in Cotterdale, Wensleydale, and at Toft Hill, Stanwick, near Richmond, Yorkshire, N.R. At Stanwick, a prominent point, Toft Hill (NZ 185116), had been converted into a defensive hill fort, and one of the leaders of the fort builders was buried there, his body accompanied by his chariot. Many ornaments of bronze, some with stylized horse-head motifs, buried with him, were from the harness and chariot trappings. Another hill fort was made at Almondbury near Huddersfield, from which a long line of princes ruled a confederacy of the north Pennine population which the invaders had subdued into a tribal group which we call the Brigantes. This confederacy formed a minor kingdom stretching from the Calder to the Tyne and probably farther north, and in some places extending to the west coast. The use of iron gradually spread among the Brigantes, who became by culture a true Iron Age people drawn from the mingled late Bronze Age 'native' stock. By the first century A.D. they had, according to Ptolemy, nine 'towns' or principal settlements which included among them those which later became Binchester, Catterick, Aldborough, Ilkley, and York. The ancient names of these towns were Vinnovium, Caturactonium, Isurium, Olicana, and Eboracum.[9]

The climate had become cold and wet, on an average worse than our present climate, and the bulk of the population outside these 'towns' occupied the better drained limestone pastures well above the swampy and wooded lowlands. In the Pennines north of Stainmore Iron Age settlements are very rare, the limestones being too thin to form the great terraces and extents of limestone pasture which are such a prominent feature of Yorkshire and the southern part of Westmorland.

On these limestone areas the traces of the Iron Age population are abundant, mainly in the form of small groups of irregular fields and of hut circles, but with a few 'villages' of Romano–British age (Plate 23). A good area in which to see these remains is between Settle and Grassington, in Yorkshire, where Malham Moor has many groups of huts and enclosures which have been stripped of turf and overgrowth, and can be seen with ease. In upper Wharfedale nearly every terrace has a number of huts and enclosures, the clearest being those on Lea Green and High Close, immediately north of Grassington (between SE 003648 and SE 004660). The fields there are rectangular, with a few huts scattered among them, and cover more than 300 acres. Quarter of a mile away at the north end of Lea Green (SE 995662) there is a group of huts within a surrounding wall, large enough to be the village from which these fields were worked. Excavation has provided material which dates from the second to the opening of the fifth centuries.[10] Similar areas of fields and huts are to be seen in Wensleydale near Woodhall (SD 982904) and on Greenber Edge south of Addlebrough (SD 952870), where they are built of rough sandstone, irregular in outline but well preserved, stretching in a complex group for half a mile along the hillside. Field groups with huts are also found in Swaledale and Ribblesdale. In south Westmorland the limestone areas of Ravenstonedale and Ewe Close have many similar settlements. The walls of fields and huts are generally rough dry-stone structures or strong gravel banks with many large stones, on which timber fences and walls could be based. In a few of the best-preserved huts which have been excavated, post holes

61

in the bank or wall show where short, stiff posts were set up to form or carry the roof. Little now remains in most of the huts, but occasionally fragments of bone, pot, or iron give us a glimpse of the life the people lived as pastoral farmers and hunters, with sufficient technical skill to spin wool and to weave woollen cloth. Although this is called the 'iron age' iron was still expensive and by no means common, bone and even flint still being used for a great many everyday tools.

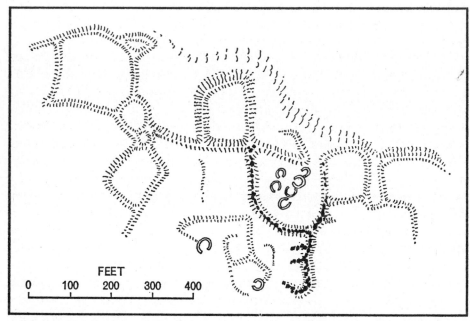

Diagram 4 *Small Iron Age farm settlement of huts and fields in Upper Wharfedale.*

Before the later settlements can be properly understood the Roman occupation of the Pennines must be described, as the two are intimately connected in the Romano–British story. During the first century A.D. when the Romans, having subdued the south of England, moved against Wales and the north, they came in contact with the tribes of the Welsh and the Brigantes, both of whom had made horses and cattle important in their way of life. Piggott could speak of these tribes as 'the Celtic cow-boys and shepherds, foot-loose and unpredictable, moving with their animals over rough pasture and moorlands, (who) could never adopt the Roman way of life in the manner of the settled farmers of the South'. The many small fields with only a single hut, or occasionally just two, are often near more massively walled enclosures, oval or irregular, which have probably been cattle pounds; narrow gullies between limestone cliffs are often crossed by massive rough boulder walls which could have served to enclose horses or cattle.

In the Roman campaign in Britain, Governor Ostorius Scapula in A.D. 47–48 moved troops towards Chester to drive a wedge between the Welsh tribes and the Brigantes of the Pennines. Three years later the native leader Caratacus fled to Brigantia, but its Queen Cartimandua surrendered him to the Romans. Her husband, Venutius, a native Brigantian leader, quarrelled over Cartimandua's increasing dependence on Roman protection, and organized a powerful resistance movement. Cartimandua seized his brothers and relations, and divorced him. For ten years the Romans helped her to suppress the guerrilla attacks of the Brigantes. As these increased she accepted Roman protection in the Romanized town of Aldborough near Boroughbridge, and Venutius drew the Brigantes together in the western dales.

The summit of Ingleborough is protected by a massive encircling wall, within which the foundations of many circular huts can still be seen. For a time this hill-fort summit was the capital of the Venutian revolt. As the revolt grew stronger the Brigantian families gathered around Ingleborough–a development which accounts for the abundance of roughly constructed and probably temporary hut and enclosure foundations on all parts of the limestone area of west Craven.

In the following decade it became clear that the Romans would attack Brigantia, following one of their common tactics to divide it. There was an ancient trade way across Stainmore from the Lake District, and a road from York could use this way into the Vale of Eden and forward to Carlisle. A road from York by Catterick could also drive up the eastern side of the Pennines, towards Gateshead. In A.D. 69 Venutius called in the help of other tribesmen, even some from Scotland, to help in the construction of great defences at Stanwick, a position within the junction of the Stainmore and eastern road.[11] At Toft Hill (NZ 185116) there is a 17-acre site surrounded by a bank and ditch, the bank rising up to 24 ft above the ditch bottom. Around this a second ditch and bank enclosed 130 acres and in A.D. 72 a further 600 acres were defended by a high bank and a ditch 33 ft wide and 15 ft deep. Such a vast work needed an army of labourers, and Brigantes from all the dales must have contributed men and food, grain, and animals. Much of the population may have been moved into temporary camps in the dales south-west of Stanwick – an area in which there are large numbers of small promontory earthworks and rough fields and huts. As part of the works to prevent or delay attack from the south, the great rock-cut Ta Dyke at the head of Scale Park (SD 985756) would safeguard the easiest way over from Wharfedale. The road from

63

Kettlewell into Coverdale cuts through the Ta Dyke at its mid point, on the very edge of the summit. On the limestone hill of Gregory in Grass Wood near Grassington (SD 989653), overlooking the entry of the through valley between Airedale and Wharfedale, a massive stone fort was built, which could act both as a forward post against any approach via Wharfedale and as a refuge for the local population. The many entrenchments across Swaledale around Fremmington and Grinton are probably part of this plan, either to protect Stanwick against a rear attack or to safeguard a line of retreat.

In A.D. 74 the Romans attacked and Venutius was defeated. Many of his followers were able to retreat into the dales but some of the captured Brigantes were doomed to work as slaves in the lead mines of Greenhow near Pateley and Hurst in Swaledale. The most interesting evidence of this Roman mining is provided by pigs of smelted lead which carry the name of a Roman emperor. In 1735 two such pigs of lead were found near the track down Hayshaw Bank between Greenhow Hill and the ford over the Nidd, roughly on the line of a road to Aldborough, the town which the Romans made into Isur-Bragantium, the capital of the conquered Brigantia. On the base of each pig was the cast-on inscription IMP.CAES.DOMITIANO.AVG.COS.VII. and on one side BRIG and EX ARG. These can be translated as showing that the lead was from the silver mines of Brigantia, cast in the seventh consulship of Domitian, A.D. 81 or 82. Another pig of Trajan date (97–117) was found just west of Greenhow, buried among the stones of the moor, and one found in Swaledale was of the reign of Hadrian (117–138). From the places where they were discovered it seems probable that the lead had been stolen by the natives or the carriers, then hidden, to be collected on some later occasion.[12]

The great earthworks at Stanwick form one of the most important and impressive monuments in the North Pennines and should be visited as the site of one of the decisive events of our early history. The area is in the care of the Ministry of Works and access is obtained from the village of Fawcett, eight miles north of Richmond.

In A.D. 78, when he became Governor of Britain, Agricola began a large-scale plan to control the Brigantes by building roads from York and Chester to the Tyne and Solway, using a labour force of prisoners and conscripted natives. Between these western and eastern roads lay much of surviving Brigantia, and this was divided by a permanent road over Stainmore on the line of the one Petillius had laid out. On the north and south there were roads along the north flank of the Tyne valley, and across the Pennines from Manchester through Castleshaw and Slack. Another cross-road was built from York to Ribchester by Skipton with

Centre fields in the valley bottom.

10a *The donkey which used to bring down the budgets of milk from pastures near Castle Bolton.*

10b (left). *Old Dales knitter, Appersett, Upper Wensleydale.*

11 (right). *Blanchland, Northumberlan[d] The nearer part of the village is built [on] the foundations of the conventual buildin[gs] The chancel and north transept of t[he] priory church now form the parish chur[ch] the priory was Premonstratensian.*

12. *Lynchets in Thorpe West field, Wharfedale. Note that some run across the contours, and that all are arranged in many distinct groups.*

forts at Ilkley and Elslack, and a cross-road from Aldborough by Ilkley to Manchester. It is along these cross-roads that some of the best preserved portions are
still to be seen. There was an important road from Ribchester on the Ribble, north
across Bowland by the Hodder valley, west of Slaidburn, and over the fells into
the Wenning valley. From here it continues by the Lune valley through Casterton
(SD 628798) and by the east side of the valley to the Rawthey junction. Then the
road goes on to the west flank of the Howgill Fells to the fort of Low Barrow
(609012). From there it continues north to Old Penrith in the Vale of Eden and
then to Carlisle.

The north-east was controlled by a road from York and Catterick which crossed
the Tees at Pierce Bridge and at Binchester on the Wear, to continue by Ebchester
(NZ 103556) to Corbridge on Tyne. When the Roman Wall was built early in the
second century the forts at Corbridge, Ebchester, and Binchester were given up
and a new one built at Lanchester (NZ 159469), roughly half-way between Pierce
Bridge and the Wall. The road over Stainmore had forts at Greta Bridge (NZ
084132) and Bowes (NY 992134), then at Brough in the head of the Vale of Eden,
forward by Kirkby Thore to join the western road at Brougham. A cross-road
which was much later used as a drove road, and is still a fine green road for much
of its length, is that which was made over the Cross Fell range from Kirkby Thore.
Crossing the summit of the range at 2,250 ft above sea level, the road goes down
the north-west side of the Black Burn valley to the fort of Whitley Castle (NY
695488) (Plate 14) down the South Tyne valley to join the Wall at Carvoran. With
the completion of this road system the 'pax Romana' began its uneasy existence.
The natives were to keep their own peace within the framework of these roads
and be supervised by 'police forts'. They were to refrain from forays, pay agreed
taxation in money or in kind, and provide a quota of army recruits and of
labourers.[13]

A period of relative prosperity followed, and by the end of the first century
bronze working was well established at Brough and at Kirkby Thore, and somewhere in the Settle district. Some of the Brigantes, possibly the bronze workers,
were inhabiting caves in the Settle area, from which fine examples of enamelled
bronze brooches and other articles have been excavated. Most typical of the
'native' skill are the 'dragonesque' brooches and carved bone. These and some of
the plate or disc brooches are enamelled in colours. Other 'trumpet' brooches
occur with them, mostly of the type which Collingwood recognized as being
Romano–British and belonging to the first quarter of the second century. Articles
of bone are very numerous and include a group of 'spoons', or spoon-shaped
fibulae (dress fasteners), which are often elaborately carved and which all have

perforated 'bowls'. These various dress fastenings support the evidence of the weavers' combs, loom weights, and spindle whorls, that there was a Romano–British skill in cloth-making.

The first phase of the *pax Romana* was broken off by widespread uprising around A.D. 155 all over the north and down into Derbyshire. Many of the forts were destroyed, and one of the tasks of the next few years was the rebuilding of the more important ones, such as Ilkley, Bainbridge, Melandra and Brough in Derbyshire, and many others. The old conditions were resumed, with the Brigantes still occupying the country and with tolerated police forces of Romans at the forts. These soldiers had time to enjoy country sports, the Pennine moorlands providing fine hunting grounds.

During 1945 two shrines were found on the side of a small stream, East Black Sike, just above its junction with the Ellerbeck. This is on the wild Scargill Moor about two miles south of the Bowes fort, at NY 998105. One shrine is a small rectangular building 12 ft 8 in. by 6 ft 3 in. inside, with walls 2 ft thick built of partly-dressed grit stones, and still standing in part to more than 3 ft high. The wall towards the stream has been destroyed by erosion. The floor was flagged and the burnt remains of a thatched roof covered it. The second shrine was of similar structure but was circular, 17 ft in diameter. At the middle of the back wall of each was an altar, and in the circular shrine the bases and fragments of six other altars, with some coins and pottery. The altar in the rectangular shrine has an inscription

VINOTONO
SILVANO.IVI
SECUNDVS
COH.I.THRAC.
V.S.L.L.M.

and this can be translated 'To Vinotonus Silvius Julius Secundus Centurion of the First Cohort of Thracians gladly and willingly fulfilled his vow'. The inscription on the altar of the circular shrine can be read 'To the God Vinotonus, Lucius Caesius Frontinu prefect of the First Cohort of Thracians from Parma, gladly, willingly, and deservedly fulfilled his vow'.

Silvanus was the god of the wild uncultivated land and of the wild creatures in it. At Scargill, the first altar identifies him with Vinotonus, the god of stream and place. The altars belong to the early part of the third century and the pottery suggests that the shrines were used intermittently into the fourth century, when the Roman officials felt like thanking the gods for a successful hunt.[14]

66

In the wild moorlands of Bollihope, tributary to the Wear valley, an altar was erected to Silvanus Invictus by Gaius Tetius Veturius Micanus, prefect of the Sebosian cavalry regiment, who gave thanks 'after catching a lovely boar which previous hunters had hunted in vain'. In Weardale at Eastgate (the gate-house of the Bishop of Durham's hunting park some centuries later), Aurelius Quirinus, a prefect of the first cohort of Ligonians, and commandant at Lanchester, erected an altar to Silvanus between A.D. 234 and 244. It may well be that natives found employment or were conscripted into the hunt, driving, carrying, tending horses, and acting as general followers, or possibly by their local knowledge and skill contributing to the success of the hunt.

At the end of the third century a unit of cavalry, mainly time-expired men from Suebia, was stationed at Lanchester, and it was probable that they continued to enjoy the hunting and sport of the northern moors. It was during this time that many of the larger 'camps', hutments, and field systems came into use by the native population, and the miscalled 'villages' such as that on Lea Green, Grassington (SE 003650), and comparable settlements around Selside and Souther-scale on Ingleborough, and in other dales, were developed by several generations of peasant farmers.

Agriculture spread, and fields were cleared on much of the limestone upland terrace in the Yorkshire dales. Pottery from east Yorkshire kilns and some few Roman articles were traded for hides and meat, and the fourth century saw also a growth of civilian settlement near the forts. Bainbridge and Ilkley, for instance, have civilian settlements outside their walls, and markets may have been held in these places from which many Roman goods could find their way into the upland settlements. The wealthier Romanized native could go into towns like Isur-Brigantia at Aldborough, or could settle in a villa farm like those at Gargrave, and Middleham, or Old Durham farther north. This period of peaceful contact between the Romans and the natives is generally known as the 'Romano-British'.

During the fourth century some of the Roman forts which had been deserted were reoccupied by the Roman army. In A.D. 367–9 the Pictish raids from the north and the Saxon pirates on the east coast were the prelude to the final scenes. Brigantia was wasted by the Picts. On the coast a system of signal stations was set up to give warning of raiders, and others were built across Stainmore. In A.D. 383–8 the Wall was destroyed and the Romans withdrew their frontier to Stainmore, leaving the north part of Brigantia to look after its own defence. Under the protection of its own people Brigantia became prosperous and most of its larger settlements were occupied and its fields tilled. Many of the settlement sites have fourth-century pottery and a few have fragments belonging to the early fifth century also. By A.D. 395 Roman rule in the north was practically at an end and the final withdrawal of all Roman troops followed their revolt in 407. A long period of three and a half centuries of imposed military rule was ended, and, with the Romans gone, the natives settled mainly into the lowlands where the Romans had built cities and created farms, while a few were banded together in small Celtic kingdoms.

4

Settlements
and early history

The natural feature which has had the most effect in shaping the life of the dales people is the overall pattern of the long, deep valleys separated by high moorland ridges. The ridges have been crossed by few regular tracks and even today the roads from valley to valley are few and far between. Some of them like Park Rash, Kettlewell, are steep enough to be used nowadays for motor test trials. The roads are unfenced across the high moors and are often buried under deep snowdrifts in a hard winter. The lines of snow poles along their margins speak of the days and sometimes weeks when all other sign of the track is lost in a wilderness of snow, and when a traveller who strays from the track faces grievous risk to his life in snowdrift or bog hole.

Because of these natural barriers movement in the dales for centuries was mainly up and down the length of the valley, to and from the principal market and the feudal courts at the mouth of the dale. With the exception of the shorter dales of the northern and western edges of the Pennines, the pattern of the valleys has influenced the settlement and has been responsible for much of the present distribution of villages and hamlets. The Pennine summits were wooded at the time of the forest optimum, but by the time of the Romans the higher moorlands were peat covered and thick woodland was confined to the heads of all the valleys and their encircling slopes. Thinner woods occupied the middle and lower dales and reached up the valley sides to between 700 and 800 ft above sea level.

The lowlands of the Vale of York had, over wide areas, been cleared and brought into cultivation by a population working with or under the direction of the Romans. The Northern Command centred on York made great demands on a wide area for corn, which the province was bound to supply under the terms of the Roman rule. The extension of villas even as far north as Old Durham and west to Gargrave indicates something of the pressure of agriculture on good land. The villas were highly organized farms, and two more, at Well and Middleham, were settled on the Pennine foothills. The younger generations of the Brigantes were attracted by the life of these farms and lowlands, so that their settlements on the Pennines were reduced or deserted and the uplands became almost empty country, open for reoccupation by any adventurers. One exception to this desertion was an area of the lower part of the valleys of the Aire and Calder where a native kingdom of Elmet persisted until the seventh century. The boundaries are not at all clear, but Barwick in Elmet, Sherburn in Elmet, Leeds (Loidis) and a few other names help to suggest its extent. This Celtic people occupied the 'forest of Elmet', living in scattered hamlets, cultivating small clearings, and herding cattle. Very little is known about them, but over the north of England, after the Romans left, the Celtic people organized themselves into a number of very small kingdoms, some of which confederated into the large kingdom of Strathclyde in the west. Until its conquest in the seventh century Elmet was a real barrier against the early penetration of the Anglian invaders into the valleys of Airedale and Calderdale.[1]

Only a few of the Celtic groups have left evidence of their location, but there are several place names, particularly of hills and rivers, which were given by them – Pen Hill, Penyghent, Pendle, Chevin, Tyne, Derwent, Wharfe, and many others were passed on to those who followed the Celts and are still in use as place names.

After the Roman Wall had been destroyed by raiding Picts and the Romans had withdrawn to a temporary frontier across Stainmore, the larger Romano–British settlements, almost villages, with their large areas of 'Celtic fields', were fully occupied, and around many of the Roman forts a civilian population remained in being within a native 'town'.

The more prosperous north, without the barrier of the Wall, was now subject to increasingly frequent raids by the Picts, and at the same time Scots from Ireland harried the coasts of the north-west. Saxon pirates attacked on the east coast and penetrated the larger river estuaries of the Humber, Wash, and Tees and attacked far inland, reaching York and even farther west. It was about the middle of the fifth century, when these raids were becoming fiercer and more penetrating, that a figure, later to become legendary, entered the struggle and rallied the Britons against their attackers. He was Arthur, probably the son of a Romanized Briton of the south-west. The *Historia Brittonum* says of him 'Arthur fought against them (the Saxons) with the kings of the Britons, but he himself was *dux bellorum*'. He commanded a small army of cavalry and was not bound to any locality, but was mobile, able to move quickly to any part of the country to give his help where it was most needed.[2]

Most of the hill country was forested, and as one of the small British (Celtic) communities was attacked by Saxon invaders the appearance of Arthur and his armed horsemen from the darkness of the forest must have seemed to be an almost magic deliverance. With no rigid plans, and appearing when least expected and most hoped for, at places scattered over the country, always in a time of dire need, there is no wonder that he and his men became figures of legend. It was Geoffrey of Monmouth who used Arthur as a literary hero and converted his followers into knights and Arthur into a king; from this stemmed the long cycle of Arthurian story with little or no basis in fact. It was the small groups of people who had benefited by his help against the pirates, who created the true Arthurian legend.

The people of Brigantia later, though mistakenly, claimed him as one of themselves, placing his birth at Pendragon Castle in Mallerstang and making him the son of Uther Pendragon. In their legends he is associated with the vast northern forest of Reged. Richmond Castle stands on its high rock towering above the Swale, and within the rock it was widely believed that Arthur and his knights lay sleeping. The sword Excalibur and the bugle were close at hand. The sleeping host waited for the day when Britain's need would be so great that some man more bold than the rest would find his way into the cave and, by drawing Excalibur and blowing the bugle, would waken Arthur and his knights to become the saviours of the country.

Local legend has it that a simple man, Potter Thompson of Richmond, did once upon a time find his way into the cave, saw the knights and King Arthur, but lost his nerve at the last moment. Thus Arthur remained asleep. Many times afterwards did he and others search for entry to the cave, but to this day it has not been rediscovered.[3] Yorkshire children are told that Arthur and his knights still sleep beneath the castle of Richmond, waiting for the day when the need will be great enough to bring them forth. Arthur and his knights are said to sleep beneath many castle rocks and wild places, like the Sneep on the Durham Derwent, and it may not be too wild an idea if we think that in some cases these are places or districts where in the middle years of the fifth century Arthur did indeed appear from the forest and give sorely needed help to a population which has enshrined his timely help in this folk-legend.

The sporadic raids by Saxon pirates were followed by a more determined and planned larger-scale settlement by Continental Germanic invaders, of whom the Saxons were one branch. Jutes in the south-east and Saxons in the east had their counterpart, in the northern area, in the Angles.[4] These were all closely related people with a common culture. While the British kingdom of Elmet still flourished in the mid sixth century, the first Anglian permanent settlements were being made in east Yorkshire. From these footholds on the Wolds, the Angles soon spread westward to York and Ripon and the valley lands of the Ouse. Some settlement was made farther north along the coast of Northumberland, and the rocky mass of Whin Sill at Bamburgh became the castle and seat of the Anglian king Ida, king of Bernicia, in 547. In honour of his wife Bebba he named the rock Bebban-burgh, from which the modern name is derived. A kingdom of Northumbria, from the Tweed to the Humber, was for a time ruled from Bamburgh but at first was divided roughly along the line of the Tees into Bernicia in the north and Deira in the south part. Edwin, king of Northumbria (616–32), attacked and destroyed the British kingdom of Elmet and opened up the way for an expansion of the Angles towards the west, enabling them to pass up the rivers Aire and Wharfe and to penetrate the Pennines by the Aire Gap westward into Craven (an older Celtic name) and as far as the Ribble valley. During the seventh century their settlements spread from the east into all the lower dales of Yorkshire, where they cleared space in the woodland, these places being named in their dialect with a suffix -*leah*, now recognized in place names as -*ley*; for example, Otley, Wensley, Ilkley, etc. The woodlands were thickest on the gritstone soils, and so it is not surprising that a map of the distribution of place names in -*ley* shows a close correspondence with such soil areas.

Such a map (Map 5) shows that the -*ley* names are concentrated in a few areas. The most numerous lie in the Vale of York and the lower dales, particularly over the whole area which we suppose to have been the kingdom and 'wood of Elmet'. The western fringe of this group appears in the map mainly in Nidderdale – Ripley, Pateley, Bewerley, and Darley – and the country between the Nidd and lower Ure – Stainley, Grantley, etc. – with Wensley as a solitary outlier farther up the valley of the Ure. To the west of these there are three more outliers, one at Drebley in Wharfedale, one at Bordley near Malham, and another at Bradley near the head of Coverdale. These three must have been the homes of venturers into a wild country.

The largest group is in the north-east, to the west and south-west of Newcastle upon Tyne, and over the ground between the Derwent and the lower Wear. This is land made up of the lower Coal Measures and part of the Millstone Grit, which by soil and elevation was suitable for the support of a forest cover. In this patch there are about thirty hamlets with names ending in -*ley*, representing quite a large invasion by the mouth of the Tyne and a spreading outwards by the Tyne and Derwent over this piece of country. Again there is only an isolated hamlet or two

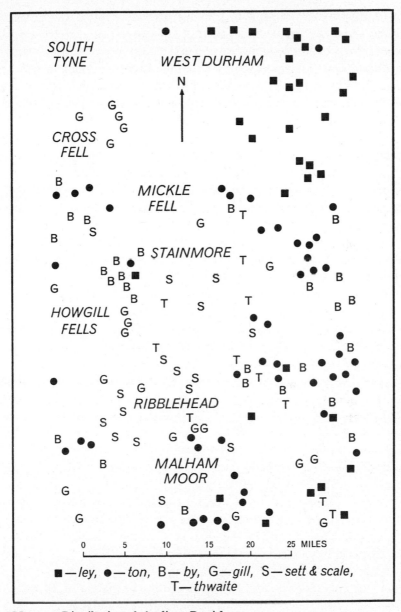

Map 5 *Distribution of Anglian, Danish and Norse place names (see opposite page)*

farther west along the Tyne and, near it, Ridley and Langley. All the west of the country on and across the Pennines is empty of -*ley* names.

There is a very early type of place name which may in fact mark the penetration of the pioneers of this settlement, the names being compounds with -*ing* or -*ingham*, like Wolsingham in Weardale, in which -*ham* indicates a homestead. On the Tyne there are Ovingham, Bellingham, and Eltringham, in north Yorkshire Barningham, and to the south Addingham.

A second much wider settlement is recognized by the affix -*ton*, a farmstead or fenced homestead. The use of this suffix continued for some centuries and many of the places named in this way originated as daughter settlements from earlier ones, made as population increased and elder sons left to set up on their own account. Occasionally the connection with an early settlement is clear, as in Oving*ton*, close to Ovingham on the Tyne. The -*ton* names have a wide scatter on the lower ground at the mouth of the dales of Yorkshire and also penetrate farther up the dales than the -*ley* names. The westward movement of the people using this form of name was up Airedale and through the Aire gap into the Craven Lowlands and the valleys of the Ribble and Wenning, and eventually into the Lune valley, where they are very numerous. They cross Stainmore into the head of the Vale of Eden but are rare farther north except for a few in Teesdale as far up as Eggleston and Middleton and a few in the Tyne valley.

No hard-and-fast rule can be made, but generally the farmers of the -*ley* villages lived in small communities based upon a common field agriculture, with outlying common pasture and some grazing of cattle and pigs in the woods. The heavy work of clearing forest and breaking up and tilling arable ground was more than a single family could manage, so the -*ley* villages started as communities, probably of nine or ten families, basing their life on holding and working the land in common.

The earlier -*tuns* were probably each the farm of a single family basing their life on a pastoral cycle, mainly sheep farming, with just enough arable for their immediate needs. Inevitably, as population increased, the -*tuns* became the nuclei of small hamlets or villages, and more arable was brought into cultivation, so that by the eleventh century many of the -*tuns* were not very different from the -*ley* villages. In general the -*ley* villages are located on the Millstone Grit and Coal Measure sandstone areas in the Pennines, which would carry the heavy woodland, while the -*tun* villages move farther west on to the limestone lands, where there would be much more open pasture and thin scrubby woodland.

The spread of the -*tun* hamlets continued for several generations, and indeed a few of them may be as late as or even later than the eleventh century. For Yorkshire, where the Domesday survey record is available, most of the -*tun* and all the

-*ley* villages are mentioned, so we can accept their pattern as being established in the seventh to tenth centuries.

During the Anglian settlement the Christian church became established from two sources.[5] In 625 Edwin, king of Northumbria, married a Christian, Æthelberht of Kent, and promised to respect her religion. Paulinus, a Christian missionary, came north as her chaplain and in 627 Edwin was baptized by him at York in a wooden church on the site of the later Minster. Paulinus became bishop of York and as a missionary baptized great crowds of converts in the river Swale at Catterick. In 632 Cadwallon and his Mercian allies devastated Northumbria, Paulinus fled to Kent, and the whole area lapsed to paganism. Cadwallon was defeated in 633 and Northumbria was restored by Oswald, son of Æthelfrith of Bernicia who had been converted to Christianity by the monks of Iona. On his invitation a company of monks under Aidan came from Iona in 634 and settled a monastery at Lindisfarne with Aidan as their bishop.

The Mercian victory destroyed most of the mission work of Paulinus, and the recovery of Christianity in the north followed the efforts of Aidan and therefore took a Celtic form and ritual. The Roman usage of Paulinus, however, had probably never become extinct – James the Deacon of York seems to have kept alive a Christian community in the country between Leyburn and Catterick, though its precise location is not known. Later, under the leadership of Wilfred and Benedict Biscop, the Roman form gained enough strength to challenge the Celtic ritual at the Synod of Whitby in 663, and to secure the decision for the Roman church. In the following year Wilfred was made bishop of a great part of western Deira with his church and monastery at Ripon. A few years later he became bishop of York with most of the north under his influence. He established a church at Hexham on Tyne in 678, which later became the seat of a bishop and the centre of a large monastery.

The settlement of church affairs seems to have been the prelude to a peaceful period during which much of the expansion of the population was accommodated by the westward movement into new farmsteads, the -*tuns*. Many of these developed into hamlets, and the country below about 800 ft OD, with the exception of west Durham, was fairly well settled. The peace was broken at the end of the eighth century by pirate raids on the east coast. The *Anglo-Saxon Chronicle* under the year 793 describes the first Danish attack on Northumbria:

> Dread prodigies appeared over Northumbria, and miserably terrified the people: that is, whirlwinds beyond measure, and lightnings: and fiery dragons were seen flying in the sky. Upon these tokens soon followed great famine, and

> a little after that, in the same year, on the 6th day of the Ides of January, the heathen men miserably destroyed God's church at Lindisfarne, through robbery and slaughter.

Jarrow and Wearmouth were also destroyed within a few years. However, no serious further raiding took place until 834, from which time it increased in intensity and frequency, at first mainly along the southern and eastern coasts of the country. In 865 the Great Army of the Danes landed in East Anglia and for many years carried war and conquest into most parts of England. In 867 the army captured York and plundered the land as far north as the Tyne. In 876 Halfdan conquered Northumbria. A peace was made and Halfdan 'dealt out the lands of Northumbria; and they began to plough and till theirs' (that is the land apportioned to the Danish soldiers). The monks of Lindisfarne had escaped in 867–8 with the bones of St Cuthbert, and for the nine years of the troubles they had carried them over much of the north, seeking a resting place, eventually staying for some time at Chester-le-Street, then finally coming to rest at Durham in 876, where his great Cathedral was eventually built.

The settlement of the Danes seems to have formed a pattern of infilling of hamlets between and around the Anglian villages. Two place name elements are diagnostic: -*by* and -*thorp*. As a suffix -*by* appears in an abundance of names such as Thorlby, Melmerby, and Eastby, and is often combined with a personal name, Thorold's-by, or a position in relation to some other settlement, as in East-by. A small proportion of the -*by* villages may have been earlier Anglian villages taken over by conquest and re-named by the Danes, but this is nearly impossible to determine. The suffix -*thorp* has the meaning 'a secondary or dependent, outlying farm or hamlet'. This is often evident in the way a -*thorp* is in the outlying land of some parent village generally of Anglian origin, and a parish name now has the form Burnsall-with-Thorpe. This is sometimes the case with the -*bys*, as in Stirton-with-Thorlby and Embsay-with-Eastby; in each of these cases the -*by* or -*thorp* is within a mile or so of the parent or host village and shares in the same township or parish boundary. Another Danish name is *Kirkby*, 'a village with a church', and this often has another name in combination, to distinguish its location – as in Kirkby Malhamdale, Kirkby Lonsdale – or a personal name – as Kirkby Stephen, or Kirkoswald. A study of the map (Map 5) shows very clearly how the Danish settlement largely coincides with the Anglian in Yorkshire but is absent from Durham. The most striking feature of the -*by* villages is their great number in the Vale of Eden, marking a spread from Yorkshire across Stainmore to Kirkby Stephen and then down the valley. A few of these -*by* villages are late, even of post-Conquest date; for example, Glassonby in Cumberland. This very late naming was possible because many of the Danish words were adopted into common speech, and some of them remained in use for some centuries.

At the beginning of the tenth century a new invasion of the north of England began with the landing of Norsemen from Ireland.[6] The Norse had migrated from north-west Norway, by way of Orkney and Shetland, and had reached northern Ireland, settled much of its east coast, and made the capital of their kingdom at Dublin. It was the second or third generations of this migration who crossed the Irish Sea to colonize the Isle of Man and then pressed farther on to the Lancashire coasts. Before 915 the Wirral peninsula was settled and Norsemen were taking possession of much of the country west of the Pennines. During the first quarter of the tenth century most of Cumberland was occupied by Norse colonists, who had picked up enough Irish words and turns of speech to give a recognizable character to some of their place names. In the north they penetrated as far as the valley of the South Tyne, but in Yorkshire they crossed the Pennines, conquered York, and for an uneasy period maintained a Dublin-York kingdom. The last king of this kingdom was Eric Bloodaxe, who was driven out of York by the English and died in the battle of Stainmore in 954. Although the Irish–Norse kingdom had not much political significance, the invasions by which it had been established gave it a permanent place in the origin of some of our place names and dialect.

There was very little clash of interest between the Norse and the Anglo-Danish people already settled on the valley lowlands. The Norse preferred the fell lands and steeper valley heads, with upland sheep-run above the forest level. On the uplands the Norse came in contact with small groups of Celtic people, but the land in general was empty and unwanted. Because of this the pattern of their settlement kept very close to that which was normal to the dales and fells of western Norway. In that country the smaller dales had the oldest settlements near the mouth, and these were named with the personal name of the early owner, compounded with 'baer' – a farmstead – or, as the Norse were late coming in the north of England and had peaceful contact with the Anglo-Danes, they sometimes took words from them and occasionally borrowed -tun and -by. Higher up the fells near the valley heads there were 'budhir' or 'booths', smaller farms which in Cumberland and North Lancashire often have a Gaelic personal name as a compound, which suggests that these outlying farms may have been occupied by Celtic servants, brought over from Ireland, or by some of the surviving Celts. Magnus Olsen, describing the typical farms of Norway says, 'the cattle grazed in the valley during spring and autumn and were kept up among the mountains in summer, moving from spring shieling (or 'saetr', i.e. mountain pasture with houses) to summer shieling . . . and back again the cattle went from summer shieling to autumn shieling, to be let at last into the home meadows as soon as the aftermath had been mown there'. This pattern is recognizable in the north. The summer pastures where sheep and cattle were kept and milked were generally called -*erg*, a name derived from the Celtic 'airge' or 'airidh', a shieling. In its use by Norse and Norse-Celt it had many variants and is found in the place names as-ergh, -airey, -arrow, -ark, etc. The name for the spring shieling, -*saetr*, appears as -satter, -seat, -sett, and -side. From the principal farms the outlying farms were often called -*skali*, now -*scale*. Natural features were fells, becks, gills, hill riggs, cams, knipe and so on; slack, mere, moss, turf-moor, heath, and ling, are all Norse names, while -*thwaite* denotes a field sloping to a flat or lake, generally a clearing in a woody area, and often associated with horses.

The -*saetr* names have survived in Yorkshire and mark something of the Norse penetration of the upper dales. There is the wide group of Appersett, Burtersett, Countersett, and Marsett in upper Wensleydale; Lunnersett, Raven Seat, Earl Seat, and many others in Yorkshire parallel the Lake District examples of Seat Sandal, Seat How, and others. The -*scale* indicates a temporary hut or shed, used by the cowherds or shepherds, and is fairly common – Barden Scale, Scale Park, Southerscales, Winterscales, and Summerscales – but most commonly the -*scale* is part of a place name locating an ancient 'scale' – Scale Foss, Scale Beck, Scales Moor, and so on. A feature of Norse farming was pig-keeping, and the Norse word -griss, a pig, is found as Grizedale in many places.

Personal names are fairly common, some of them Irish and some Norse. Yockenthwaite in Wharfedale speaks of Eogan's-thwaite, an Irish-Norse clearing; Thorogill reminds us of Thorold, a common name; and Gunnar's saetr has become Gunnerside, in Swaledale.

Using the place names we can see that the Norse settlers entered by the west coast of Lancashire and soon spread over the southern fells of the Lake District and on the western slopes of the Pennines. They came through Garsdale and Mallerstang and occupied the upper part of Wensleydale, where there are no Anglo-Danish names to suggest earlier occupation. They crossed Stainmore and found upland and empty land in the North Yorkshire Moors of Cleveland. On the Pennine summits they spread out from Stainmore southward and into Craven and moved south-east across the moorlands into the Calder valley around Huddersfield. Their penetration is shown by long tongues of Norse names stretching down the fell ridges and by a few -thwaites on the valley sides and heads – Thwaite in Swaledale, Hunderthwaite in Teesdale, Hampsthwaite in Nidderdale, Brunthwaite in Airedale and so on – and by other peculiarly Norse names, and names of

Norse-Irish like -*cross*, in Thruscross, Osgoldcross, Reycross (on Stainmore), and Staincross.

By the eleventh century our picture of the population of the Pennine dales would appear to consist of a well-assimilated Anglo-Danish or 'English' group in the valleys and lowlands of Yorkshire, and a purer Anglian group, basing their life on arable agriculture, living in nucleated villages and clearing the woodlands in the north-east of Durham. Cattle, sheep, and pigs were incidental to their agriculture. On the hills and in the higher valleys of the west, the Norse population was basing its life on sheep and cattle, with just enough arable to provide the small quantities of grain their way of life called for. Their seasonal use of higher fells for pasture, and their need for wide spaces for their sheep, led to very scattered settlements mostly in the form of isolated farms. The Anglo-Danish and the Norse areas are very distinct, and only a narrow fringe of intermingling can be seen in a few places. The western dales of County Durham seem to have been almost unoccupied until the twelfth century.

Besides the place names, these settlements have left many traces of their life and language, in dialects, in the hamlets and villages, in a wealth of pre-Conquest carved stone crosses, and to some extent in the physical characteristics and mental aptitude of the people. The Angles brought with them a language which had nothing in common with that of the Celtic folk. There was only a small and scattered Celtic-speaking population sufficient to pass on to the newcomers the names of most of the rivers and a few of the hills such as Pendle, Penyghent, Chevin, and a few town names, Olicana (Ilkley) and Loidis (Leeds), and a place name like Elmet. The Angles were content to give names to their villages and farms and to develop their speech with little modification in the form we think of as old English. The Danes had a Scandinavian language which, though differing from the Anglian, had enough in common with it for a mutual understanding to be achieved with patience and effort. These two languages were soon amalgamated into a common speech in which many of the Danish words and expressions can still be recognized, particularly in the older dialect.

In East Yorkshire the Danish settlement was very complete, and the Danes were a large enough proportion of the population to ensure that many of their words, almost unchanged, became part of the living language and that many of these were brought on to the eastern Pennines with their westward movement. In the dialect, many turns of phrase as well as individual words have a Danish origin. The 'forend' and 'backend' of the year are a commonplace of everyday speech, and in rough and cold weather it will be said 'ther's a backendish feel abaht it' and perhaps that it is a 'hask' (keen) wind. It might be said 't'winds in a

79

poorish airt (quarter) an' it's like to rain' – 'like to' being used in the sense that rain is imminent. The Danish expression '*Jeg var lige ved at tumle*' – 'I was on the point of falling' – has the expression 'like to' and also the dialect 'tummle', to fall. This is not the place to elaborate, but anyone with a quick ear and a good knowledge of the Yorkshire dialects, along with some Danish, will find very many close similarities not only in vocabulary but in grammar and construction.

As we have seen, the Norsemen spread into the highland areas and their language is spread over the features of the topography. The shepherd wandered over more and rougher country than the ploughman, and the detail of rock and crag, moor and swamp were of an urgent importance to him. This detailed naming has become part of the ordinary speech of the west, and in the Lake District, Cumberland, and the west Pennines, fells and gills, mosses and becks, crags and clints, and a hundred other words of Norse affinity are in use today without any thought of dialect, or any idea but that they are the ordinary and correct descriptive terms.

If we look back to the seventh century we see the church after the Synod of Whitby expanding through the north with the establishment of monasteries and the enthusiastic work of Wilfred and Benedict Biscop. Wilfred and Benedict had both been to Rome and travelled on the Continent, and they brought back with them many ideas on the building crafts. At York about 690 Wilfred, moved by grief at the state of ruin of the church of York, 'strengthened the masonry, raised the roof, and when it was raised protected it from injury by storms with leaden sheets'. He also put in some glass windows. 'It is marvellous', it was said in or about 700, 'how many buildings (Wilfred) brought to perfection, with walls of imposing height . . . many by his own judgement, but also by the advice of the masons whom the hope of liberal reward had drawn hither from Rome.' About 675 Benedict Biscop founded his monastery at Wearmouth, the walls of which he adorned with figures of the gospel story and the Apostles, 'so that all persons entering the church, even if unable to read, whichever way they went, should have before their eyes, at least in image, the ever blessed Christ and his Saints'. He also sent agents to Gaul to bring over glass-workers to make the windows.

Church building in the north, in stone, was limited to a few places, and of the smaller churches only Escomb in Weardale has survived.* By the eighth century there were a few local churches, but the general organization is described by Bede as very simple. 'In those days the English people were accustomed to gather together whenever a priest came to their village, at his call, to hear the Word.' In most villages there was no church, so the priest would preach and say Mass

* See Chapter 10.

13. *Ingleborough – the summit pyramid from Lead Mine Moss limestone pavements.*

Ramparts at Whitley Castle, South Tyne Valley

before a temporary cross. The cross was commonly his staff of wood, a staff which could be driven into the earth, and with a short cross arm would make a 'staff-rood'. In a few places the thegn or overlord might build a small wooden church, and this could be granted rights of burial, so becoming a church with a graveyard serving a wide area of 'field churches' which were little more than preaching places. The early parishes were formed around the churches with a graveyard and were very large; although they have since been divided, it is still common in the Pennines to have single parishes containing a number of 'townships' or villages. Kirkby Malham parish has seven civil parishes in it; Grinton in Swaledale has the whole of the upper dale with all its hamlets and villages; in Weardale two ancient parishes, Stanhope and Wolsingham, cover practically the whole Pennine part of the dale.[7]

Before 732 Bishop Acca of Hexham enlarged his church and about 740 was buried there. Symeon of Durham says that his tomb is known by 'two stone crosses decorated with wonderful carving, one at the head and the other at the foot' of the grave. It was a Celtic custom to mark some important places with a rough stone pillar, and here we see a combination of this idea with that of the 'rood-cross', which being of wood might well be carved. It was in this way that the use of carved stone crosses as grave memorials began in the north. In the twelfth and thirteenth centuries, when there was much building of stone churches, the crosses were regarded as crude, and possibly as superstitious, carrying as they did in some examples symbolic figures of beasts and birds. Many were broken up and used as building stone in the new church and thus paradoxically were saved, though in fragments, for our generation.[8]

Acca's crosses from Hexham are now at Durham Cathedral, but a modern replica of the main one stands at the entrance to Hexham cemetery. The four sides of the rectangular shaft are decorated with vine scroll patterns of great delicacy. The shaft carried a four-armed cross head patterned with circular bosses, and as there is some evidence that these early crosses were picked out in paint of several colours this must have been a sparkling and striking monument. From Hexham the idea of carved stone crosses spread, and part of one, showing the 'Hexham school' influence, was found at Easby in Swaledale. Two fragments of the cross were built into the church fabric and a third fragment was in an adjacent garden, but some years ago all three pieces were sold to the Victoria and Albert Museum. A plaster cast of the restored cross is now in the church. The shaft has vine scroll ornament with the addition of bird and beast on one side and a seated figure of Christ on the other. It is later than the Acca cross, but still of the late eighth century, and shows the Hexham type of carving at its best.

At Auckland, County Durham, there are parts of a great shaft and the base in which it stood. This cross is ornamented with figures of saints and angels on the broad sides and vine scrolls with birds and beasts on the narrow sides; it belongs to the eighth century. Between 850 and 1,000 a school of carvers developed at Ripon who carved, besides crosses such as the one at Wycliffe on Tees and the fragment at Wensley, small grave slabs, of which there is one at West Witton and two at Wensley. The slabs at Wensley (in the church) have names on them, and a cross. One is carved with the name DONFRID in a panel across the bottom, and has birds and beasts in the four spaces between the cross arms and the border. The other has the name EADBEREHCT spaced in the four corners formed by the cross arms.

In the tenth and eleventh centuries the infiltration of Danes and Norse brought ideas which influenced the ornament of the crosses, though it appears that Anglian carvers were still employed to make them. The main group of these late crosses in our area lies around the lower Swale in a broad area from Wycliffe (ninth-century cross, tenth-century hog-back), by Gilling (tenth- and eleventh-century crosses), Stanwick (eleventh-century crosses), Hauxwell (tenth-century cross), Finghall (eleventh-century cross and crucifix), and Spennithorne (eleventh-century grave slab). Farther south at Burnsall in Wharfedale there are several eleventh-century crosses and a hog-back. The 'hog-back' is a heavy gravestone modelled like a long house, the pitched roof often carved in a 'tile' pattern. Some have the ends of the 'hog-back' clasped by bears, this probably being a Norse feature. Among the crosses a Norse introduction was the 'wheel-head', in which the four arms of the cross are held by a circle. Examples of this are crosses at Stanwick, Gilling, and Finghall.

Early in the eleventh century Danish raids on England began again, and in 1016 war between Edmund, king of England, and Cnut, son of Swein, king of Denmark, was concluded by the death of Edmund and the acceptance of Cnut as king. His was a very mixed character but he was regarded as having brought peace to the country, given it a code of laws, and honoured its religion. He divided the country into four great earldoms. One of these was Northumbria, with Eric of Norway as its earl, to be followed by the Dane, Siward, who ruled until 1055.

One of Cnut's recreations was hunting, and many wooded and wild areas of the country became 'forest' in the sense of being reserved for the king's sport. After the Norman Conquest royal forests were created and defined in most parts of the country, and in the north large areas on the Pennines became 'forests' subject to forest law. Thus different conditions of life and occupation were imposed upon those people within the forest bounds and those who were outside. This separation of the 'forests' was made more permanent and significant by the Normans.

After the Conquest a revolt in the north provoked an expedition of William and his forces which, by its ruthless destruction of villages and population, earned the name of the Harrying of the North. The Vale of York and the lowland country north to Durham was completely wasted, and when the great Domesday Survey was made in 1086 most of the 'manors' were returned as waste and of no value, although in the time of Edward the Confessor they had been populated and worth a great amount.[9] The interpretation of the Domesday Survey is a matter of lively discussion by scholars, but the picture drawn from analysis of the document appears in part to be different from the impression gained from an intimate knowledge and study of the ground. It is claimed by some that the Yorkshire Pennines were totally depopulated and entirely waste; another scholar claims that what population may have survived in the dales was moved by the Normans into the wasted manors of the more fertile lowlands of the Vale of York, to re-create those more profitable areas. The Survey in fact shows most of the dales villages in the hands of the king's thegns, Anglo-Danes, or of other persons who had held them or near-by villages before the Conquest. The picture of total devastation and of the removal of population is overdrawn, and there is every reason to believe that the force sent by William was never large enough to penetrate all parts of the dales. The local people would have found it easy to disappear into the hills with their livestock, and, in effect, to become invisible and immune. The conditions in which a 'manor' could become totally waste and without population, such as is suggested on several of the recently published maps of Domesday England, would be impossible to attain in the higher dales. In fact, not all villages are returned as of no value: for instance, Grassington, Linton and Threshfield in upper Wharfedale are noted – Gamelbar had these, now Gilbert Tison has them. Farther down the dale, in Addingham, Gamelbar had two carucates, Gilbert has one plough there . . . Time of Edward it was worth ten shillings, now the same. No mechanism has been suggested which could account for the repopulation of these villages from which it is said all population was removed, and much of the confusion must arise from the inadequacy of the Domesday record in the dales area.

In the Domesday Survey there is, however, a very significant aspect of the distribution of the places named. The Survey does not go north of the Tees nor far into west Yorkshire. In the whole country it appears that land 'in the Forest' was, with few exceptions, quit of liability for geld or service, so that when the Survey stops short at the borders of what we know was forest at a later date we may perhaps presume that the forest was of earlier creation and already there. Such a boundary in the Yorkshire dales marks what may well have been the eastern and southern edges of Cnut's great forest in the north.

The distribution of the Domesday Survey manors penetrate only as far as Reeth in Swaledale, Askrigg in Wensleydale, Starbotton in Wharfedale, and Stainforth in Ribblesdale. All these lie on the borders of forests as defined in the twelfth or thirteenth centuries. In 1145 Count Alan of Brittany and lord of the Honour of Richmond was in a position to grant to the monks of Jervaulx confirmation of an earlier grant of the right to dig for ores of iron and lead within his forest of Wensleydale, and to take the flesh of deer that had been worried by wolves. The village of Bainbridge was built on the edge of this forest to house the foresters, and this and Healaugh in Swaledale, with Buckden in Wharfedale, were 'foresters' villages' built after the Survey. These 'forest villages' lie next up the dale to the last villages recorded in the Domesday Survey and are on the edge of the forests.

County Durham is not included in the Domesday Survey, the western dales being still almost unoccupied and of no value until the Palatinate of Durham was created about the end of the eleventh century and the dales became the bishop's forest.

Many of the Norse settlements were within the forest bounds, and they remained as small two- or three-farm groups, or even as isolated farms, their expansion into villages being inhibited by forest law and custom. Many became 'lodges' and are named as such in forest rentals. For instance, in Langstrothdale Chase, part of Litton Forest, upper Wharfedale, a survey of 1241 names the lodges as Crey, Kirk Gill (Hubberholm), Yoghamethest (Yockenthwaite), Risegile, Depedale, Beckersmote (Beckermonds), and Uhtredestall (Oughtershaw), of which today only Oughtershaw is a hamlet with more than half a dozen houses, the others having only one or two farms. In Barden Chase, part of Skipton Forest, the nine lodges, still remaining as clusters of one or two farms, each had a small area of meadow ground, with pannage of swine, pasture for cattle, and a small area to provide feeding for the deer in winter. In Barden and in Langstrothdale all the 'lodges' are Norse settlements with such names as Gamelswath, Holgill, Yockenthwaite, etc., except for one or two added in Barden, such as Ungayne and Barden itself. In Wensleydale Forest many lodges were 'saetrs', Appersett, Burtersett, Countersett, etc., and small places like Litherskew, Sedbusk, Lund, etc. In surveys some became vaccaries, and particularly in the surveys of Mewith Forest west of Ribblesdale vaccaries are reserved, again being located at places like Winterscales, Southerscales, Quernside (Whernside), etc.

We have to picture the Norse within the forest areas changing from their role as shepherds to that of cowherds and pig-keepers, as sheep grazing was inimical to the continuation of forest, and was usually most rigorously controlled. The fuller picture of life within the forest areas is well documented for the thirteenth and later centuries, and its discussion can be left for a later chapter.

5

The rural landscape

Neither prehistoric nor Roman invader made much mark on the rural landscape of the dales. The tiny Brigantian homesteads and fields were lost in the forest cover and the Roman forts were too scattered to be more than an occasional ruined feature among wild scenery. With the Anglian settlement, however, a visible pattern of farms, hamlets, and fields was spread through the valleys, and clearances were made in the woodlands so that a traveller through the valleys would at least see the nucleus of most of our present villages and towns and a beginning of the wide pattern of fields and cultivated ground which we now take for granted. Most prominent in the vales of the eastward-flowing rivers in Yorkshire, he would see near many villages sloping fields shaped with long terraces, step above step, or perhaps running side by side up and down a gentle slope (Plates 9 and 12). These terraces usually lie in groups, and they may be a hundred or even two hundred yards long and ten or more yards wide, the terrace dimensions showing regularity only within each group and often considerable difference between those of one group and another. The front 'step' varies in height with the slope of the ground, and is itself a very steep slope. These terraces are 'lynchets', the ploughing strips of the Anglian common fields. The early ploughs were often pulled by eight oxen, usually in tandem, and on sloping ground it would be impossible to keep a straight furrow, the plough tail swinging down the slope and interfering with the furrows below. The terraces were started by making part of the front 'step', which is often reinforced with boulders from the land clearance, and continued ploughing made them permanent. On the light soils of the limestone area there is a very heavy rainfall with considerable soil wash down the slopes, and the lynchets were very efficient for soil conservation.[1]

The lyncheted fields are found in the limestone valleys from upper Airedale and Wharfedale to Teesdale, the best developed occurring in Wharfedale and Wensleydale. A few scattered fields of lynchets are found near Kirkby Stephen and in the area between Settle and Kirkby Lonsdale. They are, however, a feature of the Anglian area, absent from the north-west region of predominantly Norse settlement.

The Anglian farmers had generations of village life and tradition to guide them in making a settlement under the rule of a leader, perhaps the head of a family, various members of which made up a good part of the village community. The traditional arrangement of their settlements was in nucleated groups, the houses clustering together round a central space, later to become the village green. The hamlets, in the valleys, were usually set on the river terrace above the alluvial swamp of the river flood plain and were well spaced approximately two, or more commonly about three, miles apart. The flood plain was cleared and became a well-watered meadow, and the forest clearing near the houses provided the ploughland, often in two fields, one each side of the hamlet upstream and downstream. On first coming, the settlers would strive to prepare sufficient plough land for a sustenance crop, which could be supplemented by wild fruits and by hunting. The extension into the large village common fields was achieved during a few generations, additions to common arable fields sometimes continuing to be made into the later Middle Ages. Woodland on the steeper valley slopes was grazed by sheep and cattle, and this, by preventing natural regeneration of the trees through seedlings, gradually produced pasture with thin scrub. House and farm building, fences and fuel, by their demands on timber, all helped in the reduction of the woodland and the production of the common pasture. In a number of generations the regular village pattern emerged, which we now recognize – meadow on the valley floor and ploughed fields on the gentler slope of the valley side, with the village near the mid point. Steeper slopes above the village became pasture – steadily improved as time went on – and above this lay the wilder moorland waste. The waste provided some rough pasture and gave heather for thatching, but on the whole it played only a minor part in the village economy.[2]

We have seen that the first Angles came up the river valleys and perhaps along the Roman roads. When their homestead site was chosen their first tasks were to make shelters for folk and stock and to clear enough land for their first food crop. The work was heavy and varied and needed several men for its proper performance, so we must picture a group of families, perhaps nine or ten, probably related, sharing the work among them and making their shelters close together for mutual protection. The area among the houses was often 'tidied up', particularly in the sixteenth and seventeenth centuries, to form the attractive 'greens' of today.

The Danes had a similar village pattern, and it is not easy now to distinguish a village originally Danish from an Anglian one, except by the form of its name. The lynchets which continued to be used, and possibly to be made, until the Conquest, occur in both (Plate 9). In Wensleydale some of the finest lynchet groups are in Carperby, a name of Danish origin but compounded with an Irish personal name and so of a late date. The form of the ground and nature of the soil were the chief determinants of the extent of lyncheted areas, and the Danish and Anglian traditions were sufficiently alike to make their use familiar to both.

The Anglian village had some features which contribute to the common plan – the 'hall' of the head man, common fields for arable, common pasture and meadow, and some things connected with these. The 'outgang' was a 'drift' or drove way across the arable to the pasture, now frequently seen as a walled green lane of very variable width and winding direction along which cattle were taken to and from the common pasture. The 'pound' where the pinder, a village officer, could impound stray beasts is often near the outgang. Roads go from the village across the arable common fields, and in many cases the end of this access road in one village field is linked to the end of a similar road in the next village. Because the roads were solely the concern of each individual common field, the ends very rarely come opposite one another across the boundary of two villages; this has caused what is a common feature in the dales roads, a double right-angled bend with a short straight piece between the bends, usually running along the parish boundary. An examination of any of the dale roads would show this: for example, from Grassington the up-dale road comes to the parish boundary at the end of Grass Wood, at Whitey Nook; it turns at right-angles and for a couple of hundred yards runs on the boundary, then turns across the middle of Conistone old common field, with lyncheted fields each side of it; it then crosses Conistone village and continues its line to the boundary of Kettlewell, where again it turns a right-angle along the boundary then a second right-angle to become the mid road of the Kettlewell south field. Such examples are abundant, and few of them have yet been entirely lost in road improvement.

In the north Pennines the pattern of the early church led commonly to ecclesiastical parishes which included many townships, so that the majority of the villages have no church within them, but there are 'church gates' and 'church paths' from the various townships to the mother church, built sometimes at a central point and not in a village.

In the north-west of the area, where Norse influence was strong, the type of nucleated village we have just described is rare. The typical Norse pattern is one of scattered farms, up the hillsides or along the upper fell slopes, nestling in the heads of the minor folds. The township often has a 'nominal' central hamlet which is often of a later date, though in Dentdale, Dent, a pre-Conquest hamlet, has assumed the nominal position in the Norse occupation. The scattered distribution is well seen in Garsdale and Grisedale, in South Tynedale or on Malham Moor. The farm sites carry names with a Viking flavour – Knudmaning, Thorogill House (*-hus*), Stang, and so on. Even today a consequence of this Norse pattern is seen in areas like Sedbergh and the Rawthey valley, where postal addresses over a wide area consist only of a house name, as Sarthwaite, Sedbergh; Dowbiggin, Sedbergh; Thursgill, Sedbergh; there being no nucleation of houses except Sedbergh, sufficient to provide a postal sub-area.[3]

In the Norse settlements sheep farming was the prime occupation, and the normal 'place' or 'hus' was one or two houses occupied probably by father and sons, with a few crofts and meadows immediately around them, sheep folds somewhere near, and a wide area of upland fell pasture not encumbered with near neighbours, so that flocks could graze without getting mixed up with those of the next farm (Plate 4). Much of the area of the Norse settlement was made into official 'forest' after the Conquest, with two principal effects on the life of the people. Sheep grazing was reduced in the wooded areas as being inimical to the regeneration of woodland and the farms and hamlets turned to the rearing of cattle and pigs, while services under the forest law were imposed on all tenants. The nurture and protection of deer and of the vegetation on which they fed were duties regulated by the forest courts, at which tenants formed the jury. Officers of the forest included a warden, usually a Norman of family, with foresters under him; the courts had their verderers and freeholders, who formed the Woodmote. There was a Woodward (a word surviving in personal name even today) responsible for oversight of timber; others kept watch in the forest against trespass and poaching, and some repaired and maintained hedges and ditches, lodges, and other structures. It was for the officers of the forest that our newest villages were built. In 1227 a *quo warranto* calls upon Ranulph son of Robert to say by what warrant he made towns and raised houses in the earl's forest of Wensleydale. He answered that the town of Bainbridge was raised by the ancestors of Ranulph by service of keeping the forest of Wensleydale, built so that they could have twelve foresters there, each with a house and nine acres of ground. The dwellers within the forest took oath to do no wrong to beast or trees, but from time to time the permission to 'assart', that is to clear and enclose a small area within the forest, for farming, was granted to individual tenants.

The event which changed upper Weardale from an almost empty countryside to one having an active population was the creation around 1080 of the Palatine

Bishopric of Durham, to which was attached nearly the whole county as well as small areas within Northumberland and Yorkshire.[4] In the Palatinate the Bishops had rights comparable with those of the king. The valley and surroundings of Weardale were ideal country for the sport and recreation of the Bishops and at an early date a park for deer was enclosed to the west of Stanhope. Hamlets were created in which the tenants held land by services mostly related to the sporting use of the area and to the forest. Some of the hamlets in the lower dale were of Anglian origin – e.g. Wolsingham and Hamsterley – and in these the services normal to an Anglian village were combined with forest duties, and their agriculture provided a steady render of food to the bishop. Before long, veins of lead and beds of a fine limestone good enough to be called marble were discovered and some tenants became miners and quarrymen and masons. The lead mining was later to expand and become for many centuries the chief occupation in the dale.

In 1183 Wolsingham church was built in the mouth of the upper dale, and in 1200 a church was built at Stanhope, which was the real administrative centre of the forest and park. In 1183 Bishop Pudsey caused a survey of his rentals and lands to be made, and from its connection with the village of Bolden near Sunderland it had become known as the *Bolden Book*.[5] It is relatively small, only twenty-four folio pages, but it contains a vivid picture of life at that time within the forest of Weardale. Stanhope Park was created, and Leland in the sixteenth century says of it, 'the Bishop of Duresme had a praty square pele on the north side of Were ryver, called the Westgate, and thereby is a parke rudely enclosed with stone, of a 12 or 14 miles in circumpace'. The Eastgate and Westgate have become villages, and the position of the North Gate and of Gate Castle on the south are still known and mark the extent of the Park. The Westgate Castle, the 'square pile', was the headquarters of the park keeper and other officials and the centre for the forest courts.

Turning to Bolden Book it is seen that the country had only 141 vills, with not much cultivated land and a rather scanty population. In Stanhope there were twenty villeins each with an oxgang of land – the amount, ten to fifteen acres, which could be ploughed yearly with one ox. The villeins payed a 'rent' of two shillings and gave sixteen days work each for the Bishop on his demesne lands. They also spent four days each in carting the Bishop's corn, on carts which they themselves provided. In autumn four portions of seedland were to be prepared, and two days were to be given in mowing, making hay, or carrying the corn. The tenant was given his food on these service days. Other services were the carriage of goods, as required, between Stanhope, Durham, and Aycliffe.

The Bishop's demesne land at Wolsingham was rented out to tenants, who had to return 128 bushels of wheat, 128 bushels of barley, and 560 bushels of oats from its cultivation. Some had also to give nine days' work on the land, and other tenants gave time in mowing, carrying goods, and preparing seedgrounds. Many of the services demanded of the tenants were connected with the forest and with the Bishop's annual Great Hunt, to which a great hoard of followers and visitors was brought. The men of Stanhope, in addition to the service already mentioned on the Bishop's demesne, had each year for the great hunt to prepare the kitchen, larder, and dog-kennels, provide bedding (rushes or bracken) for the hall, chambers, and chapel, and give other minor services about the temporary village which was erected for the Bishop and his visitors and for the use and entertainment of the participants during the hunt. Provisions for all these folk were to be collected, levied on many tenants throughout the county, and carried to the hunt village.

The services were very varied and were apportioned to individuals as well as to villages. Three wood-turners, for seventeen acres of land each, made 3,100 wooden trenchers each year for the use of the hunt. Tenants in Heighington provided ropes for the deer enclosures; others of Usworth, Binchester, Lanchester, and some other vills brought greyhounds, and would of course have to provide their care and keep throughout the year. William of Washington was to bring three greyhounds; if he caught any game on his way to the hunt it belonged to the Bishop, though what he caught while returning was to be his own. The tenants of Auckland erected a fence round the buildings, which included a hall sixty feet by sixteen feet, and a chapel forty feet by fifteen feet, kitchens, larders, sleeping chambers, and smaller buildings, all erected just for the occasion. Tenant service included the provision of all the materials needed for these.

Among the tenants a few tradesmen are mentioned: Lambert the marble cutter, who probably provided the lovely 'Frosterley marble' columns of the Galilee porch at Durham, Aldred of Stanhope the blacksmith, and Ralph the beekeeper. The pinders of various villages supplied 40 hens and 400 eggs each, as rent for their holdings of land. The shepherd and the gardener had twelve and five acres respectively for their services, and Ralph the Crafty of Frosterley held the whole vill in his right as falconer. In Weardale we see a multi-service holding, tenants giving agricultural boon work on the demesne lands, giving more or less onerous services to the annual great hunt, or rendering services more normal to a forest, such as forty days service in the forest in time of rutting and fawning of the deer, and other services directed by the chief forester.

The Bishopric of Durham was only one of several large feudal 'honours' which together covered most of the north Pennines. The honour of Richmond included all the country south of the Tees, with the drainage of the Swale and Ure, to the watershed of Nidd and Wharfe. Within this area the eastern part of the dales was occupied by villages with their commonfields and pastures and with tenants rendering services on the lord's demesne land and at his courts. The upper dales were forest in which were many widely scattered Norse settlements. The honour of Skipton covered much of Wharfedale and Craven, while most of Nidderdale came within the honours of Kirkby Malzeard and Knaresborough. To the west the forest of Mewith included upper Ribblesdale and across to the Lune, while the lordship of Dent took in Dentdale, Garsdale, and the Sedbergh area, in which there were dispersed settlements of Norse type.[6]

In the north and north-west Hexhamshire, which arose as the Anglian bishopric of Wilfred, covered much of mid Tynedale and the whole of the Allendales and Devilswater. The great waste of South Tyne had been added to Cumberland and was known as Aldenstane Moor, a wild area with a few scattered farmsteads.

Without attempting in the very limited space available to disentangle and define the very complex feudal pattern, it is only possible to draw a very generalized picture of the north Pennines about the opening of the thirteenth century. In the dale villages the fields had been added to by each generation so that they formed a spreading pattern of arable and pasture land set in a background of woodland. The woods reached up the valley sides to the fells, which through continued grazing were now taking on the aspect of moorland. A countryside was emerging in which the human occupation was creating a pattern recognizably the basis of that which we know today. In the valley heads and on the country of the high Pennines the picture was very different. Almost continuous forest concealed the scattered homesteads of Norse families – uplands with thinner forest cover were grazed by sheep, and instead of the wide extent of permanent field and village which covered the lower dales fields were restricted to small clearings in the forest and around the -*setts* and -*scales* which were used seasonally by shepherds and cowherds.

Over the whole area the population was segregated into a number of distinct and separate communities; within each honour the life centred on the honour courts and the service of the lords of individual manors which composed the honour. The individual had no rights and protection outside his own honour. In Durham county life centred on the bishopric and its details were determined by the demands of the bishop and his officers for service, food, and sport. Within the forest areas the forest courts made their demands, but there were more individual kinds of service and greater movement with only a thinly scattered and scanty population. There was, however, one very different community coming into being in Aldenstane (later Alston) Moor – that of a group of miners. There is some evidence of

Roman exploitation of the lead mines in the north-west, and again in the early years of the twelfth century lead ore was being mined systematically from which silver was extracted. The mine or group of mines was known as the 'mine of Carlisle' or as the 'mine of Aldenstane', and was leased from the crown by the burgesses of Carlisle. The earliest Pipe Roll of 1130 accounts for 100 shillings rent of the silver mine, a very large sum of money which could apply only to a flourishing and well-established industry.[7]

To ensure the proper working of the mines the king conscripted men as miners and in return gave them many privileges which set them apart as a special community. They were given the right to cut timber for use in the mines, smelting ore, and making dwellings and fences, and to take such timber from the woods most convenient to their mines, no matter to whom it belonged. This privilege set them apart and against the local landholders, and there were many complaints against them for destroying the woodlands. The Archbishop of York complained that the miners had destroyed his woodland in Hexhamshire, in the neighbouring Allendales. Other complaints reached the courts but in all cases the king upheld and reaffirmed the miners' rights to take timber, provided that they were dwelling together on the place where the mines were. The king took his royalty of one-ninth of the produce of the mines, but allowed the miners to appoint their own sheriff or sergeant who administered the law with a jury of miners, free of the common law of the country around. The many privileges were available only to those employed about the mines and to no others. To secure food for this community the king ordered merchants to go to Alston with food and goods, and there in the twelfth century a market grew up, and a church was built about 1200 which served all the district.

Lead mines were discovered in Weardale and were granted by King Stephen to the bishop for the use of his mint and as a source of lead so much needed for the big building programme at Durham cathedral. In the twelfth century there are accounts for smelting ore and extracting silver for the mint, and such items as '£174.0.4 in Silver of the profits of the ore and mint' show that the mining was on a fairly large scale. Bishop Pudsey was in a position to grant a lead mine to the hospital of St Giles in Durham 'for covering the church of St Mary and All Saints and of the hospital aforesaid'. Through the thirteenth century the bishops kept the mines in their own hands and used tenants for their miners, adding the carriage of ore, charcoal, and timber, and the delivery of lead and silver, to the services demanded from their tenantry.

Veins of lead ore were discovered in Teesdale, Arkengarthdale, Swaledale, and Nidderdale, most of them on the higher ground of the fell sides, and as these were exploited there grew a movement of miners away from the settled villages into more convenient settlements. In Arkengarthdale the tiny hamlets Arkle Town, Whaw, Eskeleth, etc., are scattered homesteads made by miners among the ore-bearing ground, starting as hovels with a tiny area of cleared and cultivated ground around them, and never achieving the status of a village. As well as the actual miners there were other men ancilliary to the industry – charcoal burners, smelters, ore carriers and others who, so long as they lived on the mining area, shared the miners' privileges. As population increased in the dales villages and land or shares within the common fields became scarce, other men were tempted to move into the wastes and take up small skills – thatching, fencing, and ditching, stone getting etc. – which they could practise enough to make a subsistence living. The lords of the forest became more favourable towards 'assarting', that is allowing small clearings in the forest, with the keeping of a cow or pig and the making of a garden or field, in return for a rent or for services in the newer skills. The four-teenth century in particular saw this migration of scattered population into the areas which lay outside primary settlement, and some of these gave rise to the tiny hamlets in the valley heads and on the flank of the fells. To meet the needs of such folk, St John's chapel was founded in upper Weardale beyond the limits of the bishop's park, and hamlets such as Cowshill, Daddry Shields, Ireshopeburn, and others, came into being at Wearhead.

During the twelfth century the feudal lords founded many abbeys and priories of the various monastic orders, giving some of them vast areas of land as endow-ment in return for prayers for the souls of themselves and their families, and for the more material help of money and horses to assist them on the Crusades. The land given to the monasteries was very largely located in the wilder fells and among the forests, but the recipients were skilled in taming the wild and in creating vast sheep walks which they managed from granges and farms. In the upland areas they brought prosperity to a section of the population and imposed a new pattern on the countryside. The pre-Conquest Benedictine abbeys had mostly been destroyed by the Danes, and only a few were reinstated after the Conquest. In the twelfth century a movement of reform gave rise to new orders, among them the Augus-tinian Canons and the Cistercian monks. In 1120 Cicely de Romille of the Honour of Skipton founded a Priory of Augustinian Canons at Embsay near Skipton and in 1155 gave them the whole manor of Bolton in Wharfedale, to which they trans-ferred; there they built their new Bolton Priory for a prior and fifteen canons. The canons were to spend their time in prayer at the priory and in serving the parish churches of Skipton, Long Preston, Harewood, Broughton, and Kildwick, which were presented to them. They were also to provide hospitality and alms. Workmen and wage servants were employed about the priory and on the demesne farms and granges, and officials managed the wide estates. They traded extensively in wool, bred horses, did a little iron making and lead mining, and ran many farms.[8]

The most important reform group was that of the Cistercians, who, from the parent house of Citeaux in Burgundy, brought with them a lively interest and great skill in sheep breeding and iron making. Their first Yorkshire abbey was founded at Rievaulx in North Yorkshire in 1131, and this was quickly followed by Fountains (1132), Byland (1138), Jervaulx (1145), and Salley (1148). The upland limestone areas of Craven were a great attraction to the Cistercians, and during the twelfth and early thirteenth centuries Fountains, Byland, Salley, and Furness abbeys were granted most of the fell country of Craven. Fountains had Kilnsey and the whole of Littondale with the fells across to Malham Moor, Fountains Fell, and Penyghent. Furness had a great part around Ribblehead and Ingleborough, with the Winterburn valley; Jervaulx had part of upper Ribblesdale, including Horton and Studfold, while Salley got Stainforth and most of Ribblesdale south of that village, and Byland had much of upper Nidderdale. Bolton had the manor of Malham East with much of mid Airedale around and south of Skipton. Fountains built a grange at Kilnsey with a hall and chapel and other buildings, including a corn mill and a fulling mill, and other subsidiary granges at Bordley and Malham. The Norse -hus settlements on Malham Moor became important sheep farms and a few new farms were made. Small hamlets or lodges in the old forest of Litton were enlarged into the hamlets Foxup, Halton Gill, Litton, and Arncliffe. Furness followed a similar pattern, making important farms from the older isolated Norse farms: Selside, Southerscales, Bruntscar, Birkwith, and Gearstones were such Norse farms translated into rich sheep farms, and new ones were created at Ingman Lodge, Newby Cote, Cam House, Colt Park, and so on.

Jervaulx was granted most of the upper part of Wensleydale above Askrigg; Nidderdale was shared by Fountains and Byland, and Bridlington Priory had large areas in Swaledale. Farther north, Weardale was held by Durham, and Hexhamshire by Hexham Abbey. A later monastic order originating at Premontre, and so called Premonstratensian, was less numerous than the Cistercians but had several abbeys in the north Pennines – Coverham in Wensleydale, Easby in Swaledale, Eggleston in Teesdale (Plates 37 and 11), and Blanchland in Derwentdale. Coverham and Easby had the gift of churches and land in the Sedbergh and Garsdale area, and Easby and Eggleston had estates in Stainmore and Teesdale. This order took more interest in pastoral work and in learning, had good libraries, and taught in the churches, which in fact became schools for the local youths. Like the Cistercians they were skilled with sheep and in the production of wool.

94

On the widespread Cistercian estates there was a new orientation of daily life. There was a constant coming and going between grange and abbey and the outlying farms; the Cellarer, Prior, and other officials came at regular intervals to hold courts, check accounts, and give some supervision of affairs. Wool, cheese, grain, building materials, and other produce of the granges was carried to the abbey, and wine and food were sent out to the granges. Some granges had special products – Kilnsey grange, besides a vast trade in wool, produced thatching reeds on the site of the glacial lake, and also had limekilns for builders' lime; Brimham in Nidderdale had a smelthouse (now the village of Smelthouse) for their lead mines, and also split laths from the oak saplings in the forest. Bradley near Huddersfield made iron; Jervaulx had great occupation in breeding and rearing horses at Horton and Studfold (named after the horse enclosures), and corn and fulling mills were part of many of the granges.

The granges became a regular feature of the upper Pennine dales, even within the more settled agricultural villages, but were most common in the open country of the sheep walks. The grange generally had a chapel, at which its workpeople and tenants could hear Mass. This and the refectory were in the charge of a priest-monk, and staffed by a team of conversi under constant supervision from the parent abbey. In the areas of the granges the local people would thus be quite familiar with the sight of monastic officials and servants and would have little knowledge of the feudal overlord of the non-monastic villages.

It is to the interest and labour of the monasteries and their workers that we owe the clearing of vast areas of upland, the draining of swamps, the elimination of scrubland, and the establishment of upland farms on the site of the Norse shielings and many other places. With all these went the great improvement in the quality of the upland pasture. Their flocks were the ancestors of some of the present dale breeds of sheep. In Nidderdale Fountains and Byland were both granted the rights to dig ores of lead and iron, to make charcoal, and to take timber, and in the thirteenth century the fells around Greenhow Hill were busy with the lead miners, whose ore was carried to Smelthouse for smelting or smelted at bole hills (very primitive furnaces) on the fellsides. Within the forest charcoal burners were at work for part of the year, and forges produced iron. In Wensleydale, Jervaulx had a grant of iron and lead within Wensley Forest, but never developed much activity; Bridlington were busy in Swaledale, and other iron-makers were at work in Teesdale. These miners and iron-workers were scattered through the forest areas and did not form a compact and separate community like that on Alston Moor.

Life on the monastic estates was not always peaceful. Some of the local people in and near the great monasteries and estates resented the way whole tracts of country and complete villages had been taken from them, and in particular the loss of much wild country in which some of the more prosperous folk had hunted was a sore trial. At the same time many of the monastic officials became hard and grasping landlords, not hesitating in some cases to deal with tenants in ways quite contrary to the established customs of the manor. In a time when there were no banks and when Scots raids and other unrest were almost a commonplace, the monasteries were entrusted with papers and valuables for safe keeping. It was surprisingly common for the abbots and priors to refuse to return these goods, and the Courts of Chancery were crowded with petitions seeking restitution of papers and possessions, not, apparently, with much success. Other sources of trouble were the many mills granted to the monasteries, grazing rights on commons and moors, fishing in the streams, and hunting on the wastes. Some of the cases in Chancery throw light on the state of the country.[9]

It is said in a fourteenth-century complaint by the Abbot of Fountains that several persons assembled men with weapons and threatened the Abbot's shepherds and other servants, who were beaten and wounded so that they were afraid to continue in his service. The Abbot was accused of robbing the commoners' grazing grounds and preventing their sheep from feeding. If action was taken against the offenders, 'they remove and go into dales and fells so that there may be no common law executed against them'. At another time John Preston of Malham and William Preston of Otterburn in Craven came armed to the abbey at vespers and attacked the monks with spears and weapons, and at other times they 'lay in wait for the abbot, his fellow monks and servants, in the parts of Craven'. It becomes clear that in the western dales and the forest areas there were many refuges for these wilder persons, who not only took refuge there but committed many trespasses which resulted in poaching affrays. There was a large degree of lawlessness.

At Cogden in Swaledale, one John Robynson was tenant of the Priory of Bridlington, having a farm of '22 acres and more with common and other properties'. When John Robynson died the Prior refused to show the copy of the court roll by which the farm was held, turned out John's heir, and took the farm for his own tenant. At Ramsgill in Nidderdale a petitioner says that servants of Byland Abbey marked two lambs from another farm with the petitioner's marks, 'planted' them in his flock, and so attempted to secure a conviction of theft and eviction from the farm. In Richmond Henry Cogell bought land on the side of a 'water' or stream, and built two mills with a dam, at a cost of more than £80. John, Prior of St Martin at Richmond, claimed that the water to midstream belonged to

15. Ingleborough, Penyghent, and Whernside from Great Whernside looking across Littondale. The fell in front of Penyghent is Fountains Fell, and the crags in Wharfedale (foreground) and Littondale, in black shadows, are, from left to right, Kilnsey Crag, Arnberg Scar, and Skoska.

16a (left). *Cattle mart at Bentham, West Yorks.*

16b (centre). *Leyburn Market.*

16c (left). *The Pennine Way Pioneers.* (left to right) *Barbara Castle, Fred Willey, Arthur Blenkinsop, George Chetwynd, Tom Stephenson, Hugh Dalton, and Julian Snow. Birkdale House, Teesdale, 1948.*

the Abbot of St Marys of York, and so pulled down the dam. The miller then paid the Abbot £4 13s. 4d. for the full use of the stream, but again the prior 'in peaceable manner pulled down the dam . . .' and stopped the mills.

In 1221 an appeal about Langcliffe mill went to the Pope's Legate, who degreed that Furness Abbey, having built the mill on land of the manor of Langcliffe, should surrender it to the lord of the manor, but that as part of the dam and pool was on their own land the Abbot should keep the whole pool and the water. Thus began a war of more than a century. In 1279 there was trouble in Littondale: 'moreover for the violence and damage done by the monks and lay brothers of Salley to the Abbot of Fountains mill in Litton . . .' a fine of £10 was laid 'and because the dam of the mill partly extends within the common of the Abbot of Salley, he and his tenants of Litton ought to grind at the mill'. With parish and manor boundaries mostly at the mid-line of a stream, it was inevitable that mill and mill-dam quarrels should be a perpetual theme in all the courts.

In the northern Pennines, however, mill quarrels were rare because of the paucity of monastic holdings and the existence of the few very large single estates. With practically the whole of Weardale in the hands of the Bishop of Durham, with the Northumberland Pennines in the sub-county of Hexhamshire, and Alston Moor almost in one ownership, there was very little cause for the kind of quarrel which enlivened life in the Yorkshire Pennines. None the less the northern areas had troubles thrust upon them from outside.

From a very early date the border area (in present terms the Scottish Border counties) was in constant turmoil. Besides a number of clan wars, the area was impoverished and depended very largely on raids and forays into the richer lands of England for the regular supply of cattle, sheep, horses, and money.[10] Raiding was the great and prime occupation of the Scots for a few centuries. As early as 1070 raids on a large scale took place. Malcolm, king of Scots, raided through Cumberland and over into Teesdale, then continued ravaging and burning his way down Tees into Cleveland, destroying all in his path. The people of Hunderthwaite made a stand against him but were defeated and mostly killed. Cattle and livestock were driven back into Scotland. In 1138 William, son of Duncan and nephew of David king of Scotland, raided with an army through the Vale of Eden and over the fells and valley heads into Craven. The chroniclers say the whole land was laid waste and 'no rank or age, and neither sex was spared'; children were killed and women carried off as slaves to Scotland. However much the violent account is reduced by critical examination there is some evidence of these very large-scale raids, and there are the accounts of the battle of Clitheroe when

Stephen opposed William Duncan, and persistent traditions of other battles in Craven, such as the one at Sweet Gap in Conistone near Gargrave.

After Bannockburn in 1314 Scots raids became very common, coming down through Durham, raiding in the dales, and then returning by Stainmore. Some came down the Cumberland valleys and into the Yorkshire dales – all the abbeys and priories suffered, and some like Bolton were deserted for several years. It is said that 'whatever places the Scots and men of Galloway reached were full of horror and cruelty'. One of the biggest raids was perhaps least successful. In 1327 an army of 4,000 Scots knights and squires with 20,000 light horse under the Earl of Moray and Sir James Douglas crossed the Tyne and began to ravage the dales of west Durham. Edward III came to Durham but could not find them and Thomas Rokeby earned a knighthood and land of £100 value by leading the king to oppose them at Stanhope in Weardale. After some days without engagement the Scots stole away at night across Yad Moss at the head of Teesdale, leaving behind great quantities of cattle and goods which they had stolen. It would only spoil the story to be too critical of the figures, but we can be sure that this was one of their large-scale raids.

One of the later raids was the subject of a ballad, the 'Rookhope Ride'. The raid occurred in the sixteenth century, after the Rising in the North, when the moss-troopers of Tynedale (North Tyne and Cheviot) thought that Weardale would have lost most of its men and would be an easy prey. With a hundred men the raiders reached Wolsingham and then turned up the dale, driving six hundred sheep and many cattle and horses before them. A small band of shepherds and farm servants, led by local yeomen, set off in pursuit and overtook them at Neukton Edge, where after an hour's battle the hundred Tynedale men were defeated by the forty Weardale folk, who had the advantage of knowing every yard of the difficult ground. Four raiders were killed and eleven were taken prisoner. All this is related in a ballad of thirty-seven halting verses,* some of which are not easy to follow –

> Thir Weardale men, they have good hearts,
> They are as stiff as any tree
> For, if they'd everyone been slain
> Never a foot, back man would flee.
>
> And such a storm among them fell
> As I think you never heard the like,
> For he that bears his head so high
> He oft-times fall into the dyke . . . etc.

* See Chapter 11.

98

In an attempt to check this very widespread raiding a large number of castles were built, the main group being in Northumberland in an arc down the east flank of the Cheviots. In the fourteenth and fifteenth centuries small defensive towers were added to many of the farms, strong and square, the ground floor providing a strong place for horses and stores, with a defended yard for cattle around it. The first and second floors provided accommodation into which several families could crowd for safety during a raid. Almost every village and hamlet had its 'pele tower' and no outlying farmstead was secure which was not built round such a pele.*

The basic plan of defence rested, of course, upon the Norman castles, but many smaller ones were added as further raids showed up weak points, until by the the fifteenth century the plan was complete in outline, and only a few fortified houses and peles were added between 1415 and 1541.[11] After the extensive raids of the early part of the fourteenth century, licences to crenelate houses were granted in large numbers and from these came many of the peles and a few of the smaller castles. A strong line of castles defended the Tyne valley and the mouths of the tributary valleys, by which an entry could have been made into the dale country. Near the bend where the South Tyne emerges from the Pennines and turns east there are Blenkinsopp Castle (a strong tower) and Thirlwall on the north flank and Bellister and Featherstone castles in the angle of the river. The Allendales are protected by Langley Castle and Staward Pele, and Burnlaw in the West Allen is a strongly fortified hall. Thornton Tower north of the Tyne is a pele. Near the entry of the North Tyne, a favourite route from Scotland, Beaufront, Aydon, and Halton castles defend the eastward way along the Tyne's north bank. Farther east are Bywell on the north bank and the big and very strong Prudhoe Castle on the south. All these prevented raiding along the Tyne valley and protected crossing places over the river.

The next great route was Stainmore and the lower Tees valley, by which the rich Vale of Mowbray and North Yorkshire could be attacked. At the west end the Vale of Eden has Dacre, Penrith, Brougham, Kirkoswald, and Appleby in the vale, then Brough and Augill Castles at the opening of Stainmore, with Hartley, Lammerside, and Pendragon castles to close Mallerstang and the way into Garsdale and Wensleydale. On the east Bowes and Barnard Castle are supported by Cotherstone, Scargill, and Streatlam, and down the east flank of the Pennines, overlooking the richer land of the mid-Durham dale, there are, from north to south, Brancepeth, Witton, Raby, Ravensworth, and Richmond (Plate 35).

* See Chapter 9 for a more detailed architectural description of peles and castles.

Mortham Tower near Scargill was built after one of the serious raids to afford protection for Rokeby, and other peles were built in south Durham. By the sixteenth century, however, the pattern of raids was changing, and the moss-troopers gradually grew into the more peaceful drovers, who reversed the flow of cattle, bringing northern beasts to the markets in the south instead of driving southern stock north.

6

The growth of
towns and markets

The Scots raids were a source of intermittent troubles in the dales for more than two centuries, but they never equalled the disaster of the Black Death of 1346 to 1348, in which the population was reduced in some places to less than half. In the Scots raids the attack had been directed mainly at the monastic houses and properties, and cattle and sheep had been driven off, but most of the people had taken to the hills and kept out of the way of the raiders. The Canons of Bolton Priory had dispersed, some to other Priories farther south, and a few into the protection of Skipton Castle. Some attempt could be made to reduce the seriousness of a raid: cattle could be driven into the hills, and, though living might be very hard, much could be saved, only a very small part of the population losing life or total property. In the Black Death the pestilence struck all; there seemed to be no escape from its attack, and in some disastrous places all died, while in others more fortunate only half or even fewer perished. In the remoter and healthier Pennine dales the deaths were not so overwhelming as in the towns and the more thickly populated lowlands, but none the less they reduced the available labour to an amount not sufficient to keep all the cultivated land in heart. With the struggle to keep and secure at least their own necessities the peasants broke from their feudal servitude and many eventually achieved the position of wage labourers. Recovery, however, was rapid, and after thirty years the countryside was again fairly prosperous. The levy of a 'poll tax' by Richard II in 1379 has provided a census of the population, each adult of sixteen years or more being named and taxed according to his status or occupation. Villages vary, but in the Yorkshire dales for which the returns are complete[1] the villages fall into members of a pattern – most of them were occupied almost entirely by labourers, with perhaps a steward of the manor or a bailiff, and the average size was somewhere about thirty households. A labourer and his wife were taxed 4*d*. Craftsmen, weavers, tailors, sutors (shoemakers) and so on paid 6*d*., and others according to status or rank: a hosteller, or inn-keeper might be taxed 1*s*. if his inn was more than an ale-house, a merchant might be taxed 2*s*., whilst stewards, franklins, gentlemen and so on paid on an ascending scale. A few villages had an undue proportion of craftsmen: for example, Appletreewick in Wharfedale had 19 labourers and 11 craftsmen. The craftsmen included weavers and a dyer, and there were also 13 servants, many of them probably assistants to the craftsmen, as all were single folk. In some of the towns, like Skipton and Ripon, merchants and shopkeepers congregated. In Ripon the population included 74 craftsmen and merchants, 23 of them concerned with leather and leather working, and 38 of them with wool, cloth, and clothing. This reflects a market town with fairs, to which wool and cattle were regularly brought, with a group of craftsmen based upon the ample supply of wool and hides. In Skipton there were 23 craftsmen with many shopkeepers and some merchants. There were two weavers from Brabant, millers, and a fuller, and evidence that in this town and round about there was developing a small textile industry, as we have already seen in the dependent village of Appletreewick.

The most prosperous villages and towns were those with markets. The feudal system and the monasteries contributed much to the necessity for, and the growth of, markets. The military garrisons and the large retinues of the feudal overlords represented a considerable amount of labour withdrawn from production, accompanied by a very big demand on food sources. While the lord's demesne and the food rents and services of some of his manors, berewicks in particular, could generally supply his household, there were armies of paid mercenary soldiers and servants and the fairly large numbers of craftsmen necessary for the work and maintenance of the garrison who for the purchase of their food needed a local market. The lord also was dependent upon merchants, who would only make a profitable journey to an established market or fair. It was profitable in more ways than one for a feudal baron to obtain the charter for a market under the protection of his castle. He was able to collect tolls and fines from the market, and merchants were willing to come under his protection and to bring within his reach luxuries of wine, fine cloths, special arms and armour, and articles which otherwise he would be unable to obtain.

Monastic communities needed markets, both as buyers and sellers; some received tithes and other dues in kind in greater amounts than they could use, and also needed goods not produced on their estates. In Skipton a market was held in the wide street leading to the castle gateway, and before 1189 Alice de Romille 'gave the canons of Bolton this liberty, that they and their men should be quit of all dues and tolls in the town of Skipton and without it, wherever toll is paid in her lands, however they may buy and sell, whether in markets or without'. As in many other markets, the monastic community of Embsay, and later of Bolton, being made free of market tolls, came to take an important part in its trade. In 1203 a Fair was granted to Skipton to be held on the eve, day, and morrow of Trinity. This would attract merchants from farther afield than the weekly markets, and would soon be fitted into their journeys round the principal fairs of the north country.[2]

The earliest markets were these established under the walls of the Norman castles, where there was the nucleus of a non-agricultural population under the protection of a powerful overlord. The Earls of Richmond secured a royal charter for a market before 1144 and its tolls were a steady source of income to them. The list of tolls in the fourteenth century cover a remarkable variety of goods – cattle, sheep, horses, grains, wool, cloth, and hides; also wines, fish, silks, lampreys, garlic, woad, salt, cheese, butter, lard, and honey. Other goods also paid tolls, such as wood, faggots, iron, lead, and coal. These tolls were sufficiently valuable for them to be sequestrated for a time for the repair of the walls of the garrison of Berwick-on-Tweed.

Barnard Castle was the creation of a Norman lord. King Rufus, at the beginning of the twelfth century, granted the forest of Teesdale to Baliol, whose son Barnard chose a place for a castle on a rock overlooking the river Tees in Marwood, in the ancient parish of Gainford. This 'Barnard's Castle' became the feudal centre of the whole district and gathered around it a small town with a market and many craftsmen. There was eventually a bridge over the river, and the old street under the castle walls is still called Bridgegate, though the bridge replaced a ford which was the only crossing for many centuries. The Roman road from Bowes to Binchester crossed the Tees by a ford which gave its name to the near-by hamlet on the south of the river and opposite the castle, Startforth. This name of Startforth has grown by slow change out of the older name of Straetford, or 'the ford on the street', most Roman roads being called in earlier times 'streets'. The line of this road is followed in Barnard Castle by the Galgate, the main street of the town. Between Galgate and Bridgegate there is the Market Place, in which there stands a fine eighteenth-century market-hall, but markets have been held in the street from the foundation of the town.

It was at Auckland, on the Wear, that the powerful Bishops of Durham had their castle-palace, and a market grew up there to serve Weardale, Bishop Auckland soon becoming a market town. In the Tyne valley there is an apparent exception to the general rule, for the powerful castle of Prudhoe, a possession of the Percies, developed neither town nor market, and these arose at Hexham around the Abbey. The topographic position of the towns, when compared, suggests what was probably the chief influence in this unexpected development. Hexham is eleven miles west of Prudhoe at the junction of North Tyne and the Tyne, not far from the Allendales, and near or on two ancient roads. From Alston, where a church, parish, and market had been created in or before 1154 for the benefit of the community of 'kings' miners, who had the king's protection, there was a road across the Allendales to Hexham (still a main road, 6305 and 686). The Roman road from Pierce Bridge by Lanchester came to the Tyne at Corbridge, an important Roman town and later a royal town or 'burgh' of the Angles. Corbridge, however, because of its position, had not grown, so that near-by Hexham, only three miles away, with its Abbey and bishopric had become in effect the head of this road, meeting there the way that was later to become a principal drove road and raiding road from Scotland, by the North Tyne. The bishopric servants and the large monastic community, with the big areas of mines and forest to the south-west, soon brought Hexham to the position of an important market centre even though it had no castle.

Ripon was a town in some ways comparable with Hexham – just off the Roman road, having no castle, but with an early bishopric and a very important minster community; close by was the great and rich monastery of Fountains Abbey, and behind it the dales population in Nidderdale and parts of Knaresborough Forest. On the east it had the rich arable lands of the Vale of York, and so was admirably placed – where the Pennines declined and the dales opened out to the lower lands – to be the ideal market between them. These feudal markets were visited by merchants from far afield, even from the Continent, and associated with them were annual fairs, usually lasting three days or more, which attracted foreign merchants. For the everyday needs of the countryside population, however, the major markets were almost inaccessible, some of them a day's journey away, so that in the thirteenth century a large number of more local markets were established, mostly by charter, which could serve a group of manors or a forest area. The number of these more local markets is very large, and the villages where markets and fairs were held in almost all cases grew beyond their neighbours, and many became the nuclei of the smaller market towns of today.

A market and fair was granted to the village of Wensley in 1202, and this served a wide area of Wensleydale as well as Middleham Castle for at least a century. In 1305 Carperby was given a market charter, and in 1387 Middleham secured its own market and fair, which soon became of great importance, fairs for cattle and pigs continuing there for several centuries. Under the protection of Jervaulx Abbey, East Witton had a market from 1307. Today the two great markets of Wensleydale are at Leyburn and Hawes, but these were not established until 1684 and 1700 and their rise may be connected with the disafforestation and the decline of the feudal castles and the monasteries, after which many of the smaller markets declined seriously. The growth of freeholders and their increased mobility made the two new centres of Hawes and Leyburn the focal points of a new population.

Askrigg is a market of somewhat different kind. The upper dale constituted Wensley Forest, for the service of which, as we have already mentioned, the foresters' village of Bainbridge was built. Within the forest there were at the most only tiny hamlets and scattered assarts with the minimum of arable land. The forest population needed a market, and one grew up by custom at the nearest village to the forest boundary, Askrigg. In 1587 the ancient customary market was regularized into a market by charter and the grant of a fair. Wensley market had died out by 1563, and in part Askrigg took its place. Wensley had suffered badly in the Plague in that year and never recovered. In the Parish Register there is a note: 'The reason as some think that nothing is found written in the Register in the year of our Lord God 1563. Because that in that yeare, the visitation or plague was most hote and fearfull so yt many fled and ye Towne of Wensley by reason of the sickness was unfrequented for a long season. As I finde By one old writeing dated 1569. By me Jo. Naylor.' 'Forest' markets similar to Askrigg grew up in other villages bordering the several forests: for instance, Kettlewell on the boundary of Langstroth and Litton forest, whose market died out with the disafforestation in the time of James I. Grinton market, soon transferred to Reeth (Plate 21), served the forest of Arkengarthdale and Swaledale; Middleton in Teesdale market served the forest of Teesdale, and Stanhope market the forest of Weardale. Few of the forest markets grew to any great size, nor did they persist much beyond the seventeenth century.

Corn and cattle markets at strategic positions in the mouth of the dales, between the rich arable lands and the upland pasture, captured the increasing traffic, and it is among these that the present-day flourishing market towns are found. Masham is an example of the rapid growth of a market in such a position. A charter, probably regularizing an older market, was granted in 1250, giving to John de Worton, Lord of the manor of Mashamshire, a market on Fridays and a fair on the eve, day, and morrow of the Assumption of Saint Mary. Another market on Wednesdays and a four-day fair was granted in 1328, and still another fair and market was granted in 1393. In 1632 another fair was granted for every other Wednesday between 8 May and Michaelmas, for corn and cattle, with a Court of Pie Powder.

As none of these markets and fairs were granted with tolls, and trade there was toll-free, other markets soon suffered by their competition, and even a secure market such as Richmond was affected, the townspeople there complaining that their town had suffered severely and that their property was depreciated in value by the loss of tolls in their market. Masham market and fairs served the larger part of Nidderdale, and people came from great distances, carrying away their

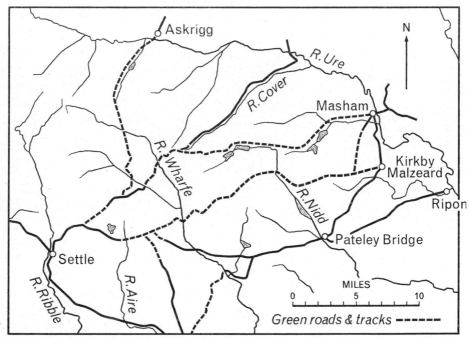

Map 6   *Market roads*

goods on pack-horses. Cattle was brought from much of the upland country, and soon, like many of the more important markets, a network of trackways was made across the fells, leading to these towns, used alike by cattle drovers with their stock, pack-horse men, traders, and customers. These networks of 'market roads' survive as green lanes, and though of very mixed date, not capable of complete identification, they are in the main very early. They form a pattern of roads distinct from any other, and have little kin except with the drove roads of the seventeenth and eighteenth centuries[3] (Map 6).

The roads to Masham survive today as green tracks over the moors, and only within the last few years, in a scheme to assist the farms in upper Nidderdale, has one of these tracks – from Ramsgill to Masham – been converted into a motor road, reopening the communications with this important market. Some of the early market roads extend for great distances and link up not only the countryside but the principal markets and fairs of a region. We can take one or two examples from the abundance which can still be recognized. Settle was granted a market charter in 1249 and was an important focal point for Ribblesdale and much of the rich Craven Lowlands. An application for additional fairs in 1708 says that Skipton is the next nearest market town and that from ancient times the market has had so much trade that extra fairs have been held, besides the one originally granted. The market had been for corn, meal, wool, yarn, hides, and other commodities, and fairs were held for horses and geldings, sheep, lambs, cattle, beasts, and all kinds of goods and merchandise. The appeal resulted in a royal grant of seven more fairs additional to the first one. 'There hath been an ancient weekly market held in Settle in which wheat, beans, barley, peas and oate meal (but chiefly oatemeal) have been openly and publicly exposed for sale . . . every week quantities of oate-meal are bought at Settle markett by persons living in the Dales and other parts of the Country, they growing little or noe grain in those places. . . .'

One of the many roads to and from this market can be traced from the market place, climbing Constitution Hill, a green track for a mile, till it joins the modern road from Langcliffe. This continues the same line across Winskill and Cowside to meet after two miles an ancient road, now modernized in part, which comes from Helwith Bridge, crossing Malham Moor where it becomes Mastiles Lane. This is part of the monastic road from Fountains Abbey to its Malham Moor estates and then onward into the Lake District. The Settle track crosses this road and continues to the north-east with no change of direction, but it is now only a faint footpath over the flank of Knowe Fell, once the forest of Gnoup. At Tennant Gill its line is now taken up by the modern road to Arncliffe. After crossing the Skirfare at Arncliffe the line becomes a green bridle track over Old Cote Moor to Starbotton on the Wharfe, where once there was a stone bridge, then continues as a bridle road across Cam Head, called Starbotton Old Road, through the col between the Great and Little Whernsides, and so down Nidderdale. It is joined by green lanes from Kettlewell and Middlesmoor in Wharfedale and Nidderdale respectively.

This link from Middlesmoor is part of a nearly parallel road from Malham by Conistone, the Sandgate, and How Stean to Middlesmoor, a road which became busy at the time of the Malham Moor fairs. After some miles along the flank of Nidderdale the track, running now more east-north-east, runs over Pott Moor to Masham. A branch keeps farther down Nidderdale side then goes from Ramsgill across Fountains Earth and the head of Dallowgill to Kirkby Malzeard, the capital town of the Honour of Kirkby Malzeard and the castle of the Mowbrays, the centre of a very ancient and important market (Plates 16a & b). The general pattern is very complex, with a web of local roads linking the market town with all the villages of its immediate region, but also with remarkably direct roads across the fells between it and other important markets and fairs tens of miles distant.

As wheeled traffic gradually took the place of or supplemented the pack-horse, and the bulk of goods traded greatly increased, roads with gentler gradients became busier and new lines of traffic, sometimes between different markets, became the main routes. In the seventeenth century, although traffic by horse and pony continued over the Settle–Masham road, another less direct but easier road was being improved, with connections between Settle, Skipton, Ripon, Kirkby Malzeard, and Masham. This road was made possible by the extensive repair of bridges and the replacement of some fords or ruinous timber bridges by new bridges of stone. This was largely the activity of Quarter Sessions, which made many records in the form: 1631, Hebden Bridge. . . . 'between most parts of Craven and the markett townes of Ripon Knaresborough and the cittye of Yorke', and which levied money on the wapentake or on the whole West Riding for the repairs which were in question.

A surprising example of this 'market road' bridge repair is perhaps the bridge at Hubberholme at the head of Wharfedale, repaired in 1659 at the cost of the whole of the West Riding, which was charged with £300. It was reported by the magistrates as 'beinge on the high roadeway leading between the markett towne of Lancaster in the countie of Lancaster and the markett towne of Newcastle upon Tyne and other places in the countie of Northumberland'. The road thus suggested would in fact be fairly direct by Clapham, Helwith Bridge (repaired in 1611), or perhaps High Birkwith, Greenfield, Hubberholme, then Wensleydale, Richmond, and Durham.

These very direct roads across the fells and between two ancient market centres are to be found over the whole of the dales, and though a few are now adventurous motor roads, great parts of them are still green roads or tracks. Stanhope is linked with Hexham by such a road through Blanchland, and southward another road across the fells links Stanhope with Barnard Castle, by way of Eggleston and a mountain crossing above 1,200 ft above sea level. Both these are now modernized.* The movement to more lowland lines of transport with roads more suited to wheeled vehicles was active in the seventeenth century, and the older upland

* See Chapter 12.

tracks were left to the use of 'broggers', 'badgers', and 'drovers'. Just a few green roads belonged to another group of occasional usage, those which were 'salt roads'. It is difficult to separate these except in their early sections where they fan out from the salt-pans on the coast; within the northern dales the market roads generally served the salters. There are a few places, however, where the place name 'Salters' Gate marks the road, and 'salt pie' in or near a village marks the salt market.[4]

The 'broggers' were licensed by the Halifax Acts of the sixteenth century to deal in small parcels of wool collected directly from the dales farms and villages for .carriage to the larger markets. The 'badgers' were pedlars or hucksters, licensed to carry corn from markets to sell in small quantities in the countryside and to deal in all kinds of small goods and produce, and they have left their name in Badger Gate, Badger Stile and so on. The 'badger' was the country packman, either carrying his own pack or using a pony for the job. His visit to the outlying farms was no doubt as great an event then as it still was at the beginning of this century. The packman came into the big farm kitchen to open and spread out his wares: lace, ribbons, sewing materials, perhaps perfumes, simple medicines, and sometimes even spices and flavourings. His most valued commodity was news and gossip, liberally dispensed over the refreshments taken when business was done. His customers were not only the farmer's wife but often the nearer neighbours who were invited in, with the servants and others, to avoid a repeated opening of the pack. His visit was in this way a social event.

The Pennines between Stainmore and Tyne are more sparsely populated than the Yorkshire dales, and there are fewer villages (Middleton-in-Teesdale, Wolsingham, Stanhope, and Alston) and rather more hamlets, though the principal settlement pattern is one of scattered farms spread widely along the valley slopes. The greater part of the area is over 700 ft above sea level, and scattered farms are occupied up to about 1,500 ft OD. The medieval arable common fields found in most of the Yorkshire dales are hardly represented except in the mouth of the valleys near the Durham plain. The emphasis in agriculture has been much more pastoral – sheep and cattle, milk and cheese, with only such oats or barley as could be grown in small crofts and enclosures. The mid and lower parts of Weardale and Teesdale below Middleton contained the greater part of the arable cultivation. This dependence upon stock was widespread in the north, and for many early centuries was the background of the border raiding which was almost the normal way of life for many northern and Scottish families.

Throughout the Pennines the seventeenth century was a period marked by a very extensive change in land ownership occasioned by the break-up of the common-field holdings. The desire to improve land was deepseated, and even from the thirteenth century there had been from time to time an attempt to achieve this through enclosure by getting an exchange of dispersed strips in a common field, so that a single parcel of a bovate (ten to twelve acres), was held, 'if the monks should wish to have the land of the said bovate together'.* After the Reformation, with the growth of the yeoman farmer, this process went on apace – strips were exchanged between different furlongs, either acre for acre or with a money adjustment, but the final effect was that fields in our modern sense were created. Many of the fields in the dales are long and narrow, and of the reversed S-shape, resulting from bringing together half a dozen or so plough strips. This exchange of strips was still going on in the eighteenth century.

Many of the new fields in the seventeenth century were used for rearing and keeping dairy cattle, as the dales villages became freed from the necessity of subsistence farming and could buy their corn from the markets on the edge of the Pennines, adjacent to the richer corn lands of the lowlands to the east. The increasing use of good land of the lowlands for corn reduced the amount available for stock pasturage, and a useful exchange of meat, cheese, and butter for corn suited both the dales population and the market traders. A major change followed developments in Scotland, where in the sixteenth and seventeenth centuries cattle raiding across the border had almost been a regular occupation. The hills of Scotland were ideal ground for breeding cattle, but were not good enough for the best fattening. The English counties could breed the good quality dairy cattle, and the extension of breeding reduced the supply of meat cattle in the Midland and Southern markets. This shortage could be met by importing Scotch cattle into England, fattening them on the northern hills, and sending them south through the large cattle fairs which soon grew up.[5]

A small trade in cattle and sheep sent to England had been prohibited in 1598 but in 1611 it was resumed, though heavy tolls were to be paid at Kirk of Graitnay in Annandale, Jedburgh, and Dunns, on goods crossing the West, Mid, and East Border respectively. The market in England was good and by 1663 over 18,000 beasts a year were coming into Carlisle. Yorkshire graziers felt the competition of the Scots cattle and asked for heavy duties against them, 'the cattle being fed, maintained, and fattened with farre less charge than can possibly be done in England, they filled and quitte the markets and undersell those of English breed'. In 1672 the tolls were abolished and the movement of cattle from Scotland into the north of England became an established trade. Cattle from the Highlands and

* *Fountains Chartulary.*

even from the Hebrides were assembled at the great fairs or Trysts, at Falkirk, Crieff, and Dumfries, and from these were taken by drovers to the Northumbrian grasslands and the limestone dales of the Pennines. The herds of cattle were brought by ways which avoided the towns and the cultivated land, keeping as far as possible on the fells and open moors, crossing streams and rivers near their source or by well-established fords. The drover had perhaps a boy and two dogs for his company and herded forty or fifty beasts. Companies of drovers would sometimes bring one or two hundred cattle, with a man to each forty or so, and possibly with a mule or two to carry provisions.

Along the drove routes progress was gentle. The cattle would eat occasionally on the way, and were found a good resting place at night after a day's march of ten or twelve miles. There was generally a halt at midday to graze a little, and in the early evening a sheltered grassy hollow, with water, would be reached. Long usage brought these places into a fine grass, and some can be recognized, forming what the drover called a 'stance'. In the later eighteenth century small enclosures near a solitary inn or cottage were sometimes used for a small fee. There are several of these drovers' inns, though very few retain their licence, and on the hills some of the later 'stances' with their now broken enclosure walls can still be recognized. The repeated passage of hundreds of cattle by the same routes created green ways, often twenty or thirty yards wide on the open fells, and cut deep as sunk ways on the hill breasts. Graziers attended the Scottish Trysts and bought cattle there, then made their arrangements for the droving, a dealer often having a few drovers in his regular employ. It was not uncommon, however, for drovers to bring cattle to be offered for sale at the local fairs and markets, and to be entrusted with the price in cash to be carried back to their masters.

At the northern English fairs the cattle were mostly bought by graziers, who either owned or hired land on which they could fatten the stock for a season, before they were sent to the southern markets, or sold to the butchers at more local meetings. A good example of a drovers' meeting-place is the Gearstones at Ribblehead, formerly an inn. Green tracks approach this lonely spot from all directions, and around it there are small enclosed fields for stock. In the district there is not far away another former inn, Newby Head, which was the favourite meeting-place for the butchers who attended the Gearstones markets.

One of the largest gatherings was on Great Close on Malham Moor, at which Hurtley, the Malham School master, records great gatherings. Great Close is 'a prodigious field of enclosed land, being upwards of 732 Acres in one Pasture; a great part of which is a fine rich soil, and remarkable for making cattle both expeditiously and uncommonly fat. This Great Close . . . was many years rented by

Mr Birtwhistle of Skipton, the celebrated Craven Grazier and on which you might frequently see 5,000 head of Scotch cattle at one time. As soon as these were a little strengthened, notice was dispersed among neighbouring markets and villages that a Fair would be held on this Field on a particular day, and lots being separated by guess as nearly as could in such manner be done to the wants or wishes of any Purchaser, so much was fixed immediately by the eye upon that lot, or so much per head, taking them as accidentally they were intermixed upon an average. . . . As soon as these were disposed of, a fresh Drove succeeded, and besides Sheep and Horses frequently in great numbers, Mr Birtwhistle has had Twenty Thousand head of Cattle on this field in one summer. . . .' Hurtley goes on to say that as well as Birtwhistle, who often had ten thousand cattle on the roads at one time, many other Craven graziers now, in 1786, also go to the Highlands and send back great droves.[6]

Only three miles away on Boss Moor another similar, though smaller, fair sprang up, with its enclosures round the now ruined inn, Lane Head, known in earlier days as the Waste Inn. Many of the cattle bought here were taken to Skipton market; some of them to Ripon or Masham. The blacksmiths of Grassington did a great trade in cow shoes at both these fairs.

It might be profitable to follow one of these drove roads at least from the Borders right across our area. Some of the cattle from the Falkirk Tryst were brought through the Southern Uplands to Newcastleton, and by a road now largely modernized to Bewcastle in Northumberland. From here the line of the Roman road was followed to Birdoswald near Gilsland for a crossing of the river Irthing. Sir Walter Scott knew the drovers well and describes their trade and training in his introduction to the *Two Drovers*. In the course of the novel he tells how his drovers travelled along the road we are now describing. They had crossed the part 'emphatically called the Waste' but now were descending towards a fertile and enclosed country which needed 'previous arrangement and bargain with the possessors of the ground . . . as a great northern fair was upon the eve of taking place and both Scotch and English drovers expected to dispose of part of their cattle'.

In *Guy Mannering* he has a note on Mump's Ha' (Beggars Hall). 'There is or was a little inn called this, near to Gilsland . . . It was a hedge ale-house where the Border farmers of either country often stopped to refresh themselves and their nags, in their way to and from the trysts in Cumberland, and especially those who came from Scotland . . . through a barren and lonely district, the Waste of Bew-castle.' 'Charlie' in the story had been at Stagshaw Bank fair with sheep and cattle and called here on his return journey.

(left of top centre), a former pothole. Areas of limestone pavement are seen on the right of the picture.

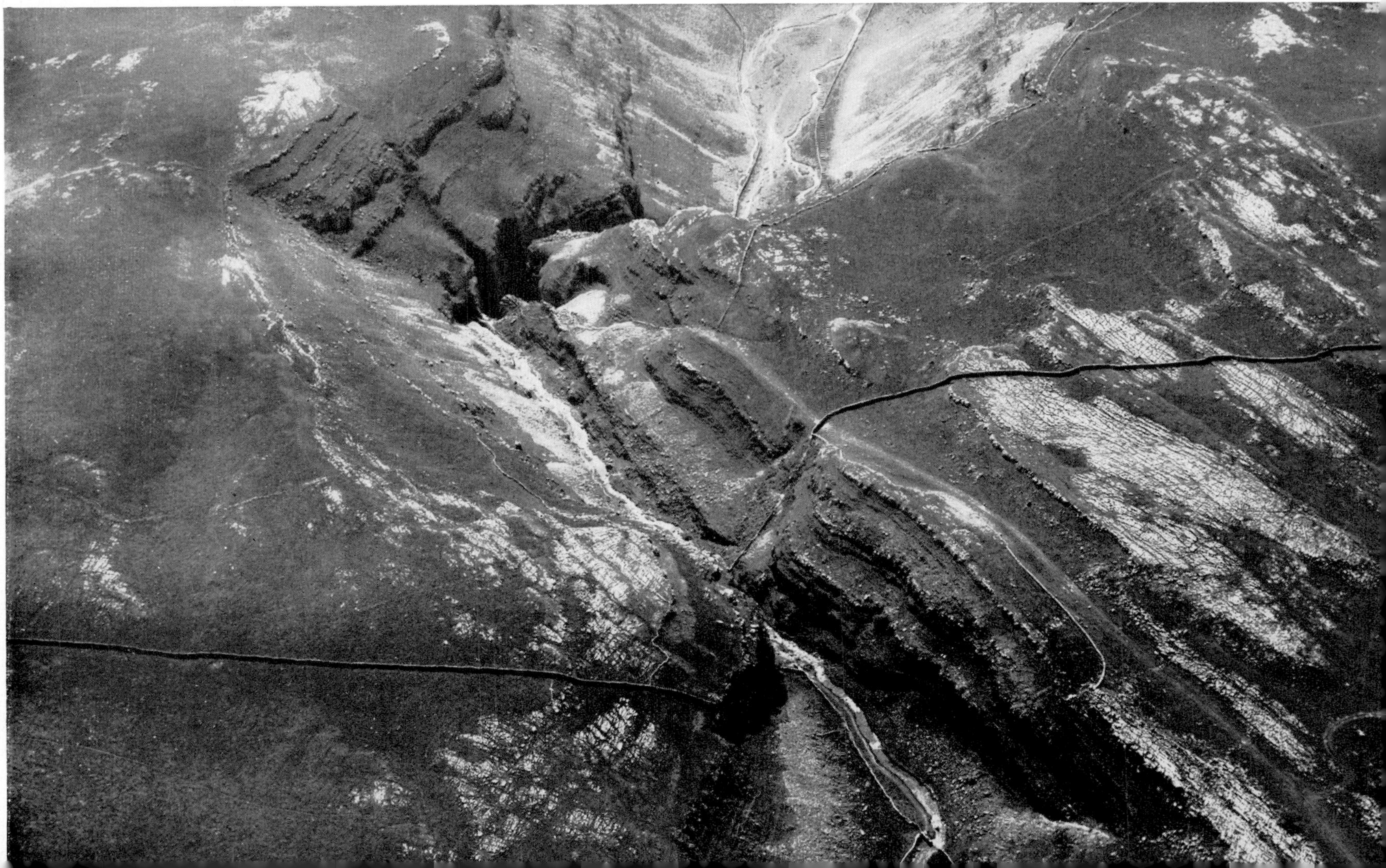

18a. *Sheep on the road towards Tan Hill.*
This is typical grazing moorland with mat grass and heather.

18b. *Sheep sale at Kilnsey.*

19a. *Muker – an earlier mining village, now with houses modernised, some farms, some retired people, and a growing tourist trade.*

19b. *Semer Water – and the (River Bain) outlet which runs into the River Ure at Bainbridge; Upper Wensleydale, North Yorks.*

From the Irthing valley the track climbs through Todholes across Blenkinsop and Featherstone Commons, rejoining the Roman road, the Maiden Way, at the Hartley Burn and Burnstones. For a few miles it keeps along the fell side to Whitley Castle Roman fort, which made an excellent 'stance'. From there two roads diverge. The Roman road, Maiden Way, used by the drovers, climbs over the Cross Fell range at just over 2,000 ft OD on the south flank of Melmerby Fell, then down the scarp to Kirkland and forward up the Vale of Eden to the great Brough Hill fair, Kirkby Stephen, and eventually into Craven or Lancashire.

The other branch keeps to the west side of the South Tyne right to its head in the col between Calvert End and Bellbeaver Rigg, just over 1,800 ft OD. It crosses the young Tees at Hardshins, goes by Nether Hearth and Moor House, both ideal 'stances', then along the east flank of Dufton Fell to cross Maize Beck at the ancient ford of Birkdale. The many small enclosures round Birkdale must have given rest and shelter to thousands of weary cattle in their time, while the house provided refreshment for man and dog. As 'Man Gate' the road now continues across Cronkley Fell and by well-marked fords over all the intervening streams to Holwick. It now turns south, keeping to the west of the village, crosses Lune Moor, and then descends to Grassholme in Lunedale. The ford over the Lune is submerged in the reservoir but a bridge carries the road on its southward line into Balderdale, then over Cotherstone Moor to Pasture End on the Roman road from Bowes to Brough. Across the Greta by God's Bridge it turns slightly west to Sleightholme before crossing into Arkengarthdale and down by Dale Head to Eskeleth. Here it fords the Arkle Beck and goes in a remarkably straight line over Reeth Low Moor to Featham on the Swale.

Over Whiteside Moor and Askrigg Common the road to Askrigg was macadamized early in the nineteenth century. It crossed the Ure either near Bainbridge at Yore Bridge or by a ford near Worton. The last portion of this road crosses the Stake as a green road, down to Buckden in Wharfedale, then Arncliffe on the Skirfare, and so to Malham Moor and Settle. This, from Gilsland to Malham, is only the southern part of the way, but is over seventy miles across mountains and valleys.

From Scotland a second road followed the west side of the North Tyne, making for Hexham and Stagshaw Bank fair. The road south from Hexham goes by Blanchland and Stanhope to Eggleston on Tees, and joins the one already described, or keeps down the Tees for Barnard Castle and then across to Richmond. There are many other drove roads linking the older cattle fairs, some of them near the lines of the still earlier market roads, as those which link Malham Moor with Kirkby Malzeard and Masham. From Kirkby Stephen the ancient road is by

Nateby, then along the side of Mallerstang, by Garsdale and the 'Driving Road' round Widdale Fell to Gearstones, or by Appersett and across the fells to Malham Moor.

The droving trade died a natural death in the nineteenth century when new markets grew up which were served by the new and competitive railways. York, Northallerton, and Darlington became the great market centres on the east. On the west Carlisle, Penrith, and Appleby made the high Pennine routes unnecessary. Malham Moor was replaced by Skipton with its rail connections. Alongside this diversion of routes sheep grazing took on a new importance, and in some places, like Malham, the highland cattle fair on the Moor was replaced by the sheep fair in the village, where great numbers of Dales-bred sheep and lambs are gathered annually.

One marked effect of the droving trade is evident throughout the Pennines: the improvement and 'intaking' of the hill pasture. The improvement of rough pasture was mainly brought about by the generous use of lime and heavy grazing, and no part of the Dales lacks its abundant limekilns with their concomitant 'coal roads'. The many thin coal seams in the Yoredale and lower Millstone Grit strata were hunted out on the fells, and small collieries opened on them. Coal was bought at the pit mouth then carried by pack-horse or occasionally by small wagon to the limekiln. The kiln was strategically placed near a limestone outcrop so that it required the minimum carriage of the bulkiest raw material. The position was usually lower than the coal pit so that coal was carried downhill, and then again it was above the land to be limed so that between kiln and land was again downhill carriage. There is nothing haphazard about the siting. Most farmers with limestone on their land had their own small 'field kiln' which they could 'burn' in the quieter autumn season. Where such field kilns were not easy to obtain, larger 'land sale' kilns were set up by professional lime burners at a place to serve a limited district. Great quantities of lime were used – for instance one farm, Pickering End in Wharfedale, in recovering in 1822 some rough moorland pasture, used 3,088 loads (pony) of lime.[7] Limekilns are so numerous as to become in some parts a feature of the landscape. In the upper parts of Wharfedale, Wensleydale, Garsdale, and Dentdale, there are still to be seen along the hillsides more than three hundred kilns, and the other dales northward to the Tyne have large numbers, though not quite so many as the Yorkshire dales (Plates 31a and 31b).

In many of the upland parts traversed by the drove roads of which we have spoken there are occasional glimpses of abandoned and often ruined buildings, spoil hillocks, faint tracks leading to deserted mining sites or shafts which are the only remains of a once thriving industry. On the valley sides and in areas like

Greenhow Hill, Grassington Moor, and in much of Swaledale, Teesdale, and the northern dales, these remains are an inescapable element of the scene (Plate 27b). The traces of the earliest mining are rare and have now to be sought out and disentangled from the great mass of nineteenth-century activity. None the less the

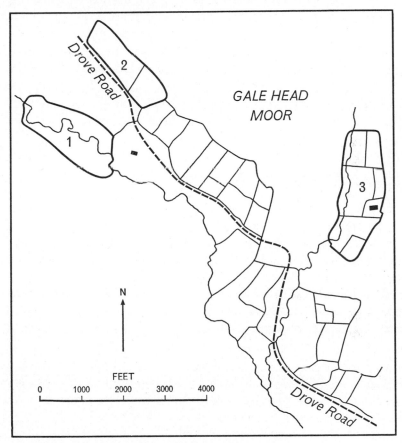

Diagram 5 *Intakes – 1, 2, 3, – and old enclosures along a drove road all above 1,300 ft* OD.

miners have left their mark in one clear pattern impressed upon the areas in which they wrought. Between the farmland which occupies the valley bottom and the lower hill slopes, and the uncultivated moorland, there is usually an irregular belt or zone of small fields and enclosures with a few scattered cottages, now almost all in ruins or used only as shelters for hill cattle and sheep. The fields are generally in poor condition, rough pasture with invading sedges or bracken, with fence walls broken down and uncared for. Some of this land is now treated almost as part of the moor. These fields are almost all of them 'intake' and many of them were produced by the hard labour of the lead miners. Mining was always a chancy occupation, as well as being unhealthy. The close confinement in bad air often made worse by the fumes of gunpowder, and the constant presence of dirt and water, soon attacked the miners' health and made chest infections very common. Much of the mining was paid by bargain, a form of piecework which made it possible at any time to let work in the mine stand for a few days. The miner could then exchange the underground conditions for outdoor work as a seasonable help on a farm, at haytime or sheep-shearing, or could go beating at grouse shooting. These spells of outdoor life were very beneficial and it was natural that many miners sooner or later longed for a bit of ground of their own. Landowners allowed miners to build cottages on the edge of the 'waste' of the manor and to take in a small area of land from the rough, clear, and reclaim it, and so make a smallholding. This intake, as it is called, is very widespread and has taken its place in place names – Intake Lane, Intake House, High Intake and so on are common all over the Pennine dales[8] (Diag. 5).

On Greenhow Hill, in the seventeenth century, a new settlement was made when miners who lived in the neighbouring valley of Nidderdale, having a weary walk up the fells to their work, were allowed to make 'intakes' on the moor. As a result of a case in Chancery, a decision was arrived at which among many other matters relating to common pasture said 'that there may be cottages erected for the miners and mynerall workmen upon the said waste and some competant quantity of ground to be improved of the said waste to be laide to them and also for keeping of draught oxen and horses for mayntenance of the mynes always leaving to the tenants sufficiecy of common'. This was the origin of the hamlet of Greenhow Hill. Many of these little 'intake' holdings provided horses or ponies for underground mine haulage and for pack transport on the surface.[9]

The London Lead Company appreciated the value of a smallholding which gave a miner some outdoor activity to offset the strain of underground conditions and to act as a great stabilizing influence. They built, and helped miners to build, cottages, and added to them land on the edge of the moor – six acres to some – a cow-house and pig-sty, and some rights to pasture sheep on the moor. This policy, which in some form or other spread to all the mining areas, created the very extensive belt of intake which is now an essential part of the mining landscape.

Returning to our earlier viewpoint on the edge of the moorland we cannot help now picking out this element in the scene. Meadow and good grass creeps up the valley side, with outlying barns scattered among the well-fenced fields. The picture is a mosaic of bright greens and greys. As the valley slope steepens fields become smaller and browner, their walls very ragged and tongues of moorland insinuated among them. This is the marginal intake capable of being recaptured and improved and equally capable with continued neglect of reverting to the moor. It is the land of the small farmer, doing another job for survival, in the past a miner but now perhaps a quarryman, roadman, or odd-jobbing waller, carrier, or labourer, though this type of smallholder is now almost extinct. The 'farm' reared a few calves and sheep and took a little hay for winter, kept a few hens, and fattened a pig. All these were jobs in which a wife and children could give very material help. It was a hard life for all but there was a degree of independence, a contact with the land, and an offset to the miner's unhealthy life, that made it the ambition of every miner. Intake was a slow, intensely laborious process, and a reasonable smallholding may well be the result of the toil and sacrifice of two or even three generations. During the period of the cattle droving a man with intake could, even in the absence of capital, take in a few Scotch beasts for feeding and over-wintering. This 'ajistment' was a reliable small source of cash income.

In the nineteenth century, as mining, especially the ore dressing, became mechanized and more miners came on to wage earnings and more regulated shift-working, intakes were neglected, and many partly reverted to moorland. Most of them are now only rough pasture, and many are marked out mainly by the remains of fences and an occasional patch of better grass, a watering place, or a ruined shelter.

The lime-burning contributed to a larger-scale recovery of rough pasture, partly through mere spreading to neutralize acid soils, and partly by means of 'paring and burning'. By the end of the eighteenth century this was fairly widespread in the north. A piece of ground to be recovered was walled in, then the sod was 'pared' off in a thin skinning of only a few inches thickness. This was piled and dried, then burned, and the potash-rich ashes spread over the ground, followed by heavy liming. This new ground was then ploughed and frequently, if not too high, cropped with turnips followed by corn (oats), and finally, after two or three years, sown down to grass. Some very good ground in the valley heads was made in this way, and it was generally counted that the cropping with turnips and corn would give enough profit to pay for the winning of the ground.[10]

7

The recent past: 1750-1900

As the eighteenth century entered its last quarter the Pennine dales experienced the first effects of the Industrial Revolution, effects which heralded an important change in the life of many places. The exploration of the harnessing of the power of steam had been paralleled by improvements in water-wheel design which had for some decades maintained water power as a prime source of energy for the new machinery of the textile industry. At the same time the water-wheel was applied to mine pumping from greater depths and to many processes in ore dressing which were capable of mechanization.[1] The possibilities of the improved overshot water-wheels converted many dales streams into important sources of power. The pressure of trade and industry had encouraged the development of canals and turnpike roads so that cross-country green tracks and the pack-horse trains which used them declined, and quicker movement by wheeled vehicles, along better roads which were built with easier gradients, took their place.

At the turn of the century there was a widespread spinning industry housed in little mills throughout the dales, but already it was differentiated, some spinning worsteds, others spinning woollens, cotton, or flax. The bulk of the weaving was still done on hand looms in the homes, and the clack of the loom must have been a common sound in many of the villages. In the dales of the mid Pennines there was a great industry based upon knitting yarns, which were spun in many small mills between Richmond and Kendal.

The tradition of wool production so nurtured by the monasteries persisted after their dissolution. The export of wool declined but the 'broggers' of Halifax, licensed pedlar dealers, soon took the place of the monastic servants in buying and collecting wool from the outlying farms. Besides the raw wool taken to market, the

118

broggers encouraged home spinning, and much wool was scoured and carded or combed before being spun up on the hand spinning-wheel. Some of the yarn was bought in for the weavers, but much was redistributed in the dales, to be used in knitting. A survey made near the end of the sixteenth century mentions that there are several villages around Richmond where there are found 'above 1,000 knytters wch doo make about 166 dozen every weecke . . . ther is made every fortnight 14 or 16 packes and every packe contayneth 40 dossen pare'. '2,000 knytters after the rate of 2 pare every one a weecke amounteth to 333 dossen every weecke. . . .' These figures refer to long stockings. A century and a quarter later Defoe tells us of Richmond that 'here you see all the people, great and small, a knitting; and at Richmond you have a market for woollen or yarn stockings, which they make very coarse and ordinary. . . .' The stockings were then sold, in the smallest size for children, at 18d. a dozen pairs. This glimpse by Defoe of every one, great and small, knitting, is born out by artist and commentator for most of the dales. Walker, the artist working at the opening of the nineteenth century, has a water-colour of the knitters of Hawes, where the old grandfather, his daughter and granddaughter, and the shepherd following sheep, are all knitting stockings. Men as well as women knitted while walking about their work, and among the miners of Swaledale and some other dales it was common to knit while having a rest, so much so that an expression was widespread describing such a rest as having 'six needles' as a measure of the time.

This trade stretched through the dales across to Kirkby Stephen and Kendal, and at one time, besides stockings, great quantities of knitted woollen caps were sent to Holland and the Netherlands for seamen's wear. Around Kendal in the later part of the eighteenth century a trade developed with finer wools brought from Leicestershire and Durham, and it was estimated that about 5,000 people were employed in fine-stocking knitting. There were around Kendal about a hundred and twenty wool combers, who could each keep at work five spinners, themselves in turn supplying yarn for four or five knitters. They were said to make 550 dozen pairs of stockings a week, or 28,600 dozen a year. Being of fine wool these stockings, of knee length, were high priced – as much as three shillings a pair. All these stockings were at that time collected and sent to London. Much of the transport was by pack-horse and at one time 354 horses in different gangs were employed at Kendal. At the opening of the nineteenth century a report on Kendal estimates that the hosiers collected weekly from Ravenstonedale 1,000 pairs, from Sedbergh and Dent 840 pairs, and from Orton 560 pairs of stockings. About that time a byword became common which is still remembered over most of the north: 'the terrible knitters of Dent'.[2]

There are just a few houses both in the dales and in the Lake District still to be seen with the feature called a 'spinning gallery'. This is generally a wooden gallery with attractive ballustrade, roofed over and often approached by an outside stair of stone. It is built as part of the house and generally faces on to the yard, and here the spinning-wheels could stand and spinners work in shelter. There is a fine gallery at Adamthwaite farm in the Howgills, and a few others are still seen here and there in north-west Yorkshire and in Westmorland. The knitting industry was transferred in part to small factories, but as a hand occupation it has lasted in pockets until recent times. When the railway over Ribblehead and Dent by Garsdale to Carlisle was being built, many of the navvies took up stocking and cap knitting as an occupation for leisure hours.[3]

Arkwright's spinning jenny was the first textile machine to be adapted to a power drive, and soon after 1770 small mills were being built in which could be concentrated the spinning of yarns which for generations had been spun in the homes, wool being distributed and yarn collected by the 'putter out'. In the seventeenth century the Birkbecks of Settle were wool dealers collecting their wool from a large area of the dales, sorting it and putting it out to be spun in the homes in a 'cottage industry'. Before 1800 they took an old corn mill at Giggleswick, buying it to get the water rights, and with an improved water-wheel set it up as a spinning mill. In 1794 we hear of them at Skipton with a warehouse to which 3,000 packs of wool a year were brought, and after 'sorting and combing it is spun at the Company's mills, at Linton and Addingham . . . and made into stuffs, viz. shalloons, calimancoes, and all sorts of double goods'. They also had interest in other mills. Some families, like the Claytons, bought mills for the water rights, as they did the mill at Langcliffe near Settle, and introduced cotton spinning, while a little later flax heckling and spinning was brought into Nidderdale.[4] Progress was rapid and in the opening years of the nineteenth century various areas were well defined – upper Airedale and Wharfedale had over twenty cotton spinning mills; around the upper Nidd and the Washburn there were about fifteen flax mills, while in Wensleydale, Swaledale, and the north-west knitting wools and knitting processes occupied several mills. At Barnard Castle an interesting development, based upon the coarser wools, was the spinning of carpet yarns and carpet weaving.

The spread of the mills can be seen in Wensleydale, where the mill at Aysgarth Falls on the Ure was built in 1784 to take power from the river. About the same time other mills were built at Askrigg, Hawes, and Gayle, though these were on tributary streams. These mills were at first spinning cotton, but later turned over to woollen yarns, some for the knitting industry and some, like Hawes mill, for weaving horse cloths, plaids, and rugs. At Low Row in Swaledale the Knowles family established a putting-out business and later built a mill to spin knitting yarns which were used mainly for the production of seamen's jerseys, along with some coarser yarns for carpet-making. In Craven there were cotton spinning mills at Arncliffe, Kettlewell, Hebden, and Malham, and several around Skipton and Settle, with a few around Sedbergh. Near Sedbergh the Farfield mill and Rawthey Bank mill were employed in making horse cloths, but at Hebblethwaite Hall a woollen mill was built in 1792 to make yarn for the knitters. It was built by a Quaker, Robert Forster, for the better employment of the poor, and had a school for their education. Knitted caps, gloves, and stockings were the main products of the yarn. Many of the smaller mills had only a short life, but a few remained active in the middle of the nineteenth century. In the parish of Linton mills at Linton, Grassington and Hebden were active until about 1860. In 1851 there were more textile workers, mainly women and children (427) than there were miners (229), although Grassington was considered to be the centre of one of the most flourishing lead-mining areas in Yorkshire.

The two necessities for this textile industry were of course power and labour. Within limits rivers and streams could provide the power, and labour was largely that of younger women and children. The enclosures of common pastures and the moors and commons which were taking place everywhere at the end of the eighteenth century were reducing the condition of those who were called 'the labouring poor', and from many parts where sheep and hill cattle were replacing arable crops as the mainstay of the farmer there was a steady migration of population. Archdeacon Boyd was able to say of Arncliffe: 'this depopulation was less noticeable in Arncliffe for the flour mill was transformed into a cotton mill about the year 1820, and this afforded for some years employment for the youngsters of the village at home.' Low wages in mining, diminishing employment in other areas, and the loss of commons on which could be grazed a few geese or a cow, made it essential for the youngsters of a family to help the family income. The application of the steam engine to textiles and the development of better transport to the towns by canal and turnpike road soon tempted manufacturers to establish larger mills in towns where cheap coal could be obtained. These town mills, with a growing demand for labour, sucked whole families out of the countryside, and even the few specially advantageous villages failed to resist this process for more than a decade or two.

In most of the dales area the early common fields had been enclosed by agreement – strips of arable land by purchase or exchange had been acquired side by side to make a small field on a few of which the yeoman farmer could establish his position. The wide-ranging common pastures and moors had, however, been un-touched, and almost every family, however poor, was able to supplement meagre earnings by the produce of common right grazing and by fuel and other small products collected there.

The mining areas suffered heavily in the depression of 1828–31 and many families which had managed with the help of their children's labour on a small 'intake' holding, or by means of spinning either in the mill or at home, were brought to a state of pauperism.[5] Food prices were so high that Poor Relief was not sufficient to maintain a family, and there was widespread migration into the expanding coal-fields or into the textile towns. Between April and May 1832 Alston lost 124 persons by assisted emigration to Canada, and over the years of the depression a total of more than 2,000 left the parish. In 1831 the census recorded 150 empty houses in Alston, but in the Poor Law Commission Report of 1832–3 there were 500. A similar movement took place from Weardale and Swaledale, mainly into the Durham coalfield and the Lancashire towns. The second quarter of the nineteenth century was a time of severe poverty throughout the Pennine dales area, except perhaps for some of the farmers who were able to profit by the high prices of corn and meat. A few upland areas were brought under plough and oats were grown for some years, but as prices fell these were abandoned and can now only be recognized by the faint plough rigs on a patch of rather better grass. As poverty increased, the Government allowed parishes to make further collections and levies to assist emigration overseas, and with this help many dales families left for Canada.

The desire of farmers and landowners for the improvement of land and rents and for a better control of trespassing animals led to the enclosure of common pastures in nearly every township in the dales (Plate 40). In west Durham this enclosure started at an early date on the Bishop of Durham's estates, and by 1800, in Weardale alone, 60,000 acres of pasture had been enclosed, though it provoked much anger among the workers and a great increase in poaching and so-called 'lawlessness'. These enclosures and the decline in trade, with their consequent impoverishment of families, was the cause of many small intake and squatter holdings being abandoned, and the many ruins of cottages and small fields along the moor edges date from this depopulation[6] (Plate 22).

Within the general decline there were a few small areas of relief where a second-ary industry gave employment to some families. We have mentioned the parish of Linton, where three well-placed water-powered mills provided employment until about 1860. In Nidderdale and the Washburn valley the flax mills flourished and multiplied through the nineteenth century, though the Washburn mills by the end of that century were at a standstill, and West End, where many of them clustered, was being drawn and described in the guide books as 'the deserted village' and is now submerged under the waters of a reservoir.

Stanhope and Dent were two villages where new industries offset to a slight extent the general decline. In Dentdale the limestone strata include a few beds of hard, black limestone and a good quality grey bed, both being capable of taking a good polish. These beds, when worked, became the 'Dent Marble'. The beds of 'marble' were thin but by the deep nature of Dentdale they are exposed at many places along the steep valley sides and could be won in a number of small quarries there and in neighbouring Garsdale. The quarrying was all done with crowbars, since explosive would have cracked and spoiled much of the rock. The large blocks were cut to size with hand saws and kept flooded with water and a sharp sand. The cut surface was then polished with water and many grades of fine sand and finally with 'rotten stone'.[7]

About 1780 a small woollen mill with water-wheel had been built in Arten Gill on the north side of Dentdale, but about 1810 it was taken over to become the High Mill, a 'marble mill' where the limestone could be sawn with the aid of the water power. Another mill for polishing was built at the foot of the same gill and the ruins of this are alongside the road at Stone House. The wheel at High Mill has special interest, as it was seen and examined in 1835 by a young Newcastle solicitor who had just become a partner with Armourer Donkin. The young man was William George Armstrong. Out of interest he made measurements of the wheel and of the stream and decided that only about five per cent of the available power was used by the wheel. He turned to study the more efficient use of hydraulic power and from these studies came his departure from the law and the formation of the great engineering firm of Armstrong's on Tyneside, building up at first on hydraulic cranes and small machinery for the docks and navy yards, then on hydraulic gun mountings, and later on every side of heavy engineering.

The Dent marble was used for fireplaces and smaller ornamental articles, and the products, in addition to local sales, were sent to London and Newcastle and sold from warehouses there in large quantities. The carriage of these heavy goods by carts or pack-horses, over the fells to Newcastle or Stockton on Tees for shipment to London, or to Gargrave on the Leeds and Liverpool Canal, provided employment, even if part-time, to many horse-keepers and carriers. There was also much carriage of limestone blocks between the quarries and the marble mills.

When the railway came to Dent, the trade was stimulated by the easier transport and probably reached its greatest extent in the few years after the opening of the railway. The import of Italian marbles and the great demand which the local industry made on hard labour and strength in quarries and in handling caused it to decline, and by 1900 it had ceased.[8] In upper Weardale some of the limestones had been quarried for many centuries. The limestone which corresponds geologically with the main mass of the Dent marble is the Frosterley marble, and this was used in Durham Cathedral and in many Durham churches from the fourteenth century. In the Bolden Book a 'marble cutter' is mentioned. Probably the best known slab of this rock is that which covers the tomb of the Venerable Bede, in the Galilee Porch at Durham. The limestone at Stanhope was used for more mundane purposes, being burnt for lime or used in the ironworks. To its exploitation we owe one of the early and exciting railway lines, the Stanhope and South Shields. To plan a railway at Stanhope was very natural, as Tyneside had been familiar for a century with the 'tramway', first of wood then of iron, and the steam locomotive had been working on various lines since 1808. The Stockton and Darlington line of 1823 must have fired the imagination of many local people. However it arose in 1831, the double possibility of Stanhope limestone for the coalfield and Medomsley coal for Stanhope and the Tyne encouraged Cuthbert Rippon of Stanhope Castle, with Wallis of Westoe and Harrison of Monkwearmouth, to make a partnership to survey a railway. Rippon and Wallis soon withdrew but Harrison, with new partners, completed the line. Quarries were opened and a bank of limekilns was built at Stanhope, and from it a line of rails was laid, up which the wagons were hauled by a stationary engine. From the loading point at about 800 ft OD the incline rose 327 ft at 1 in 8 to Crawley, then along more long pulls to the summit at Park Head, 1,474 ft OD, the highest-but-one railway point in Britain. From the summit the line by inclines, both steam- and gravity-operated, with some sections horse-drawn, reached the fantastic Hownes Gill near Consett. Here the wagons, one at a time, were lowered sideways down one side and pulled up the other side of a ravine 106 ft deep. More inclined planes took the wagons to the Tyne. There was a total of 11 miles of inclined planes, 3 miles of self-acting inclines, $10\frac{1}{2}$ miles of horse-drawn line, $4\frac{1}{2}$ miles of branches, and $9\frac{3}{4}$ miles of steam locomotive way. No other line in Britain could show, in $37\frac{3}{4}$ miles, so much variety and engineering ingenuity.[9]

At Consett the Derwent Iron Company founded iron furnaces in 1840, based primarily on the local iron ores which they mined. In order to use the Stanhope limestone and some of the Weardale ores, they bought the upper part of the railway and in 1856 replaced the Hownes Gill inclines by a viaduct which is still one of the grandest industrial monuments in Durham. The discovery of the Cleveland iron ores, however, brought the local mining at Consett to a low ebb, when the Company found that these Yorkshire ores, in spite of the long transport, were cheaper than the local ones. With them the works expanded and soon employed a much larger number of workmen.

Iron had been worked in a small way by forges in the forest of Weardale since the fourteenth century, and in the lead mines above Stanhope more and more veins were being discovered or developed where in parts there were considerable deposits, particularly in flats, of iron ores. These were grouped mainly around Cowshill and Ireshope, but later were found through most of the valley from Stanhope upward towards the head. In 1845 a blast furnace was built at Stanhope, with limestone and ore at hand and good transport by the railway for coal. The Weardale Iron Company was formed, but after only a year of the Stanhope furnace they built six at Tow Law, eight or nine miles to the east and on the edge of the coalfield. The furnaces and mines together soon employed about 1,700 men, and the carriage of ore between the mines and rail head employed many more as carriers. As the lead mines declined the quarries and ironstone mines absorbed some of the displaced men, so that although there was some migration of families from Weardale it was not on such a large scale as in some other dales. The demand for limestone developed with the increase of the iron industry in County Durham, and quarrying soon became a permanent industry of the dale.

In the Yorkshire dales the mining had very variable success. In Swaledale and Arkengarthdale there was depression in the first half of the nineteenth century, with the consequent migration of families into the Durham coalfield and the growing cotton towns of Lancashire. In Wharfedale a reorganization and mechanization of the mines was carried through between 1790 and 1820, and this served to delay the migration. At the same time in Linton parish, which includes the mining townships of Grassington and Hebden, mills were extended on the river, and there were soon three textile mills finding work particularly for young people from ten to twenty years of age, and for a number of men and women, mostly up to the age of thirty but a few older. In Nidderdale the expanding flax industry and the expansion of the Greenhow Hill mines shielded the villages from the worst effects of the depressions.

During these industrial changes one might well ask, 'what of the farmers?' The Industrial Revolution had got into full swing and the towns of Lancashire and Yorkshire, Teeside and Tyneside, were increasing their populations at a fantastic rate. Leeds had a population in 1801 of 71,000 (to the nearest round figure), but by 1851 this had increased to 233,000. Bradford increased from 13,000 in 1801 to 104,000 in 1851. On the Lancashire side of the Pennines, Manchester grew from 95,000 to 401,000 in the same time, and Oldham from 22,000 to 72,000. All these vast populations had to be fed, and some of the food, particularly meat, cheese, and butter, could come from the dales area. In the north the population increase was not so large, as the principal industries were mining and engineering, but Tyneside had still increased from much less than 100,000 to over 200,000 between 1801 and 1851.

At the opening of the nineteenth century the drovers were still bringing cattle from Scotland to the fairs and markets of the north, and many farmers were engaged in feeding these cattle for the butchers' markets which supplied the south and the new industrial areas. Some improvement of the enclosed meadowland and also of the breed of cattle helped to create a dairy farming tradition in the lower dales, and even in the upper dales most farmers combined a few dairy animals with their sheep and store cattle (Plate 2b). In the extreme north-west of Yorkshire, in 1794, we have a picture of what was happening in Dentdale:[10] the surveyors of the Board of Agriculture reported that there was 'a considerable quantity of butter salted in this tract, and disposed of at Skipton . . . Few cattle are fed but great numbers of milk cows are kept, and large quantities of butter and cheese produced.' The picture of Nidderdale is one of great bustle and business: 'Paitley is a fine thriving place: it being market day when we were there, the town was much crowded, and the shambles presented a sight which declared that the inhabitants were in no danger of starving for want of butcher meat. A great deal of linen is manufactured in this place and neighbourhood . . . Much butter is also salted here, and sent to York for the London market. One person alone exports 700 to 800 firkins annually of 56 lb per firkin. . . . A number of hogs are fed upon oatmeal, and sold to the Lancashire manufacturers at 7s. per stone of 14 lb. The hams are generally sent to the London market, as nothing will do with the Lancashire people but the fattest part of the beast.' In Wharfedale and the other dales the story is the same. Such ploughland as existed was mainly growing oats, and the cheese, butter, and meat was going to the growing markets such as Barnard Castle, Bishop Auckland, Richmond, Ripon, Skipton, and others within the dales like Leyburn and Hawes. One traveller says, 'Settle fair being upon the day we were there, had an opportunity to see a great show of cattle of country breed. They are universally long-horned, and seem in shape, skin, and other circumstances to be nearly the same as the Irish breed.'

It becomes apparent that while there was terrible poverty in the mining areas there was still some measure of prosperity among the farmers and more particularly with the market dealers. The small farmer could make a living with his dairy herd and sheep, but the dealer could make far better profits. In the late eighteenth and early nineteenth centuries the poverty and never-ending labour in the heaviest tasks of mine and quarry, a life where everyone, man, woman, and child, had to work to the limits of strength, provided a rich soil in which the Methodist evangel could flourish. The Church was the special preserve of the employer and landlord, with the officials and the larger farmers joining them on the fringes of the privileged classes. The forceful message of Wesley offered something which gave dignity and importance to the poorest and which created a democracy in the chapel 'Society' in which service and character counted beyond all worldly position. The emotional relief of the wholehearted singing of the robust hymns of Methodism, the close-knit unity of the congregation where most of the preachers were drawn as 'local preachers' from among themselves, and the class leader who might be a miner, quarryman, or any earnest person who by study and dedication had prepared himself and been approved by the leaders of the local circuit – these were a fore-shadowing of the glorious life and liberty to come.[11] The chapel provided the centre for a community with an intimate life and activities in which all could share. The local preachers spoke their own language, most often the local dialect, and drew their illustrations from the life lived by their hearers. The preachers walked many miles to and from remote chapels each Sunday to preach, crossing wild moors by ill-defined tracks in all kinds of weather. The stories of their adventures, persever-ance, and endurance, and of the vigour and homeliness of their sermons, are still treasured by the older men and women of the dales.

The ground in which Methodism flourished had in some degree been prepared in the seventeenth and early eighteenth centuries. The companies of 'Seekers' who were numerous in Swaledale and the country towards Sedbergh were ripe for the message of George Fox, and out of these groups a strong Quaker following was established by 1700, with many meeting-houses over most of the Pennines. The Quakers were drawn from shepherds, small farmers, artisans of all kinds, and miners, and with no paid ministry they formed a close-knit community in which all had an equal part and responsibility. The coming of the London (Quaker) Lead Company into the northern lead-mining area, and their work there until 1905, brought much of the social attitudes of the Quakers into industrial relations, even if most of their workpeople were Methodist.[12]

In Weardale there was an interesting area of Presbyterian faith and practice occupying much of the head of the dale. It is said that many Covenanters, from about 1645 onwards, found a refuge from persecution in the nearly empty lands of upper Weardale. A small Presbyterian meeting-house was built in 1687 at Ireshopeburn, to which a school was later added. By 1720 there were 150 members drawn from Kilhope, Wellhope, and Ireshopeburn. Some of the Scots founded a settlement in the Alston area, and a Presbyterian chapel in Garrigill was for many years served by the minister from Ireshopeburn. There were many Independents too in upper Weardale and in Teesdale, but these, along with the Presbyterians, were largely drawn into Methodism either by Christopher Hopper, the first Methodist to visit Teesdale and Weardale in 1749, or by John Wesley, who started the great revival in 1752 at Westgate. The first Methodist chapel was built at Ireshopeburn in 1759, near the Presbyterian Chapel. Methodism quickly became the religion of the dale, and nearly every village soon had its chapel.[13] Among the miners of Alston Moor and the Allendales, Teesdale, and Weardale, the same revival brought Methodism into a position of great strength.

In Swaledale the influence of Philip Lord Wharton had introduced Independency or Congregationalism, and a chapel was built by him at Smarber in 1691, to be followed by other chapels at Reeth, Keld, Low Row, and Thwaite between 1785 and 1863. John Wesley, visiting Swaledale in 1768, writes: 'The evening congregation in Swaledale was far larger, and equally attentive; and the society was one of the most lively which I have met with in England. Many of them do rejoice in the pure love of God, and many are earnestly seeking it.' Many Wesleyan chapels were built during the nineteenth century, most of which have survived.

Farther south the Independents had arisen around Airedale, with the early Independent chapel at Winterburn, supported by Lady Lambert, and with the powerful influence of the itinerant preacher, Oliver Heywood, and the Rathmell Academy founded by Dr Frankland. Richard Frankland had been a Presbyterian minister at Auckland St Andrew, County Durham, but in 1662 was ejected from his living. It may be the independence of the people of the Pennine dales which has traditionally made them receptive to the reformers. When Benjamin Ingham, friend of Wesley, began his new movement – which still persists in the Inghamite churches – he found his supporters in the western dales – around Clapham over into Wensleydale, at Sedbergh, and near Warcop in the head of the Vale of Eden. Nonconformity has been a major influence in the life of the people of the north Pennines for three hundred years.

The chapels had a place in life which extended beyond the religious services of Sunday – many had a mid-week evening service and all had class meetings during the week. The class meeting was a time of serious religious instruction and testimony and an essential basis of church membership. Other groupings were to be found as well – Young People's classes, Mutual Improvement societies, Mothers' classes, Choirs, and many other associations. 'Efforts' to raise funds, even joint 'efforts' to build a chapel by volunteer labour and finance, drew the members together in activities and a shared life. Each chapel had its Anniversary, a day of services of thanksgiving attended by great crowds. Sunday-school scholars practised special hymns for the occasion, and in smaller rural chapels one service

on which the market was held. Arkengarthdale is the valley behind.

22 (above). *Upper Weardale looking north-west across Ireshopeburn and Wearhead. The pattern of enclosure is well seen.*

23 (left). *Part of an area of Romano-British 'Celtic' fields on High Close, Grassington.*

24a (above). *Bringing in a sick sheep,*
Park House, near Keld, Swaledale.

24b (below). *Escomb Church.*

of song might be held outside as a 'Stand-up' to which folk came from chapels round about. There is no doubt that in the nineteenth century the chapel stood at the centre of life of the dalesfolk, claiming much of what little time they had free from work.

Throughout the nineteenth century 'chapel' on Sunday was a great event for the whole family, and even in the early years of our own century this attitude was not wholly lost. People would arrive some time before the service, even when, as was often the case, they had to walk a few miles to get there, and a great exchange of greetings and news would take place. Children shared the Sunday-school into which they moved from chapel before the sermon. In areas of widely scattered population the evening service was often brought forward to early afternoon following a picnic lunch, so that families could get back to their distant homes in daylight.

In the mining areas there was an interest in reading and study, to which many chapels contributed with a small library. Mining demanded a constant exercise of judgement, of evaluation of evidence and the planning of work by this evaluation. In the evenings miners gathered in one another's houses to discuss and argue their problems, and in most gatherings the flagged floor before the fireplace would at an early hour be covered with chalked diagrams of the run of veins, special problems of working places, the theory and practice of mining. This interest often widened to geology and natural history and even to philosophy. To meet these interests subscription libraries were formed at surprisingly early dates. In 1788 the Westgate Subscription Library had 21 members, who subscribed 4s. each; 42 volumes were bought, including of course Wesley's and Fletcher's works, as well as others on geology and other subjects. Before long this library had over 400 volumes and over 100 subscribers, nearly all miners. Other libraries were established at Stanhope and Newhouse, and in the later years of the nineteenth century these became centres of evening discussions and debates, where visiting lecturers introduced a wide variety of topics. In Teesdale and Alston Moor the London Lead Company provided Reading Rooms and Libraries for their workers, as did the Beaumont Company in the Allendales and parts of Weardale. In the Yorkshire dales the Mechanics Institutes spread to many of the villages, and the 'Mechanics', as it was generally known, provided a library, discussions, lectures, and meeting places.[14]

During the seventeenth century many dalesfolk, particularly the younger sons of yeoman farmers, left the area to become merchants or to enter the church. Several of them, making fortunes, remembered the place of their birth and endowed a school, sometimes a 'grammar school', at which the sons of poor men were to be educated free, and in some of these schools further endowment included that of scholarships to the universities. There were a few even earlier schools, arising from the dissolved chantry schools of the sixteenth century, and a few of these survived to be extended by seventeenth-century endowment. In Sedbergh, one, Roger Lupton, had built a school just before 1527 and endowed a chantry, the priest of which was master of the school. The endowment included six scholarships to be held at St John's College, Cambridge. At the dissolution of the chantries the inhabitants of Sedbergh successfully petitioned the king and in 1552 obtained a royal charter as a grammar school. This provided a good education for many dales children, and among them many famous men had their start in life; people like Adam Sedgwick, geologist, John Fothergill, physician, and many church dignitaries and scholars. At Burnsall in Wharfedale, William Craven, born in the parish but as a youth removed to London, where in due course he became a wealthy merchant and Lord Mayor, in 1605 transferred to trustees land and a school in Burnsall, with endowments, to be a free grammar school (Plate 30b). The boys were to be taught English and Latin, with writing and arithmetic added for a small charge. In the adjoining parish of Linton a free grammar school was endowed by the will of Matthew Hewitt, Rector, in 1672. This school again was to teach English and Latin, and had four scholarships to St John's, Cambridge. This school and the one at Burnsall eventually became public primary schools, while Sedbergh became a select public school. Early grammar schools at Richmond, Kirkby Ravensworth, Wolsingham, Dent, and a few other places had a development in two directions. Some like Dent and Kirkby Ravensworth declined and were taken into the State education system later, while some like Richmond became large and flourishing country grammar schools. All, however, in their early days shared a long list of eminent pupils, and the number of bishops and archbishops, professors, mathematicians, and other learned figures produced in them would, if space permitted to print it, surprise many people.

For the poor children many small schools were formed, some, like those in Weardale, provided by former residents. Bishop Barrington in 1819 established endowments for schools for poor children in Heathery Cleugh, St Johns, Wearhead, Westgate, Eastgate, Rookhope, Stanhope, and Frosterley in Weardale, though in some places schools had already been built by public subscription much earlier.

The mid-nineteenth century was a period when the prosperity of the emerging middle classes encouraged an interest in holidays, in which the railways helped to transport people cheaply into the countryside. 'Tourists' were discovering the Lake District, journeys were being made into Scotland, and the works of poets and artists were arousing an interest in, and appreciation of, natural scenic beauty. History which had been in the hands of the leisured gentry and the country parson mainly concerned with the titled and landed families was now acquiring a topographical sense. Villages rather than manors, and life and occupations rather than pedigrees, occupied the new writers, who, drawing their skeleton of formal history from great volumes of scholarly writers, combined it with their own observation of the countryside and the everyday activities of its people. 'Tours' and 'Guides' appeared in the bookshops, and anecdote and personal encounter with the countryfolk and their lore took precedence over 'prospects' and eulogies of the larger country seats. People from the towns found a new world to explore in the country. The younger and bolder men took 'walking tours'; a few families spent their holidays at a farm, often returning to the same one year after year, and found recreation and a complete change in sharing in an amateurish way the life and work of the farmer. A highlight of the farm holiday was provided by the farmer's weekly trip to market.

This for the farmer was a day of combined business and recreation – the careful business of getting his beasts to market in time and condition for the auctions, the excitement of the auction ring after a long and careful appraisal of the stock on offer, the hopes placed on a new milker or on a number of store beasts to eat off his grass. After auction the farmers' 'Ordinary' held at a customary inn was a social meal served to a company who came for it week after week, so that the dinner-table became almost a family party or a club, and in fact was often presided over by an elder member of the group. News of farms and families was exchanged, stories were told, and sometimes enough drink was taken to make a few farmers 'market merry'. Farmers' wives accompanied their husbands to market, and for them the customary stalls and benches were first a place of business where their load of butter, eggs, chickens, or cheese was converted into cash which later in the day enabled them to 'shop' round the stalls of the fent merchants, the dealers in pots and pans, groceries, clothes, and carpets, and all that townsfolk would seek in their shopping centre. News, gossip, and friendly meetings took place over cups of tea and sandwiches in homely cafés while their men took their leisure at the 'ordinary'. Market was the nerve centre of the whole district, the steadily recurrent meeting-point of friends and neighbours from a wider circuit and more varied background than that afforded by the chapel or village group (Plate 16c).

A factor which contributed to the opening up of the dales to the visitor was the development of the branch railway lines, mainly planned in connection with mines, quarries, and farming produce. From Darlington the railway reached

Richmond in 1846 and soon became used for the moving of lead from the mines which was brought to the railhead instead of the former long overland haul to Stockton. In 1856 rail from Northallerton on the main line reached Leyburn, and, twenty years later, the head of the dale at Hawes. The Tees Valley–Barnard Castle line was opened in 1856 and taken forward to Middleton in 1868. The Haltwhistle–Alston railway was opened in 1852, and a line from Hexham to Allendale in 1868, so that before the last quarter of the nineteenth century Wensleydale, Swaledale, and Teesdale were in close contact by rail with the industrial populations of Teesside.[15] Wharfedale above Bolton Abbey remained aloof until 1902, but was well served by wagonettes from Skipton railway station from about 1860.

The first quarter of the twentieth century was probably the heyday of the bicycle. Schoolboys looked forward with healthy ambition to owning one, and a mark of emancipation was to own a 'fast' model and to be a member of a well-known cycling club. In the Pennine dales this was the time when the yellow C.T.C. sign (Cyclists' Touring Club) was a genuine welcome to good food and clean beds. The cyclist learned the country as the motorist cannot. Today the motorist fears to meet the harassed cavalcade of a cycling club, but for all right-minded people such a procession of young folk exploring the country under their own power and earning their pleasure by hard work brings nothing but encouragement and hope. The bicycle carries no threat to the peace of the countryside and the cyclist gives little encouragement to the urbanized 'road-house'.

8

The recent past:
1900-1960

The 1901 Census revealed that the population of the northern dales was at, or only just past, its lowest ebb, and in nearly all places the next ten years showed an increase far greater than was explicable merely by natural increase. Part of this change was due to the growth of the habit of having a 'weekend cottage', easily possible when abandoned miner's cottages could be had in many villages for rents as little as sixpence or a shilling a week, when rail fares were very low, and when transport by trap or wagonette from the railway station to the more remote villages was equally cheap. In 1890 carriage proprietors in Grassington could advertise 'Horses and carriages to all Places of Interest in the Neighbourhood. Parties of five and upwards met at Skipton (ten miles away and the nearest railway) at any hour, fare 1s. each'. Airey of Grassington advertised a daily horse-bus from Grassington to Skipton 'conveying passengers to trains for Leeds, Bradford, Manchester, Liverpool, Lancaster, Settle, Carlisle, etc.' . . . with two return buses in the late afternoon.[1] Chapman also had a daily bus, with another going right up the dale from Skipton to Buckden. All spoke of 'post horses and conveyances for hire'. With the opening of the railway branch line from Skipton to Grassington in 1901 and an excellent connecting train between Skipton and Bradford, Grassington entered upon its new and increasing role as a dormitory area for people working in Bradford in occupations which did not demand an arrival at the office before 9. a.m. Cottages were 'improved' and two terraces of orthodox town houses were built not far from the station; several semi-detached groups were also put up, shops opened, and a definite bit of 'Bradford by the Wharfe' established. This connection of Grassington with Bradford has continued even after the closure of the railway in 1930, by which time there was a motor-bus connection with Skipton station and the 'Bradford businessman's train', though this is now, and for many years has been running between Bradford and Morecambe stopping at Skipton. Among all the reductions of bus services in the upper dales, this connection between Grassington and the Bradford train and its evening return has remained.

The trend of population was reversed in a way that is almost dramatic. For Grassington, which is not in any way exceptional, the census returns show the population as being in 1851, 1,138; 1881, 617; 1901, 494; 1911, 567; 1921 988; and in 1951 a complete recovery to 1,151. The bulk of this recovery was due to the incoming population from Bradford, and, since 1921, the effect of the Rural District Council housing programme, which allowed many young people to move into Grassington from higher up the dale. Grassington had the benefit of a train service, then later a bus service, to Skipton, where there was a growing demand for young labour in offices and shops. Farther up and down the dale the increase after 1901 reached its peak thirty years later, but has declined slightly in the last thirty years, largely due to the closure of the railway with its service related to Skipton business times, and the substitution of a bus service catering primarily for the summer visitor traffic with Grassington, with the first bus from the higher dale only reaching Skipton at 9.20 a.m., too late for most employment.

This has been the trend throughout the dales, and today, while the older generation using the family car can get to work outside the dale, the younger folk, dependent upon bus services, are cut off and are driven to move into the towns. While their numbers are sufficient to ensure a local 'life' in the dales, if they can be retained, they are not enough to provide a pool of labour sufficiently large for a local industry. Boys can find some local work on the farms or at the quarries but girls have little outlet other than helping in the home. It is the towns on the fringe of the dales that are big enough to provide employment for young people – Ripon, Skipton, Hexham, Richmond. These are the towns where the professions congregate: doctors, lawyers, banks, agents, the larger repair garages, who serve a very wide rural area and are located there not singly but in numbers. Shops and offices in great variety, local government offices, both county and rural area offices, with their own urban services and industries, all these offer employment, some of which could be satisfied from the dales if rural transport were arranged so that young folk could get to these centres in time for business opening hours. The habit of travel is already there, since children and youths from the dales travel in to the grammar schools by transport arranged by the transport companies or the education departments. The main bus services, however, are related to the holiday season traffic and to the shorter distance runs (Grassington–

Skipton, for example) which can be economically run. Beyond this radius early buses would not pay. For lack of a public transport system which would include the well-being and life of the rural population as an item in its auditing the rural areas are being drained of their young folk.[2]

The coming of the motor-bus was only one aspect of the revolution caused by the popularization of internal combustion engine transport. The motor-car, which in 1910 was making its adventurous way from the towns into the country, after 1920 began its phenomenal expansion of popularity, and after 1945 became a torrent, a swarm, an invasion not yet under control. The cars which now move in the countryside in their thousands are divisible into two distinct groups. There is a very small minority which we might be forgiven for calling 'native', belonging to farmers and residents in the dales. The ubiquitous Land-Rover was at first essentially the farmer's car. Recent years, however, have seen a change. It is now much more an extension, and a very essential one, of farm mechanization.

The great majority of cars which use the dales roads now belong to weekend and holiday invaders – urban cars seeking pleasure. Unfortunately one can still see a goodly number parked on the roadsides, on open spaces, or near village greens.[3] An ever-increasing procession of larger and longer cars pours along the country roads, enjoying what can be seen of the countryside between the frustrations of slow traffic ahead and the impossibility of overtaking. The 'run' may be 50 or 100 miles up and down two or three dales and will probably include a big meal at one of the larger inns, but walking will in many cases be limited to a rather aimless saunter around the village. These folk are often the customers for whom the arty-crafty souvenir shop exists, the shop which makes it more difficult for the real local craft shop – blacksmith, potter, woodworker, and such – to find his proper market. There is, however, some sign in recent years of a change; the true craftsman is being more appreciated, and his work is finding employment and outlet for a few of the rural youths who have any creative gifts.

The changes due to the internal combustion engine are not confined to the vast increase in the numbers of visiting cars. Cars and cattle wagons have been a means of changing the pattern of farming. A farmer's market radius has increased. No farm is too remote now from a market, and sheep and cattle are quickly transported over long distances in comparatively short time and in good condition. Farmers in Airedale can quite easily attend markets in Hexham in Tynedale if they wish, and some of them do so. On the farm new machinery has gone into the fields, and, with the baling machine, has brought to an end one very picturesque feature of farming life. For almost a century the extra labour needed for hay-making and harvest has been provided by Irish labourers. After the famine years in Ireland an army of labourers each year would set out for England to reach Midland areas for the earliest part of harvest, find employment for a few weeks or a month, then move farther north. For year after year some of the labourers went to the same farms and became in time almost a part of the family.

In spite of a decline in population in the dales area – a decline which is de-creasing – there has been a livening and expansion in the towns on the fringe of the lowlands and at the valley mouths. With the increase in the number of motor-cars, a town like Settle, which for centuries had a small but very important market mainly deriving from its position on the Keighley–Kendal highroad, has now become the commercial and service centre for upper Ribblesdale and for most of Settle Rural District and Bowland. Throughout the week it is a busy, bustling place providing a distributing centre for groceries and farm provender, carried over its area by a fleet of vans and wagons. Motor and machinery agencies and repair shops provide a most essential service without which the life of its wide rural area would be seriously affected. There is a second influence at work on the town: it is the very convenient and attractive stopping place for the in-creasing tourist and holiday traffic from the industrial west and south-west to Morecambe and the Lake District. Nearly half-way from the cities to the seaside or the Lakes, it is a natural calling-place. Car parks, cafés, antique and souvenir shops, 'country' shops of high quality and the quaint attractiveness of the old town are increasing assets, and the town now has the problem, by no means insoluble, of combining these new demands with the basic functions of a rural market town without losing its unique character.

To some extent Settle is linked with the larger town of Skipton, where cattle and sheep markets are large and from where services such as law and banking are regulated. A welcome development will be the expansion of Settle and a strength-ening of its own regional character, a process which has already started and holds out great promise for its future. Another small town which has a potential as a regional centre is Sedbergh, in the very north-west of the West Riding of York-shire, focus of Dentdale, Garsdale, and all the Howgill Fell country, with part of the Vale of Lune and Rawthey.

Since the completion in 1818 of the Kendal–Lancaster Canal, Kendal, only ten miles away, has become the major market and service centre and has delayed much development in Sedbergh except as a town from which workers can be drawn into Kendal offices. There is a great local pride and loyalty, however, which carries the assurance that Sedbergh is conscious of its proper place in the rural pattern as the centre of its large Rural District. It has a wealth of interest and beauty in the Howgill Fells and in the dales which focus on the town; it has its large public school, and, in spite of its apparent remoteness as seen from Wakefield, the administrative centre of the West Riding, it is on the important main road between Newcastle, Teesside, and Blackpool and Lancaster. It will be near the new motorway which is being built along the Lune valley. It is the centre of a very fine area of Pennine country and the natural head of the very attractive north-west portion of the Dales National Park.

The Pennine dales are curiously ringed round with these towns, most of them with markets which have increased considerably in importance with the coming of the motor-car and with motor-bus services. The few markets and larger villages within the Pennine area have declined, with only one or two exceptions, and the population think now of their shopping and business centre as being not within, say, 4 or 5 miles but within easy reach by car or bus. Road distances have lost much of their significance in the last thirty years. This has taken away from the roads one great feature of the nineteenth and early twentieth centuries the large droves of sheep and cattle which converged by every road on the market town. Drovers, boys, and dogs made up a noticeable element of the market population, but they are now almost gone, their place taken by the large cattle wagons and their drivers.

During the wars much effort was spent to make the upland farming more productive, and though there was no very radical change in the overall pattern there was some improvement in detail. A small acreage of the higher dale land was ploughed for kail and oats, though for oats there was in some years a difficulty on higher ground in proper ripening. As soon as possible the ploughing for grain was stopped and ploughing for re-seeding with good grasses took its place. This was part of the move towards a better breeding and feeding of beef cattle and an increase in dairy herds. The farming pattern, however, is very clear. Arable is negligible within the Pennines, and the main mass of the Pennine dales area divides approximately into the rough upland grazings, with around 50 ins of rainfall a year, a lower belt, mainly the hill slopes and valleys, with between 50 ins and 30 ins of rainfall, and the lowland. In the highland rough grazing dominates, concerned with breeding and rearing sheep. Cattle increase in the land below this zone, with cows in milk which a better quality of land and good hay production increases. Some stock fattening for beef is combined with this dairy farming. In most villages sheep and cattle far outnumber humans, and much of the working life centres on their care and maintenance.

The seasons are marked by 'lambing', 'clipping', and 'lamb sales', by the dates when cattle are turned into the fields after their winter sojourn indoors, by haymaking, by the opening or closing of the meadows to stock, and by other events

137

in the animal routine. Human activities and events are integrated into an age-old rhythm which gives a sense of stability and continuity which no kind of urban life can afford.

Since the decline of lead-mining, limestone, after farming land, has become the major economic potential in the dales. In the south-west of the area the vast outcrops of the Great Scar Limestone and, farther north, the scars of the Great Limestone (about 60 ft thick) which is seen in most of the Alston Block, have drawn envious appraisal from the lime and iron industries. Before the 1914–18 war the increase in motor traffic soon overtaxed the capacity of the road system which had been adequate for the preceding century of horse traffic. The dry macadam surfaces, easily mended with a load of crushed rock, and the light road foundations were unsuited for the higher speeds and heavier loads of the new transport. A smoother surface with greater cohesion and easier drainage was provided by tar-macadam. A vastly increased programme of road improvement gave the impetus to a limestone quarrying industry which was soon transformed from the widespread, former small-scale, quarries serving local limekilns and local road repairs into an industry with a fresh location for fewer quarries of a vastly increased size. The roadstone industry, with its demands for crushed rock of high quality and of regular standardized grading, called for quarries with a large and steady output and with mechanical plant on a large scale. The increased use of concrete needed rock aggregates, which in turn stimulated the quarrying of limestone, whinstone, and the older slate and grit rocks below the limestone.

After the First World War attention was turned to making our grasslands more fertile, and it was soon found that one of the more serious defects was a re-markably widespread lime deficiency. The evidence of this accumulated from many areas, and by 1937 a Land Fertility Scheme was introduced by Parliament, granting considerable financial aid towards the provision and spreading of lime. This subsidy was largely for the use of finely-ground limestone rather than burned, but burned lime of high quality was coming into increasing demand for the chemical industries and the net effect had been a very rapid upward trend in demand. Limekilns of new patterns had been erected at many quarries and crush-ing and grinding plant installed, sometimes at the same quarries as the kilns, sometimes at new quarries where there was no burning. Finally, the increase in blast furnace capacity gave a correspondingly great demand for raw limestone as a flux. All these accumulating demands resulted in the extension of old quarries and the opening of many new ones, their work based to a large extent on mecha-nized handling and on outputs of the order of from 25,000 to more than 100,000 tons a year from a single quarry. In this development a few large pockets of quarrying around particular areas retarded, or even locally reversed, the migration of population from the area.

By the topography of the ground, the nature of the outcrops, transport, and other factors, the quarries have tended to concentrate on six or seven localities with a grouping of quarries in each. In Weardale below Stanhope, the Frosterley Marble (limestone), which was used from medieval times, was now sought out as the location of several quarries producing roadstone and ground limestone for agriculture. Above and around Stanhope there arc at lcast four quarries with outputs between 50 and 100 thousand tons a year, two of them almost entirely roadstone, one of them flux, and one of them burned limestone. A recent development too is the establishment of a largc ccment works near the valley head. All this has brought a big demand for labour and has restored much of the lost mining population, with its demand for housing being met by Rural District Council housing schemes, services, improved educational facilities, and all the activities of a thriving community. In Teesdale there are again three quarries turning out limestone for roads and for agriculture, and some large quarries in the Whin Sill for roadstone and aggregate. Lower Wensleydale, between Redmire and Leyburn, has a large-scale quarry industry connected with the iron industry of Teesside.

In Wharfedale the Skipton to Grassington railway opened the way for the large quarries, with their banks of limekilns, at Swinden and Skyrethorns (Plate 31b), where both lime (hydrated in part) and ground limestone as well as crushed roadstone are produced. Giggleswick and Horton in Ribblesdale had already opened alongside the London to Carlisle railway line up Ribblesdale, and, connected with the older line by Ingleton, the limestones and slates of Ingleton were soon developed into a large industry. Another large-scale development has taken place more recently around Brough and Kirkby Stephen in Westmorland, at the head of the Vale of Eden, with very big quarries providing roadstone, burned lime, and ground limestone for agriculture. In addition to these there are developments at Greenhow Hill, for roadstone and artificial building stones, and a few quarries around Alston in Cumberland.

This industry sets a number of problems for the area, among which there is the great spread of dust and noise from the crushing plants, smoke from the kilns, and the mass of buildings. The greatest problem comes with the closure of railways and the movement of all these vast loads, many hundreds of thousands of tons in total, by motor lorries, over the dales roads. This heavy traffic is demanding widening and upgrading of roads, and is sadly at variance with the desired quiet and beauty of the countryside. The return of much of the quarry load to the railways would have saved much of the peace of the dales, and more adequate rail service to the developed quarrying areas may yet be the best solution to an urgent problem.

The effect of the lime subsidy for farming has been an improvement in much of the pasture, not yet so widespread but quite as effective as that of the late eighteenth and early nineteenth centuries. Both hill farms and dairyland have benefited, and milk production has greatly increased.

In the nineteenth century a constant seasonal occupation for the farm wife and daughters was cheese-making. This on a large scale has been a feature of dales life from monastic times onward. Most of the monasteries had one or more granges where the flocks of ewes were milked and cheeses made for the use of the parent house. In the accounts of Bolton Priory as early as 1290 to 1300 the sheep-house on Malham Moor was sending regularly to the Priory, large amounts of cheese, sometimes as much as 20 stones, with occasional parcels of butter. Cheese was sent from Kilnsey Grange to Fountains Abbey, and other houses too had cheese-making as a regular part of the work on their estates. It is generally believed that the cheese-making recipes of Jervaulx Abbey remained in use in Wensleydale after the Dissolution, and that they are the basis, along with the quality of the local milk, for the special place given by most people of discrimination to Wensleydale cheese. In Teesdale the local cheese is Cotherstone, which sometimes claims an early connection with the dairies of Egglestone Abbey. Around Sedbergh there is a fine Dent cheese, but they are all closely related in type though having qualities which are unmistakably their own.

It was probably in the nineteenth century that the shorthorn cow took the place of the Wensleydale ewe as the source of milk for cheese. Rennet was still unknown and 'keslop' was in use, prepared by drying the stomach of a young calf, boiling a small piece, and cooling and straining the liquor. Cheeses were entirely a farm-house product and were made during the months in which the cows were out in the pastures, that is between mid May and the end of October. No cheese was made in the other seven months of the year. In 1897 'factory cheeses' began to be made in Wensleydale, these being the regular cheese of the farmhouses, for convenience made in bulk at a central place to which the milk was brought. This change was made in order to secure, if possible, a more uniform quality for the cheese factors. Edward Chapman, who collected cheeses from the farmhouses and sold them at Yarm Fair between 18 and 20 October, started the cheese factory at Hawes, and was soon followed by Alfred Rowntree at Masham, Coverham, and Thoralby. Factory cheese was made and stood in the market alongside the farmhouse cheeses until the changes imposed by the 1914–18 war began to affect the whole industry. The sale of liquid milk to the towns of Durham and Yorkshire and to the rapidly growing milk-buying companies who even sent milk by train to London, proved an attractive alternative to the labour of cheese-making in the home and offered more leisure to the farm womenfolk. Industrial depressions in the 1920s and '30s were often reflected in broken or reduced milk contracts, which, although they left more milk for the cheese factories, involved them in the loss due to falling prices and reduced demand. A looming failure of the industry was averted in 1933 by the setting up of the Milk Marketing Board.[4]

Although this did not at once restore the industry and though many factories had to close for part or all of the Second World War period, the Marketing Board was firmly established and became a normal and necessary part of present farm life.

The twentieth century has been marked by the spread over the country of many 'movements', new social groupings and organizations which have effected a broadening of contacts in rural life. The place once occupied by the Mechanics Institutes was in part taken by the Workers' Educational Association and by evening classes organized by the Local Education Authorities. These classes provided many opportunities for the study of non-vocational subjects of a very wide variety. In Workers' Educational Association classes, and with the excellent and rather more general work of the University Extension Lectures to supplement them, many academic subjects became available, and from time to time students from the rural areas were able to secure scholarships to universities, such as to Ruskin College, Oxford, or to Agricultural Colleges. The total number of these successes is high and rewarding. The Local Authority classes and the Evening Institutes, as they are now known, are providing a great encouragement to choral and music studies, to many craft classes, art, pottery, as well as to more domestic subjects as cookery, soft furnishings, glove- and dress-making and so on, which provide a new meeting-ground for the women of the dales.

The Young Farmers' Clubs are popular for their social gatherings as well as for the very excellent programme of lectures, farm demonstrations and visits, which have brought a wealth of new understanding and methods into farmwork. Along with these activities, the married women have found a new life in the Women's Institutes which are now found throughout the rural areas, though usually several smaller villages combine to run a single Institute group. Originating in Canada in 1897 as an offshoot of a Farmers' Institute, the idea was taken up in 1915 by the Agricultural Organization Society, and the first Women's Institute was formed in Wales. The movement spread rapidly under the care and encouragement of the Board of Agriculture, but in 1919 it became independent. Its aim was to educate the women of the rural areas and to improve their social environment and opportunities. The idea spread quickly until there are now few areas without a group. The regular meetings, 'efforts', events of many kinds both local and regional, have brought much happiness, friendship, and interest into the lives of women in the remoter areas. Although the farmer, with a twinkle in his eye, will tell you that the W.I. (as it is everywhere known) is mainly concerned with 'jam and gossip', he will admit more seriously that it has brought a richer life and interest for his wife, and if pressed further will admit that there may be more variety and interest about his meals, better ideas about furnishing in the house, and an increasing contentment with rural life. A wider fellowship is provided by the regular Drama Festivals held in centres such as Skipton, or at the larger gatherings of County scale where products of W.I. industry and effort are exhibited and compared. In these many gatherings the sense of belonging to a countrywide organization is very manifest.

In the larger rural scene the twentieth century has witnessed several innovations which in some degree are altering the pattern of life in the Pennine dales. Some of these changes arise from new legislation and the formation of new administrative bodies, others from new voluntary organizations and from new habits of the population at large. During the war of 1914–18 the country was made acutely aware of the insufficiency of our resources of native timber. Plantations and woodlands disappeared and any mature timber was likely to be felled to meet the demand. From this situation and the necessity to secure replanting came the Forestry Act of 1919, setting up a Forestry Commission with powers defined in the first and later amending Acts between 1919 and 1951. The net effect was that a State forestry service, planting and managing State forests, came into being and is now one of our large-scale industries. The Forestry Commission was empowered to buy large areas of suitable land and to prepare and plant it with an economic timber crop. In its first ten years the Commission planted over half a million acres of forest, mainly in newly created forest areas.

For the work of the Commission men had to be trained in forestry and its associated skills, and houses, and, in the larger and remote forests like that of Keilder, whole new villages, had to be built. Within the Pennine dales of which we are speaking the Forest of Arkengarthdale has produced an entirely new landscape between Arkengarthdale and the Greta valley, on 1,120 acres between Scargill and Barningham Moors. A much larger forest is that on Hamsterley Common south of Wolsingham in Weardale, covering much of the upper course of the Bedburn Beck and its tributaries. South of Hexham there is the Slaley Forest and

Dipton Woods, but none of these compares with the huge Forest of Keilder and Kershope along the Borders.[5]

A more radical change in the scenery of the Pennine Dales has been effected in the later years of the nineteenth century and during this century by the construction of a number of reservoirs, which now have the appearance of lakes, except for the embankment or dam and the overflow works. Some of them – for example, Gowthwaite reservoir in Nidderdale – have become famous as the haunt of an amazing variety of birds, and some have settled well into the landscape.

The beginning of this change was made by the two small reservoirs built on Barden Fell for the supply of part of Bradford. They were completed and began to supply water in 1864. For the years that the navvies were at work a tiny school was built for their children at Barden, and later this was replaced by a permanent school, which reached its peak of occupation about the 1870s. Through the decline in population and in the size of families, this school is now closed and the building is used partly as a National Park information and briefing centre. Leeds city, under the pressure of rising demands for water, turned to the valley of the Washburn, tributary to the Wharfe below Otley. Here three large reservoirs were built – Lindley Wood in 1875, Swinsty in 1876, and Fewston in 1879 – while now a fourth has been added higher up the valley at West End. Around the lower reservoirs there has been a good deal of plantation – not, however, as an unpleasant and unacceptable blanket covering the whole countryside – and it is probable that the whole aspect of the valley has been improved. Leeds had a scheme for several smaller reservoirs in the drainage of the river Ure, mainly in the area of Colsterdale, but only one of them was built at Leighton and opened in 1926.

Bradford experienced a rapid growth in the nineteenth century which compelled it to design an entirely new water supply system and to look for new areas of supply. Their choice fell on Nidderdale and in the last decades of the century this scheme was started with the building of Gowthwaite reservoir just above Pateley Bridge, to act as a compensation reservoir storing winter flood waters to release in summer drought and so maintain the river flow. The highest reservoir at Angram was completed in 1914 and a second, below it at Scar House, but with its head nearly reaching the Angram Dam, was completed in 1936. For these two reservoirs a 36-mile conduit was needed to reach Bradford, and this had to tunnel for four miles beneath Greenhow Hill. For the construction of the reservoirs, a light railway was built from Pateley Bridge to the head of the valley, bringing much new life into the upper dale. When the reservoirs were finished, this light railway continued in use for a time, but was later taken up, and recently the railway to

143

Pateley Bridge has also disappeared. A scheme is at present being considered to use the old railway track as a foot road and bridle way, and if this can be achieved it might set the pattern for good use of many discarded railway lines.

Farther north the two tributaries of the Tees, the Lune and the Balder, each acquired a large reservoir (in Balderdale there are in fact two, the head of the lower one meeting the dam of the upper one). A still larger one is now being built at Cow Green above Cauldron Snout in Teesdale. This impinges on part of the unique area of very rare plants and it will be long before the bitter resentment of naturalists from all parts of the world, is forgotten. The Wear has two reservoirs on its tributary, the Waskerley Burn, and a magnificent new one at Burnhope, built and opened in the second quarter of this century. There are two small reservoirs connected with the Hisehope Burn and one under construction near Muggleswick in the main valley of the Derwent. Although the South Tyne and the Allendales have no large reservoirs there are, on all the fells around them, numerous small dams and reservoirs connected with the great demand for water used by the mines for ore dressing and for power. One effect of these many reservoirs, both large and small, is that there is a rich group of visiting birds and a very large number of gulls which breed at some of the more remote waters. It may well be that with modern water purification methods some of the reservoirs may in the next few years come into use for boating and other forms of water sports.

Since the 1914–18 war two outdoor movements have come into being which have a great influence in bringing young people into this north Pennine area, to enjoy its open moors and its countryside on foot. The Youth Hostels Association, founded in the 1920s, has now provided twenty hostels in the area, which among them provide nearly 900 beds and enable walkers to make their way over the Pennine country with supper, bed, and breakfast accommodation at very reasonable cost, with another hostel within fifteen and often within fewer miles. These hostels, with their familiar green YHA sign, are providing something approaching or possibly exceeding 100,000 bed-nights.[6] The Ramblers' Association has a smaller membership but is deeply concerned for access to the countryside, for the preservation of footpaths, commons, etc., and has done a great deal of the pioneer work in the demand and preparation for the National Parks and Access to the Countryside Act of 1949. As a result of that Act, the Yorkshire Dales National Park was designated in 1954 and includes 680 square miles of the Dales, in the West and North Ridings, which all lie within the area of the country described in this book. The effect of this has been to bring an increasing number of visitors to the Dales. This has created problems of motor traffic, but the

The road climbs the opposite fellside from Bouthwaite, a former grange of Fountains Abbey.

26a. *Dalesman with 'budget' back can. Near Middleham, Wensleydale.*

26b *Looking across Stainmore from Tan Hill to Mickle Fell.*

National Park Planning committees in the two Ridings are providing better car parks and picnic spots, regulating caravans, and controlling building and other development in their areas. The effect on the life of the people has not yet been great, but the increase of visitors to the Park is beginning to bring increased prosperity. This increase will continue as the Park becomes better known, and knowledge of the Park will tempt visitors to explore those other northern Dales which have many areas of beauty comparable with those within the Park to reward the exploring traveller.

A silent revolution has been accomplished in the working life in the dales during the last few decades, more penetrating and more wide-reaching even than that of the motor-car: it is the rural electrification scheme now nearing completion and acting as the threshold between two ages, between two widely separated standards of comfort both in the home and on the farm. Many remote farms and cottages have moved from the dim light and the labour of paraffin lamps and candles, with problems of oil storage during the winter weather when delivery is always doubtful, into the comfort of a well-lit house. The farmer has progressed from the feeble light of the hurricane lamp to the clarity of a bracket light. An electric milking machine may have lightened and shortened considerably the labour of milking, and may have enabled the farmer to manage some increase in his herd without demanding more labour. In the house the farm wife now has her washing-machine and often an immersion heater to ensure the constant supplies of hot water which formerly demanded the fireside boiler or the large copper. The daily labour of trimming lamps has gone and many minor refinements of life and work have been made possible.

Along with electric power has come the possibility of television or at the least of a proper radio set. The most isolated farm is now in as close contact with news of world events as is the city dweller, and has at command a world of entertainment for what leisure the new power has helped to create.

As with all rapid changes one may look back with some amount of nostalgia to the former ways, but one is compelled to accept the great improvements of the modern age. One of the thrills of boyhood when staying on an uncle's farm was the time after tea when uncle and cousins moved away into the shippon for evening milking. The two wire-guarded storm lamps were lit, one at each end of the long row of cows standing patiently in their boose. Milking pails and stools were collected and soon the milk hissed quietly into the pails. Fodder was carried on the fodder gang and distributed to the quiet cows, milk pails carried to the milk house, and the milk 'syled' into the churns. Then cans were taken to the back kitchen of the house to be 'scalded' and polished ready for morning. Today milking is more like a factory process: pipes, the hum of electric motors, the weighing of milk from each cow, the rattle of bottle racks and the trickle of the cooler, in the clearness and glare of electric light, embodying the change which electricity has made.

Electrification is not without its problems for the planners, and the avoidance of a crazy and ugly tangle of lines and poles sprawling over the countryside has been attained only by constant care and thought on the part of the electricity authorities and conference with the planners.[7] The main high-voltage power lines striding across the country on their high steel pylons have become a major element in the landscape. They are there to stay – the undergrounding of much of those lines is not possible, and one pressing problem is the way in which these can be integrated into the landscape. The authorities are meeting this problem, and with the landscape architects are producing a countryside in which the minimum number of power lines will take their place with roads and walls, as an accepted part of the cultural landscape. We shall accept them as the symbol of a cleaner, fuller life for the rural population as well as a sign of more abundant power for industry. They indeed are the sign of the new age.

9

Vernacular architecture

A traveller coming from the South or Midlands into the Pennine dale country would notice a marked diminution of the number of buildings of more orthodox architectural interest, particularly of the larger country house and wealthy parish church. In the lower part of the dales, near the fall of the Pennines into the low-lands, monastic ruins and castles would provide an abundant scope for architectural tastes, but in the true dales among the higher fells architectural interest would need to turn to a contemplation of much humbler buildings. This need not imply a lessening of interest but only a very marked change in scale and form – the study of a vernacular architecture which has developed in response to local materials, a harsh climate, and a community with little wealth. The sheer hard practicality of house and farm buildings, of bridges, churches, and schools, robs them of the chance to display ornament or to give play to architectural fancy. A solidity in unity and balance with a natural environment gives an air of fitness and stability and imparts character to many modest buildings which would be of no note in a richer context and a kinder climate.

There is thus a great dichotomy in building throughout the dales, with little to bridge the gap. On the one hand the monasteries, abbeys, and priories exemplify the grace and beauty of the Gothic building developed in warmer climates and with greater wealth; on the other hand the small domestic buildings, ranging from cottages to yeoman's farmhouse, the school and church, are built in a style which is a local growth, born of the local people, their surrounding hills and materials, and characteristic of the particular area and not of any other. It is possible that the castles stand in part between these two, reaching out through pele towers, tower houses, and fortified farms towards the vernacular rather than the Gothic tradition. They entered more into the life of the people and the ways of their occupants were more akin to those of the peasants than were the habits of the cloistered monks and clergy of the abbeys and priories, who were mainly seen in the pageantry of high church liturgies on Saints days and holy days. The castle garrisons and servants were down-to-earth fellow peasants, many of them recruited from the peasantry and kin to them.

The basic unit of vernacular building is a hut for shelter from the weather, a place in which to sleep, with cooking, eating and work outside in the open. The earliest huts which we can recognize with certainty belong to the Bronze Age of something more than three millennia ago – circular walls of rough stone as foundation for a hut built mainly of light timber and thatch. During the Iron Age the hut diameters were generally smaller, and a low side wall of timber sometimes stood on the stone foundation and lifted the roof to comfortable height.[1] It was the Roman example which led the Romano-British Brigantes to make the exceptional rectangular huts, but remains of all types are still limited to foundations and occasional post-holes, so that the whole subject of these earliest dwellings remains an open and profitable field for research.

There are few remains, except foundations, of Roman buildings within the forts, and whatever these structures were they stand outside the line of development of our own vernacular building. It is to the Dark Ages that we owe the foundation of nearly all the present villages, though the buildings we know are all much more recent replacements, mostly over the site of the original houses, which were destroyed to make room for them. There are just a few buildings left which have sufficient material structure for us to study their form, but these are all connected with the church and tell us little of the life of the people. On Malham Moor and within a few hundred yards of the Tarn, at SD 897674, a building was excavated a few years ago to which the name of 'priest's house' has attached itself, and the features of this may reflect one of the more permanent Dark Age huts. It stands on a high shelf of the hills, about 1,500 ft OD, with a magnificent view across the upper Airedale country and over the moors of Bouldsworth beyond. The house is a rectangular building 15 ft by 9 ft inside, with two slender partition walls, one cutting off a room 8 ft by 9 ft at the south end into which there is an entry from outside at the south-east corner. The narrower room is divided by cutting off 3 ft from the south end. The outer walls are remarkable, made of a double row of limestone boulders up to 6 ft long and 4 ft wide, set on edge, making the inner and outer faces of a 6 ft-wide wall. The space between the large stones is carefully packed with smaller limestone boulders, but no gravel. The natural limestone floor of the rooms was carefully levelled with small stones, then covered with a layer of calcareous marl from the near-by Great Close tarn. There was a small hearth in one corner of the larger room and a large stone placed as a footing for a central post to support the mid point of the ridge tree. If timbers had been footed on the long walls which were about 3 ft high, they could have met on a ridge tree supported at the ends and mid point by posts, and would give a height to the house of more than 7 ft. The end gables could be made up with a thick turf wall or with wattle screening.[2]

Among the finds in the house was a cast bronze disc, head of a large pin, $1\frac{1}{4}$ ins in diameter with pierced 'Celtic' interlacing ornaments and traces of gold inlay, a simpler bronze brooch and buckle, and pieces of perforated bronze strip which could be the edging for a book cover, along with typical book ornaments. The house and material found in it are very like those excavated from the Anglian monastery which underlies Whitby Abbey. All this suggests that we have the little house of a seventh- or eighth-century priest or hermit, but it was no doubt based upon prevalent tradition, built here in stone instead of timber.

Buildings of more skilful workmanship can be seen in the crypts of Ripon Minster and Hexham Abbey, in both of which cut and shaped masonry and vaulting was used. There is also a complete church of the Anglian period at Escomb in Weardale, but these will be discussed later with other ecclesiastical buildings. Of the housing of the mass of the Anglian peasantry we know very little. Their houses were almost entirely of wood and turf, with some wattle and with thatched roofing, and had little or nothing that was durable. The few larger houses were rectangular timber-framed structures and would generally house both humans and animals. The small huts were no more than hovels and so roughly built that it is doubtful if even their foundations could be recognized.[3]

The traces of more substantial houses are probably of Norse date, belonging to the tenth and persisting into the thirteenth century. These are rectangular foundations standing not more than a foot in height, varying in size but keeping similar proportions, and ranging between approximately 25 ft by 12 ft to 40 ft by 15 ft inside the walls. The walls are of limestone or grit boulders, generally slabby and built in courses. In some houses one end is slightly apsed and the entry is usually near the end of a long side and only very rarely in the gable. The structure above these foundations would be timber and thatch. In one such house that was excavated the floor in the third nearer the door was laid with large limestone cobbles, and the rest more carefully made with gravel and marl. In this latter part there was a good deal of pottery, mostly green-glazed of thirteen- and fourteenth-century date with a few shards of earlier types, the whole dating from the eleventh to the fourteenth centuries. There was a hearth between the two sections. This building is one of several in an area which was settled by Norsemen sheep farmers, and the building probably housed the family of more than one generation. This type of 'house' is fairly common over the Yorkshire dales, where more than twenty have now been recognized, but so far they have not been seen in the Durham dales, where Norse settlement was either very sparse or absent.[4]

After the Norman Conquest we know little of domestic building until the opening of the fourteenth century, when masons trained on the castles and abbeys were becoming available to build the occasional manor house. The abbeys had granges in many parts of the dales and these set an example of stone building that was followed by an occasional secular lord. Very few remains of peasants' houses, however, can be recognized, though there is one small house within a mile of Grassington which may be a picture in stone of the arrangement of the timber and wattle huts of the serfs and poorer labourers.

This house is in Kimpergill, a slight valley on Lea Green, and the house is a building in parts standing 4 ft but mostly only 1 ft or sometimes 2 ft high. It is about 21 ft by 19 ft outside and 13 ft by 11 ft inside the 4-ft-thick walls. These are of massive slabby limestone, some stones being 4 ft by 1 ft 9 ins by 1 ft. Both faces of the walls are well built, with stones laid flat, dry-walled and coursed, with well-placed stone fillings. The corners are well squared. Part of the wall at the north and north-east seems to be the complete height, finished off at four feet. The doorway at the south-west corner is formed with two large slabs of limestone set on edge, about 4 ft 6 ins by 3 ft by 1 ft 6 ins thick. Just inside this doorway a low stone-built screen projects from the west wall, and behind this is the fireplace. Against the west wall there is a thick backstone of fine grit, very heavily burned of course, behind a flat hearthstone of similar stone on which the open fire was built. The floor is natural limestone, and many clefts in it are filled with small pieces of flagstone and levelled off, and covered with rushes would make a good floor. A timber roof frame would sit firmly on the broad top of the walls, and would be thatched.[5]

The house has an annex slightly larger inside because its walls are a little thinner and less well made. The back and front walls butt against the house on its east side without any bonding. The door is at the south-east corner and opens on a slight passage marked off from the rest by a kerb. The fact that the pottery and other remains were almost all from the room with the fireplace, and that this second room had a thin earth floor, suggests along with the quality of the building that the fire room was the 'house' and the second room an 'annex' for animals. The pottery included fifteenth-century 'Cistercian' ware, red paste with black glaze, some green fourteenth–fifteenth-century pots, and some late sixteenth-century slip ware. Articles of metal included a bronze spur, pewter spoon, iron sickle, and many fragments of iron strapping from a bucket or other wooden vessel. In the north-west corner between fireplace and wall there was a heap of lead ore, which encourages the suggestion that this was the house of Adam Cokeson, who in the mid fifteenth century was selling lead ore to Fountains Abbey from the bell pit workings on the Lea Green veins within two hundred yards of this house. A few foundations of similar size and appearance are known in other parts of the dales, but only excavation could determine whether or not they belong to the same type and date of building.

A form of building which has given rise to much discussion and to a variety of theories about its origin is that which is based upon the use of timber 'crucks'. In the simplest form a 'pair of crucks' was made by splitting lengthwise a curved tree trunk and setting up the two paired timbers as a pointed arch. Two pairs linked apex to apex by a straight ridge tree made the skeleton framework of a small building. To give rigidity a horizontal cross tie was morticed to the crucks at about half their height. The ends of the tie projected at each side to a position above the foot of the cruck, and a side wall of turf, stone, or wattle enclosed a rect-angular space. From the top of this wall, which was carried up to the ends of the ties, light rafters could span to the ridge and form a framework for a thatched roof, thus completing a high room. Usually the tops of the crucks were held by a short 'collar', and the ridge tree rested in the crossed ends of the crucks. There are of course many minor variations in detail but the whole structure of a pair of crucks with ties and ridge is the simplest form of a stable timber-framed build-ing.[6]

Crucked buildings are found over much of north-west Europe but in this country they have only a limited distribution, being found mostly in the highland zone of Wales, the Pennines, and north-west England, with some in Cleveland. Cruck buildings older than the thirteenth or fourteenth century are not certainly known in this country, but they continued to be made into the sixteenth century. A survey of the township of Cracoe, six miles north of Skipton, in 1569 describes most of the buildings in the village as being built with crucks and mentions that one Nicholas Ricroft had built 'one firehouse (dwelling) and a lath (laithe or barn) of three pair of crucks' and Richard Cockson had built a 'firehouse of four pairs of crucks of oak'.[7]

During the sixteenth and seventeenth centuries there was much rebuilding in stone, and many crucked barns which had had stone walls making the gables and side walls to the tie end level were adapted for a stone slate roof by filling the gable corners up to the new roof slope and adding a little to the side walls to bring them to the new eaves level. Barns with these features are far more numerous than others in which the crucks have survived, and many of them, particularly those in the villages, may represent crucked cottages converted to farm building when a new house was built (Diag. 6).

A house or barn of three or four pairs of crucks would be of two or three 'bays' length, and this unit of measurement, the span of the cruck feet (16 ft) and the length between adjacent pairs of crucks (10 or 12 ft), remained as the general

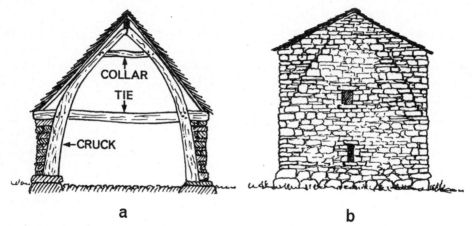

a   b

Diagram 6 a *a barn built on crucks*
   b *a 'crucked' barn altered to a trussed building.*
   Traces of crucked structure still seen in the gables.

units of dimension of dales houses right through the sixteenth and seventeenth centuries and even into the early eighteenth century. It was not until the Georgian influence was felt that a 'cruck' or 'bay' dimensioned house ceased to be built. The cruck building was increased when necessary simply by adding another cruck at a bay length beyond the gable so that the building kept the same width but increased its total 'bays' length. It was natural after two bays of house room to add one or two bays for the stock, and so create the 'long house' which is so typical of the Pennines and so close to the Dark Ages traditional house. Haymow, shippon (for cattle), and 'house place' are under one continuous roof in the long house. The principal features of the rebuilding were the substitution of stronger side walls and a stone slate roof, with its demand for much heavier timbers and a lower pitch. The roof was now held by framed timber trusses resting directly on the side walls. Some internal partitions were carried up in stone at the positions at which the crucks formerly stood, to give support to the long roof truss now in more than one section. The length of the bay – 10 to 12 ft – and its width – about 16 ft are traditional dimensions related in Anglian and medieval times to the amount of room in which an ox could be stalled and could turn itself. These dimensions enter into most seventeenth-century dales buildings; barns and shippons are usually three bays long, seen by the undulations of the roof over the trusses, and the house is often two bays, so that a very common proportion for the dales farm is about 50 ft or perhaps 60 ft long and about 20 ft wide (allowing for the side walls being 2 or 2½ ft wide).

In looking at the vernacular architecture of the Pennines it is at once obvious that Stainmore is a line of very great significance, separating the area south as far as Derbyshire where this typical 'dales' type of building is common, from the north Pennines where it is rare and where more often the houses tend to be dull and lack special features. The houses which the tourists love to call 'typical dales' have a certain unity of style – the long rectangular plan is accompanied by a stone slate roof of a low pitch, not far from thirty degrees, mullioned windows, door-ways often with a moulded and dated lintel, and in some cases gable ornaments and a well-built dressed stone chimney.[8] In Teesdale and farther north the houses are generally built of rubble limestone, and are smaller, approximating much more to a square plan. The window and door openings are plain and mullioned windows not so common, and there is no ornament to suggest date (Plate 3a). In fact the greater part of the stone building in the northern dales is later and mainly of eighteenth-century date, and because of the harder climate, poorer soil, and the greater occupation in mining, the yeoman-farmer class to whom we owe so many of the finer dales houses never developed as it did in the mid and south Pennines. These northern buildings are usually taller, and farm buildings more often cluster round a yard than share the same roof.

The mullioned windows are a Tudor fashion adopted by the local masons after a delay of two or three generations, and were soon given a local flavour in the turn of the hood mouldings, the shape of the mullions, or the chamfering of door jambs and heads. The variations are slight but one who knows the Pennines intimately and who observes with care can often place a picture of such a building with accuracy within a fairly restricted locality. The long plan has persisted from the long house of the Anglian tradition, but details such as the mullioned windows were imported from the south, probably via the larger houses which were built following the break-up of the monastic estates.

Swinsty Hall in the Washburn valley, tributary to Wharfedale, was built in 1570 by two men reputed to have come from London. It is in a Tudor style comparable with many smaller halls and houses in the Midlands and South. It has a large hall originally open to the roof but later divided by a floor, and at right angles to the hall a kitchen and parlour. The hall is lighted by long, mullioned and transomed windows with string course and hood mould above them. The porch has on its first floor a six-light mullioned and transomed window, but on the second floor and within the gable a small window of a pattern that spread during the next century into many buildings in the dales. This is a three-light mullioned window, the central light of which is taller than the side ones, and in which the hood mould is stepped in the middle to conform to the windows. Windows similar to this were built in the Wharfedale and Airedale area between 1600 and 1670. The apex of the porch gable carries a large finial which is repeated on the kneelers at the end of the gable copings. The porch at Swinsty set a fashion which was widely followed for a hundred years, and similar porches with a well-lighted room over the entry and a stepped three-light window in the gable are found on many buildings.

The long house with mullioned windows spread right across the mid Pennines and was built in many places in east and north Lancashire throughout the seventeenth and the early part of the eighteenth centuries. Another area in which this type of house occurs is the upper (southern) end of the Vale of Eden in Westmorland. Around Ravonstonedale and Kirkby Stephen and northward towards Penrith there are many long houses with mullioned windows and all the other features which mark this style, but more and more as one goes north the farm buildings tend to form a protective quadrangle in whole or in part. The four principal areas of this Tudor vernacular style are all marked by some degree of prosperity with the appearance of a yeoman-farmer class. In Westmorland, Lancashire, and the Yorkshire dales, the yeoman emerged as the small owner-farmer building up a farm by purchase of land in the two or three generations after the break-up of monastic estates and by the exchange and purchase of strips during the dispersal of the manorial common fields. In the south Pennines the prosperity was that of the yeoman clothier, who combined with his farming a dealing in wool and the 'putting out' of wool for spinning and weaving. On the whole the clothiers prospered more than the farmers, and their houses are bigger – small 'halls' rather than farmhouses – and more often keep to the earlier plan of large hall and two wings.

There is an essential difference in the plans of the 'long house' and 'hall' which seems to emphasize their different origin. The long house follows naturally and inevitably upon the simplest construction with a pair of crucks. Here the unit is fixed by the cruck pattern and by the ancient customary room allocated to a pair of oxen. Crucked buildings are easily extended by adding more crucks at regular intervals along the axis of the building. Any other arrangement would create technical problems with the roofing and with the junction of crucked elements at right angles. A small outshut could be added at one side but this could only be a low building no higher than the eaves. Such a lean-to was sometimes made but was not satisfactory until the building had been translated into stone. On the other hand the 'hall' originated in the timber-framed buildings of the South and Midlands. The main hall was built with an elaborate carpentered framing and a high roof, and one or two wings were made virtually as separate buildings, framed as the main hall was, but placed with their principal axis at right angles to that of the hall, forming an H-plan. In this type of building there was no rigid customary dimension and halls could vary in sizes suitable to the status or fancy of their owners. In the Pennine dales we have something of a common ground where northern-derived cruck and southern framed hall meet and stand side by side. Swinsty Hall, already quoted, is a typical 'hall' but its great barn (pulled down about 1910) was entirely a crucked structure.

Many large medieval houses have survived which were built on the common H-plan. In several of these the original house with a hall and two wings has been partly hidden by later additions and will not be obvious except after careful study. In the south Pennines the early halls were often of timber and the seventeenth century saw them being cased or replaced in stone but with the preservation of the plan. In the more troublous northern area, subject to the repeated Scots raids, the halls, if they were to survive, were built in stone and built so solidly with walls from 3 to 10 ft thick that any extension was made by addition rather than by rebuilding. Thus in Westmorland a few examples of these medieval halls remain, mostly built in the late fourteenth or early fifteenth century.[9]

One of the best examples is Wharton Hall, in the mouth of the through valley of Mallerstang, two miles south of Kirkby Stephen. This was the home of the Wharton family. A house of H-plan was built in the last years of the fourteenth and first years of the fifteenth century. There was a central hall lying north-west to south-east and about 30 ft by 20 ft with a screen passage across one end and a porch which opened into the north-west end of this cross passage. There is a three-storey block or tower at the north-west end of the hall and a two-storey block at the other end, making the cross lines of the H. This was the original complete house. A passage runs through the middle of the south-east block and leads to an outside kitchen. In 1540 Thomas, Lord Wharton, added a much larger hall at the south-east end, over 60 ft long and nearly 30 ft wide. This is now in ruins. The hall stood on an undercroft. At the south-east end of the great hall there is a splendid building which was the great kitchen; this is in two storeys, a barrel vaulted basement and a very high main room, 35 ft by 17 ft, with two fireplaces. In 1559 a long range of buildings was added, running nearly south from the corner of the north-west tower, and a gate-house block was built from the end of this, running parallel with the halls. A strong curtain wall with parapets completed a five-sided courtyard about 150 ft by 80 ft. Above the outer arch of the gateway there is a panel bearing the arms of Wharton and the motto 'Pleasur in acts darmys' (Diag. 7).

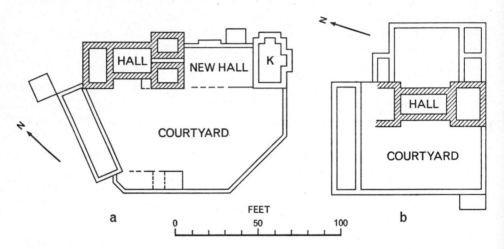

Diagram 7 a *Wharton Hall*
     b *Middleton Hall*

Wharton Hall provides evidence of the troubled state of the north in the provision of a courtyard defended by a stout parapeted wall and a secure gate-house. The same feature can be seen in Middleton Hall in the Lune valley, four miles south of Sedbergh. Here two courtyards were added in the fifteenth century to an H-plan house of late fourteenth-century date. The north wing of the hall has been largely destroyed and an outside kitchen at this end was pulled down in 1850. On the east side of the house a square courtyard was added between extensions of the two wings which were built at the same time in the fifteenth century. On the west side a much larger courtyard with a north block of stables

156

and a gate-house was also built. Much of the wall is now ruined. Both at Wharton and at Middleton the kitchen was away from the hall and this seems to have been a frequent practice. From the lack of remains it even appears probable that the early kitchens, in most cases, were built of timber and were placed a short distance outside the house.

Other houses of medieval pattern, mainly built in the last years of the fourteenth and early years of the fifteenth centuries but often altered in the sixteenth or seventeenth centuries, are to be found in the area of which we are speaking in this book. Kirkby Thore Hall, the Rectory at Asby, and Ormside Hall have each had one of the wings altered, but one wing and the hall remain. Crake Trees in Crossby Ravensworth (ruined), Killington Hall, Howgill Castle, and Newbiggin Hall, are all medieval H-houses but are best recognized by the plan, the outside being frequently 'improved'.

Houses of this type are only occasionally found in the Yorkshire dales. They are essentially a feature of the richer arable lands and of the wealthier clothier country farther south on the Pennines. The best example, still externally in its original condition, is Nappa Hall in Wensleydale.[10] This house is of the usual plan, a large hall with a cross wing at each end, the one at the west end being a tower. The house was built between 1450 and 1459 and so is a little later than the Westmorland examples we have already quoted, although it is possible that the west tower was a little earlier, built as a self-contained tower house. It is very strong and of four storeys connected by a newel stair in the south-east corner. The hall, 44 ft by 23 ft, separates the two wings, the eastern one being also a tower but of two storeys. The passage at the east end of the hall is separated by a screen and is of more than usual width with a gallery over it. The kitchen was in the east tower. In the seventeenth century a south-east wing was added, and this formed another side to the forecourt making a courtyard, though this did not have a strong defensive wall (Plate 8b).

Nappa was the home of the famous family of Metcalfe, to which many legends, true and false, attach. One of the early Metcalfes at the opening of the sixteenth century was Forester of Wensleydale and High Sheriff of Yorkshire. It is said that one Christopher Metcalfe, High Sheriff in 1556, attended the judges at York leading three hundred Metcalfes all mounted on white horses. Like most of the medieval houses Nappa has been altered and cut up by internal partitions and is now used in part as a farmhouse. However, its external appearance and main structure is well preserved, and its remarkable position just beneath one of the limestone scars and at the head of rich pastures running down to the Ure make it a lovely place. The traveller up the dale has the unique experience of viewing it first at roof level, as the modern road runs along the edge of the scar within a few yards of the house.

Near Richmond there is another medieval house, Hipswell Hall, partly disguised by a tower porch in the middle of the south wall of the hall. This porch leads into a screens passage with the main part of the hall on the east side and the kitchen-buttery on the west. In many of these early halls the dais at the end opposite to the screen was the portion used by the master and mistress of the house, the body of the hall being kept for servants and others, and it was frequently the custom to place a large window at the end of the dais in the wall opposite to that which carried the fireplace, so as to light the dais more clearly. At Hipswell this extra light is provided by a very lovely bow window, a most unusual feature. The bay is of two storeys, and has in each window five lights with a double-cusped ogee arch and a square head. The whole bay is battlemented and between the windows has a shield of arms. There are the remains of a moat around the hall.

Still in Yorkshire and only two and a half miles south-east of Barnard Castle there is one of the most attractive of all the medieval houses in a perfect setting. This is Mortham Tower overlooking the magnificent river scenery at the junction of Greta and Tees, with Brignal Banks and Scargill close at hand (Plate 8a)

Near the river junction lies the hamlet of Rokeby, which Torfin, according to the Domesday Survey, held of Count Alan of Richmond. In 1327 Alexander Rokeby got the manor of Mortham in addition, Mortham lying just across the Greta from Rokeby. In one of the many Scots raids the manor houses of Rokeby and Mortham, probably of timber, were both burned down. The house of Mortham was rebuilt in stone about 1485 to 1490 in the form of a strong tower to which other buildings were soon added. The tower stands at the north-west corner of a courtyard and is of four storeys. Windows on the south and east sides, looking to the courtyard, have two lights cinquefoil headed and with cusped tracery. The top storey of the tower is open to the sky, and its floor, covered in lead, forms the present roof. The tower is made very attractive by a turret at each corner, and all four differ in shape. The south-west turret is circular, the south-east octagonal, the north-west square and carried on corbels, and the north-east part of a hexagon and built up from ground level to contain a stair.

The hall of the house is east of the tower, 33 ft by 25 ft, with an open roof. This has blocked-up windows on the north side and small loops in the south wall. Another bay of building lies to the east of the hall, making it roughly follow the

H-plan, and is slightly later than the hall. South of the tower and forming the west side of the courtyard there is a long range of buildings which were rebuilt in the eighteenth century. The large square courtyard is completed by a battle-mented wall of considerable strength, with a fine gateway in the middle of the south side. The yard is 70 ft by 64 ft.

About two and a half miles south south-west of Ripon there is a fine medieval house, Markinfield Hall, where a licence 'to crenellate' a house was issued to John de Markingfield in 1310. The house and buildings form an enclosed quadrangle, with a gate-house giving access to a square courtyard. The present stone bridge across the moat replaces a former drawbridge. The plan of the house is in the form of an L, with the hall making the shorter leg, but partly embraced by the second limb at right angles. In the second wing there is a chapel and another room. Both hall and chapel are on the first floor, the kitchen being under the chapel. The hall windows are very attractive, two lights with quatrefoil heads and a transom. The entrance to the hall was by an external staircase at one end, of which the foundations can still be seen, along with the roof trace. The roof was an open timber one and its corbels remain, but the present roof is modern. The chapel has a good east window of three lights with geometrical tracery. The hall is extended by a lower and much later building, now the farmhouse, and each side of the courtyard is made up with recent buildings, though remains of some of the fifteenth and sixteenth centuries can be seen.[11]

The Pennines north of Stainmore have few of the very attractive mullion win-dowed farms and the medieval H-plan houses, but in architectural interest they more than compensate for this particular poverty by their richness in another group of domestic buildings – the pele towers and tower houses. These are a product of the uncertainty of life in the borderlands within reach of Scotland and its raiders. The borders for many centuries were an area where cattle and stock, and even sons and daughters, were taken by the strongest man, and where border raiding was the normal flavouring and spice of a hard life, or even the serious occupation of many families. The country of the Durham dales and Northum-berland was too poor to support a population based upon arable argiculture, or to build many defensible towns, but none the less it was excellent pasture and many of its inhabitants counted their wealth in heads of sheep and cattle. The isolated farm was easy prey for the raiders, and to build it strong and defensible was to exercise common wisdom. There developed, therefore, as a true vernacular building the strong tower with its protective fence, the true 'pele' (pale or pele means a fence), and the fortified farm in which the pele tower has become incor-porated with more buildings and a walled and strong courtyard.

The pele is essentially a very substantial square tower usually of three storeys, built in stone with walls of great thickness, and sometimes battlemented. The ground-floor compartment is roofed with a stone vault and was used for stores or in some cases as stable or byre. The living quarters were on the first and second floors reached by a stair in the thickness of the wall, or sometimes by an outside stair or ladder to the first floor. The peles date mainly from the fourteenth century when, after the devastation by the Scots before the battle of Neville's Cross in 1374, very many licences to crenellate dwellings were issued. In Northumberland they number many scores, and as a result there is a pele or tower house of some sort in almost every village and hamlet. There are also many in Tynedale and through the Vale of Eden, with a number scattered down east Durham. Many have farm buildings and later houses associated with them and were primarily, for some few centuries, a place of safe retreat on the occasion of border raids and forays, where refuge was taken until the raiders had passed by on their way to or from the richer fertile lowlands.

One of the earliest peles is Pendragon Castle in the mouth of Mallerstang, built at the end of the twelfth century probably of timber, very much in the style of a Norman keep. It passed into the possession of Robert Clifford, who strengthened the first building about 1300. In a Scots raid in 1341 it was burned out, but Roger Clifford restored it in stone between 1360 and 1370. Leland saw it in 1539 but it was again attacked and burned by the Scots in 1541. After this very troublous history it was in ruins for more than a century until Lady Anne Clifford included it in 1660 in her extensive programme of castle restorations. Both Buck and Pennant made drawings of it in the eighteenth century, although it had been 'dismantled' in 1685. It is now a ruin, standing in part to the second storey but partly buried in its own debris. It is a stone tower 64 ft square with slight corner buttresses the walls about 11 ft thick. It was formerly three storeys high. There are banks and mounds and part of a ditch which are the remains of an enclosing wall and buildings of a defence added by Lady Anne. A peculiar feature is the presence in the thickness of the walls of barrel-vaulted L-shaped chambers in the angles of the north-east and south-west corners of the ground floor and in all the four corners of the first floor. Parts of these chambers can still be seen. The few windows were round-headed of one or two lights. The entrance was on the north side, and on the side away from the river there are the remains of a deep ditch crossed by two causeways. The tower has got some measure of romance from its name and from the legend, mainly nineteenth century, that it, or its predecessor on the same site, was the stronghold of Uther Pendragon, the father of King Arthur.

27a. *Taking milk to the collecting point, Wensleydale.*

27b (below). *Gunnerside Gill, Swaledale, a mining landscape. Bunton Level on the right and Sir George Level near the stream. Woodward Level on the left and Blakethwaite Smelt Mill at the head of the valley.*

28. *Limestone pavements on Blue Scar, Littondale. Romano–British enclosures may be seen near top centre of the picture,*

Of the peles which stretch along the Tyne valley one of the most characteristic is Willimotswick, the ancient home of the Ridleys, five miles west of Haydon Bridge and on the south bank of the river. The main building is a massive square tower, battlemented and with the ground floor vaulted and used as a stable. The living quarters were on the first and second floors, and the roof formed an outlook post. Ranges of later buildings now fill the sides of the original courtyard. Now the tower is incorporated with many other buildings as part of a large and thriving farm. Only $2\frac{1}{2}$ miles away to the south-east there is another, known as Staward Pele, occupying a most romantic position on the summit of a high limestone crag forming the east side of the gorge of the river Allen. The position is one of great natural strength on the tongue of land between the Allen and a tributary stream which joins it here. The restricted summit of this spit of rock has been strengthened with a very thick curtain wall to enclose it and a strong gate tower. Most of the pele is now in ruins but nothing can detract from the impressive strength of its position and its importance at the mouth of the Allendales. An unexpected pele tower is that in the churchyard of Corbridge, a few miles to the east, which was noted in a list of peles compiled in 1415 as the property of the vicar. The tower was built in the time of Edward I or Edward II and seems to have been the parsonage from the time of building. The battlemented walls are nearly perfect, although the timber roof has been removed. The ground-floor room has a barrel-vaulted roof and only a single loop-light to illuminate it, and a pointed arched doorway. A straight stair in the thickness of the wall leads to the first floor with a stair over it to the second. The windows are small, single light, trefoil-headed. The first floor was a single room 19 ft by 13 ft, with a fireplace in the north wall. The second floor was divided into several small compartments, one of them an oratory for the parson, with a reading desk for a book in a small niche and a small window to give light on to it. There are small corner turrets carried on corbels. There was another comparable tower at the other end of the village.

The peles pass almost insensibly into the tower houses like Nappa and Mortham by marriage with a hall house, and these lead equally towards the humbler and often later fortified farm. In these, features of the pele may very occasionally be seen in a strong portion of the building and in a closed quadrangular courtyard, one or occasionally two sides of which are formed by a wall with a strong entrance, the other sides being house and farm buildings. Few of these survive as more than traces to be recognized by careful study, though Walburn Hall in Downham, Swaledale, is still a fine example in which an Elizabethan rebuilding has incorporated and preserved some of the earlier features.

If we revert briefly to the humbler farmhouses, the long house with its Tudor-fashion mullioned windows, the best examples of which are seventeenth century or early eighteenth, many of them have been disguised in a later building period dominated by Georgian influence. With increased prosperity many yeoman-farmers climbed into the small landowner class and sooner or later marked their progress by 'improvements' to their houses. Usually these took the form of re-building the front and enlarging some rooms. The new frontage was symmetrical – central doorway and window openings sometimes with a classical pediment. The doorway may have flanking columns or pilasters and a classical style. Sash windows were used and the general proportions were now vertical, and often framed with good cut masonry mouldings. Rooms were made higher and near cube proportions, so that the whole extension was higher than the earlier house. In many farms the alterations were not carried through to the back, and not only do many fine Georgian-fronted houses have a few mullioned windows left at the back but sometimes the dated door-frame has been moved there to serve as a more ornate back door.

This style, with its larger windows and greater height, was easily adapted to more modest use, and many seventeenth-century farms retain the main features of the long house structure, but with the horizontal emphasis of long mullioned windows on the frontage replaced by the verticality of sashes.

There are a few larger houses, both of Elizabethan and Georgian style, which might rank as larger yeoman houses or small country mansions, which were built in their entirety in the new periods, and some of these are among the gems of our domestic architecture; some are associated with the first planned and 'land-scaped' gardens and estates. A house like High Hall, Appletreewick, in Wharfe-dale, is a fine house in Elizabethan style, following much of the hall house plan, but built in the early seventeenth century. Friars Head at Eshton, Airedale, is another, as large in plan but much taller than the medieval hall house, being of three storeys. Both these are now farms, but were built by families newly enriched by trade and investment (Plate 30a).

For the story of Friars Head one must turn to the family of Procter, who were tenants under the Abbeys of Fountains and Furness in this part of Yorkshire for many long years before the Dissolution. There was a Thomas Procter who held Friar Head of Furness Abbey at the time of his death in 1507. The tenancy devolved upon his son Stephen, then before 1530 we find Gabriel, presumably Stephen's son, living there as steward and bailiff of Furness Abbey estates there and in Winterburn. Stephen Procter, presumably his son, was born at Friar Head in 1562 and rebuilt Friar Head in its present form about 1580–90. He made a fortune and moved to the Ripon area, and in 1596 purchased for £4,500 from the heirs of Sir Richard Gresham the remaining estates of Fountains Abbey. Among other things, he began about ten years later to build a large mansion adjoining the abbey, the present magnificent Fountains Hall. In many of its features it is obvious that Friars Head had been the prototype for this building and the two have a great deal in common, though the Hall is very much larger.

10

Monastic architecture – castles – art

One effect of the hard climate and poorish soil of so much of the northern dales area has been that arts have had little chance to flourish. They are essentially the by-product of a community with sufficient wealth to afford leisure. In the near poverty or the low level of prosperity of the northern dales, leisure has been a scarce commodity. None the less, the northern folk have developed a mastery of one of their art materials, that of stone, and in their building, both vernacular and the larger scale military and ecclesiastic, they have achieved levels worthy to rank as art forms. No one would deny a place to such a building as Fountains Abbey or Hexham Abbey in a work on art and architecture; it would be foolish and short-sighted to limit art to the softer materials of paint and paper, or to the forms of free-standing sculpture. For these reasons, we must include in this title of art what is in fact one of the skills, that of building, which has given the north Pennines and their neighbouring land a wealth of monastic buildings and castles, large and small, almost unequalled elsewhere.

We have already discussed the buildings known as pele towers and tower houses, and these are very closely linked with changes in the social policies and conditions under which castles had been built. They arise naturally from and embody in simple form some of the ideas of castle builders of the immediate post-Conquest period. The earliest castles were built as part of the imposition of Norman feudalism on the country. The earliest Norman castles were of a fairly simple structure: the *motte*, a large earthen mound protected by a ditch at the base, and a wooden palisade around the summit edge. On the flat top of the mound the only building usually present was a timber tower, square and of three storeys. The ground floor was used for stores and the first floor for living

164

quarters. The second floor sometimes provided for the retainers who used the roof as a look-out. The living quarters were extremely cramped and in most cases a large area was enclosed outside the motte, which could be protected by a ditch and palisade and within which there was plenty of room for a hall, stables, and quarters for the retainers. These mottes could be built with astonishing rapidity. It is recorded that William the Conqueror erected the castle at York, known as Baile Hill, with its tower, in only eight days; in the time of Richard I (1192), the great timber keep at York was built for £28 13s. 9d., while its successor, built in stone less than fifty years later, cost £1,927 8s. 7d.

The extended area outside the motte was the *bailey*, protected by its big ditch which joined that of the motte, and by a bank with palisade, and bringing about a quarter of the motte within its area, making in all something of a key-hole plan. There was a gantry or steep ladder-like bridge from the bailey to the summit of the motte. Within the bailey the buildings were erected against the walls, leaving a large central area for the horses and for much of the work of the community. None of the timber work of a motte and bailey castle has survived but motte and bailey was often left complete when a stone castle was built on an adjoining site. At Middleham in Wensleydale there is a very strong motte and bailey, small, but an excellent example covering about one acre. This is William's Hill, built soon after the Conquest by Ribald the brother of Alan the Red of Richmond to protect and govern his lands of Wensleydale, and to guard an ancient road from the south which came down Coverdale. The motte is three-quarters detached from the bailey and is a hill, 40 ft high, surrounded by a 20 ft-wide ditch with a counter-scarp bank 9 ft high. The summit is an area 160 ft by 115 ft, in which there is a platform on which the tower stood and a small sunk court 85 ft by 55 ft on which the first hall stood, the bailey being unusually small. The bailey is enclosed by a ditch with a 13 ft-high rampart on the inner side, within which were crowded domestic and garrison buildings. All this was abandoned when about 1190, the stone castle was built close by. At Burton in Lonsdale there is another fine motte and bailey, and excavation in the courts of both showed that they had been paved with rough stones bedding in clay. In the courts wood ashes from cooking fires, bones, knives, arrow points, an axe, and other remains were abundant evidence that all the cooking had been done outside. There is another interesting motte and bailey at Sedbergh in the Rawthey valley, where the top of a natural rocky hill has been cut and scarped to make the motte. No trace of buildings now remains but the position and shape of the hill make it a predominent feature on the edge of the town.

Until the middle of the twelfth century the castles were all of the motte and bailey type with wooden buildings and defences. Richmond Castle was the only one in 1154 to have any masonry walls and this was on a site of such natural defence that a motte was unnecessary. The Swale here is running in a deep post-glacial rock-cut gorge leaving a high rock mass between this and its pre-glacial course, now filled in with glacial debris to a lower level than the rock. A wooden palisade on the edge of the gorge and two masonry walls on the north-west and north-east enclosed a bailey or great court, triangular, 450 ft on its base, and 300 ft from this to its apex (Plate 35). At the south-east corner there is another enclosure which seems to be contemporary, the Cockpit, 220 ft east to west and 170 ft north to south. The entrance was by a gate-house at the apex of the triangular court, now covered by the stone keep built 1160 to 1174.

In the change from timber and earthwork to stone the castle retained two essential features: the tower or 'keep' and the palisade, which in stone became the 'curtain'. In Richmond Castle we have one of the finest early castles in the country. The great scale of the keep of 1160 is outstanding among contemporary military architecture, equalled only by London and Rochester. It is 100 ft 6 ins. high, and of rectangular plan 55 ft by 45 ft. The plain walls are broken up by vertical narrow flat buttresses from ground to battlement. The old gate-house entry on the ground floor was blocked up and entry made at the first floor. A central pillar supports the first floor and another makes a central support for the beams of the wooden second floor.[1] The pattern of the Richmond keep was followed at Appleby, Brough, and Brougham within the next few years, while at Barnard Castle the plan was circular.

In the south-east corner of the great court at Richmond, Scolland's Hall, named after a servant of the first earl and built soon after the keep, is one of the earliest halls of its kind. It was the dwelling place of the earl, the keep being entirely for military and not domestic use. The hall is of two storeys, the ground floor being cellars and store-rooms. An outside stair reaches the finely moulded doorway to the first floor. The hall has a solar at the east end and is lighted by round-headed two-light windows, one of those on the south wall being enlarged in the fourteenth century to give more light on the dais. A late alteration was made by breaking doorways in the west wall leading to a buttery and pantry and a central passage to the kitchen, which was farther west. There are remains of other buildings, and the small towers on the curtain wall are of interest. The present gate-house buildings are modern. This is one of the castles in the care of the Office of Works and is open to the public.

The Pennine dales are surrounded by a wealth of castles, which would need a whole volume for their adequate description. Architecturally Richmond,

Middleham, Brough, Brougham, Appleby, Prudhoe, and Barnard Castle, though all different in detail, belong to the same group of early keep and curtain wall type, with many later additions, mainly domestic, made within the original wall enclosure. Middleham may be an early example of a concentric castle, a massive and very large keep of 1190 to 1210 in the centre, having round it the other castle buildings set four-square across a broad alleyway, their outside walls being part of the square curtain wall. At Barnard Castle the keep is circular and placed, like Richmond, at the corner of the courtyard. In this castle the enclosure outside the curtain wall was divided into four wards, of which the largest Outer Ward was probably a refuge for the townspeople. This is now largely covered by part of the town. An elaborate system of walls and dry moats separated the wards. At Prudhoe the curtain encloses two wards − the east and west − and the keep, which is rectangular, 44 ft by 41 ft, and 45 ft high, is one of the smallest Norman keeps in England (Plate 3b). At Skipton most of the early castle, being ruinous, was pulled down and rebuilt in the sixteenth century by Lady Anne Clifford, so that the central defensive part is now known mainly by fragments among the foundations and lower rooms of the 'keep', which has five towers, three of them circular, linked by ranges of rooms, all domestic rather than military in their design.

Skipton could probably be described as a fortress-palace, one which starting as a castle of prime military significance was later rebuilt and extended as a baronial mansion. In this class could be put Raby, Streatlam, Brancepeth, Featherstone, Ripley, and Appleby, though of these Brancepeth was entirely rebuilt at the beginning of the nineteenth century.

Of what are now fortress-palaces Raby is the largest and clearest example. The story goes back to pre-Conquest days when King Cnut in veneration of St Cuthbert gave his mansion house with all its appurtenances as an offering to the holy shrine. This mansion house was at Staindrop on the site now occupied by the castle. When held by the Nevilles, John de Neville in 1379 was given licence to crenellate and fortify, and from this arose much of the early part of the castle. Leland says it was the largest castle in all the north country and 'of a strong building'. Pennant describes it as 'a noble massy building of its kind . . . simply magnificent, it strikes by its magnitude, and that idea of strength and command naturally annexed to the view of vast walls, lofty towers, battlements, and the surrounding outworks of an old baron's residence. The building itself besides the courts, covers an acre of land.' The exterior, a massive pile of towers, has been the least altered, but most of the interior, though retaining many of the original rooms, was greatly altered in Elizabethan times. The south front was the work of

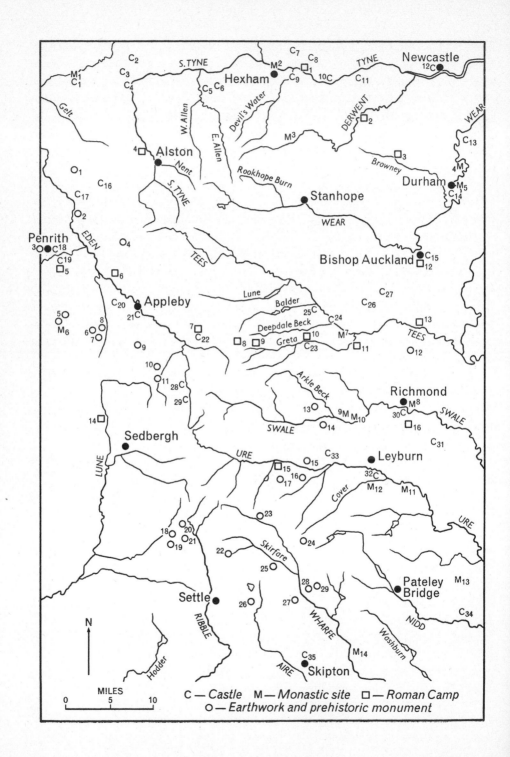

Penrith

Newcastle

Hexham

Alston

Durham

Stanhope

Bishop Auckland

Appleby

Richmond

Sedbergh

Leyburn

Pateley
Bridge

Settle

Skipton

N

MILES

0   5   10

C — *Castle*   M — *Monastic site*   □ — *Roman Camp*

○ — *Earthwork and prehistoric monument*

Map 7 *Castles, monastic sites, Roman camps, earthworks*

Castles c

1 Naworth
2 Thirlwall
3 Blenkinsop
4 Featherstonehaulgh
5 Staward Peel
6 Langley
7 Beaufront
8 Aydon
9 Dilston
10 Bywell
11 Prudhoe
12 Newcastle
13 Lumley
14 Durham
15 Auckland
16 Haresceugh
17 Kirkoswald
18 Penrith
19 Brougham
20 Bewley
21 Appleby
22 Brough
23 Bowes
24 Barnard Castle
25 Cotherstone
26 Streatlam
27 Raby
28 Lammerside
29 Pendragon
30 Richmond
31 Hornby
32 Middleham
33 Bolton
34 Ripley
35 Skipton

Monastic sites M

1 Lannercost Priory
2 Hexham Abbey
3 Blanchland Priory
4 Finchale Priory
5 Durham
6 Shap Abbey
7 Eggleston Abbey
8 Easby Abbey
9 Marrick Priory
10 Ellerton Priory
11 Jervaulx Abbey
12 Coverham Abbey
13 Fountains Abbey
14 Bolton Priory

Roman camps ▢

1 Corbridge / Corstopitum
2 Ebchester / Vindomora
3 Lanchester / Longovicium
4 Whitley Castle / Alauna
5 Brougham / Brocavum
6 Kirkby Thore / Bravonia-
  cum
7 Brough / Verterae
8 Maiden Castle
9 Rey Cross
10 Bowes / Lavatrae
11 Greta Bridge
12 Binchester / Vinovia
13 Pierce Bridge
14 Low Borrowbridge
15 Bainbridge
16 Catterick / Cataractonium

Earthworks o

1 Stone circle
2 Long Meg and her daugh-
  ters circle
3 King Arthur's Round
  Table, 'henge'
4 Hanging Walls of Mark
  Anthony (lynchets – Dark
  Ages)
5 Stone circle
6 Stone circle
7 Ewe Close,
  Romano–British settlement
8   ,,   ,,
9   ,,   ,,
10   ,,   ,,
11   ,,   ,,
12 Stanwick Park, Brigantian
  fort
13. Calver Hill, Romano–
  British settlement
14 Maiden Castle
15 Stone circle, Oxclose
16 Castle Dykes, 'henge'
17 Greenber Edge, Romano–
  British settlement
18 Souther Scales, Romano–
  British settlement
19 Hill fort, Brigantian
20 Romano–British settlement
21   ,,   ,,
22 Giant's Grave, chambered
  burial
23. Stone circle, Yocken-
  thwaite
24 Ta Dyke, Brigantian
25 Settlement, Blue Scar
26 Wide area of settlements,
  Bronze Age to Medieval
27 Hubbercove, medieval
  settlements
28 Lee Green, Romano–
  British Settlements
29 Yarnbury 'henge'

Inigo Jones and much of the castle was redesigned in the Gothic style. In 1570 it was forfeited to the crown and later was bought by the Earl of Darlington.

Not far away is Streatlam Castle, built in the fourteenth century but rebuilt by Sir William Bowes in the beginning of the fifteenth in the Norman style. Like many others, however, the castle was rebuilt from the foundations in the nineteenth century in the baronial Gothic so much favoured at that time. Brancepeth, Ravensworth, and Featherstone are other castles rebuilt in recent times, but of them, Featherstone, with its fine setting, has been described as 'perhaps the loveliest tower in the county' of Northumberland. This refers to the ancient tower portion, a rectangular tower-house of early date, on to which has been built and rebuilt a great area of Gothic castle residence, with numerous towers and battlements. The whole effect is remarkably successful as an approach to the dream castle of the story book.

Among the many other castles only two need to have special mention – Langley and Bolton. Langley Castle, on the South Tyne, is a very fine example of a tower-house, first mentioned in 1365.[2] It has a central oblong hall about 80 ft by 24 ft inside, with at each corner a large square tower. The only entrance is by a doorway with portcullis, opening on a narrow passage through the base of a small but very strong square tower near the west end of the north wall of the hall. A stair in this fifth tower is the only access to the three storeys above the ground floor of the main hall. The whole building was of one period. By 1541 it was in ruins, 'all the rooffes and flores thereof be decayed wasted and gone', but the Commissioners thought it an excellent position for defence against the thieves of Tynedale, Gilsland, Liddesdale, and Bewcastle when they raided Durham. However, it remained for the historian Mr Bates to restore it in the nineteenth century and return it to a habitable condition.

A larger version of this four-square plan is seen in Bolton Castle.[3] Overlooking much of Wensleydale and facing into Bishopdale, Bolton Castle has a wonderful position for an oversight of a wide range of country. The position, however, is hardly a defensible one – it is on the valley side with rising ground behind it and an easy approach from all sides. No natural cliff or deep ravine separates it from the open ground, nor does it occupy a hill spur or rocky promontory. Its location appears to be eminently domestic. Its plan and structure are those of the four-square toy castle of childhood. Domestic convenience was combined with strength in all the designer's plans. The castle is a rectangular curtain of apartments enclosing a square courtyard, with a strong tower at each corner, a smaller tower at the centre of the north and south walls, and a massive gate-house in the east side.

The castle is built of local stone from quarries within a few hundred yards, except for the freestone for quoins, arches, and a few special features; this came from Greets Quarry, three miles away on the Apedale moors. Timber of the sizes required was difficult to find in the dales, and according to Leland 'most parte of the tymber was gott out of the forest of Engleby in Cumberland, and Richard, Lord Scrope, for conveyannce of it had layde by the way dyvers draughts of oxen to carry it from place to place till it cam to Bolton'.

The Scrope family settled at Bolton in the thirteenth century and had their manor house there. In the late fourteenth century Sir Richard Scrope got licence to crenellate his house and used this as the excuse to cover the replacement of the old house by a new castle. In 1378 an agreement was made with John Lewyn for him to build part of the castle. The size of some of the towers, the gate-house, and principal rooms was specified, and all the rooms were to have doors, windows, fireplaces, privies, etc.; the thickness of the walls was to be 4 ft for the inner ones and $7\frac{1}{2}$ ft the outer. The northern and western parts of the present castle were built first, then the manor house on the site of the east wing was pulled down and the rest of the castle built over its foundations.

There was only one entrance into the courtyard, by the very strong gate-house, and from the yard five narrow doorways, defended by portcullis, all alike, led by tortuous stairs and passages to different parts of the castle. If an enemy penetrated the yard and entered by any of these doors there was still no direct way from one part of the building to another. Any journey about the castle involves many stairs, up and down, between passages which seem to have no plan and no regular direction, leading to unexpected rooms which have to be crossed for the continuation. The inside of the castle, except to those who have spent a long time 'learning' it, can be very much of a puzzle maze.

The rooms of the gate-house and south-east tower were for the garrison, but the rest are commodious and domestic, with generous windows and fireplaces, and the hall in the north wing, 51 ft by 27 ft and two storeys high, was nearly matched by a 'great chamber', 47 ft by 25 ft in the west wing. Sets of state apartments occupied four floors of the north-west tower, all of them of unusual size and provided with good windows and handsome fireplaces. Everywhere there is evidence of spacious comfort. Throughout the castle it is clear that we are dealing first and foremost with a 'stately home' or baronial mansion, upon which enormous ingenuity has been expended in giving it strength and security if put to the siege without its military strength being anywhere intrusive.

The Pennine dales are not very rich in ecclesiastical architecture except down their eastern borders where, in the lower dales, there are many beautiful monastic buildings. There are, however, two gems of pre-Conquest architecture in the churches of Escomb and Corbridge, and many fragments such as the crypts at Ripon and Hexham and some part of Hexham Abbey. Escomb church stands one and a half miles to the west of Bishop Auckland, on the south bank of the Wear.[4] It is the only parish church of the seventh or eighth century, in this country, still surviving in its entirety. It is small but very high and plain, and achieves a great dignity. The nave is long and high, with a nearly square chancel beyond it, separated by a chancel arch of carefully fitted well-cut long and short work. These very large blocks are probably taken from the Roman fort of Vinovia, Binchester, not far away. The windows are very small and very deeply splayed on the inside, two on the north side with straight heads, and two on the south with round heads. A few later windows have been inserted to light the building.

Not far from the abandoned Roman city of Corstopitum on the north bank of the Tyne, the early Northumbrian kings had a manor and seat which was the nucleus from which the small town of Corbridge was to arise. In the seventh to eighth centuries a church was built parts of which are now incorporated in the parish church structure.[5] The Saxon church had a west porch opening by a fine arch into a nave nearly 50 ft long and 18 ft wide. By what remains of the walls, still to be seen in the lower part of the later building, the nave was about 29 ft high, like Escomb, very high in proportion to its width. The doorway through the west gable is very remarkable, entirely of Roman workmanship, and was most likely brought from the near-by Roman town and re-erected with little or no alteration. On the porch, at a slightly later date in the eighth century, a tower was built. One of the Saxon windows remains over the west door and parts of others can be traced in the nave. Later additions to the church have created a very spacious and beautiful interior worthy of careful study. At Hexham Abbey the Saxon remains are seen in the crypt and in the foundations of Wilfred's church, of which the apse remains, along with the sculptured crosses already mentioned. Along the Tyne valley there are two fine towers of the third quarter of the eleventh century at Bywell and Ovingham.

The chief glories of the art of the stonemason are of course to be found among the monastic buildings, which with few exceptions are, like the castles, located in the lower eastern part of the dales. The best known of these is Fountains Abbey, standing in a rich setting in a narrow, well-wooded valley a few miles north-west of Ripon. The church and much of the conventual building have the walls standing almost to roof level, so the picture presented on approaching has far less the appearance of a ruin than of a lovely building, the defects and roofless condition of which are only appreciated on a closer view. The nave, choir, and Lady chapel of the Nine Altars contain some lovely Early English work. The cloister court, which is complete, requires little imagination to see it in its full original beauty. Perhaps the most striking part of the monastery is the great cellarium, the under-croft of the lay brethren's quarters. This is 300 ft long, with a roof entirely sup-ported by groining which springs from a row of nineteen pillars down the centre of the room. The groin ribs spring from floor level and spread from the head of the short straight column without the interposition of any capital or any other break. The whole lovely roof seems to grow naturally from the floor. The room is well lighted with a large window in each bay, and must be one of the most im-pressive features of monastic architecture in the north. It was used for the storage of the great wool crop from the many estates of the abbey, and gives, more than anything else, an impression of the scale of the work of the Fountains community as sheep and wool breeders. The handsome tower was a late addition to the abbey built not long before the dissolution.

In Wharfedale the ruins of Bolton Priory are very beautifully placed and have inspired many artists, Turner, Girtin, and others, by their romantic appearance. Architecturally the chief interest is in the splendid Early English front with its fine lancet windows and doorways, though this is obscured, but protected, by the unfinished abbot Moon's tower. The choir has some fine arcading of intersecting round arches, and a flamboyant window in which most of the tracery remains. The nave of the priory was retained at the dissolution as the parish church, and though it is fairly plain it offers a few features of interest. The main glory of the priory, however, remains in its position in the bend of the river and in the grandeur of the scenery around it.

To describe all the monastic ruins would take many chapters, and the only real way to appreciate them properly is to visit them. Blanchland has a part of its church retained and restored as the parish church, with its cloister garth con-verted into the village, the entrance to which is through the gate-house of the priory. Much of the conventual building is incorporated into the houses of the village, and a building with an apparent eighteenth-century exterior may present inside fourteenth-century portions of great interest. Egglestone, Easby, and Jervaulx are all beautiful both in their position and remains, but of Coverham little remains but a few arches and sculptured stones.[6]

There is in Weardale, in the Bishop's Palace at Bishop Auckland, a surviving monument of many architectural styles. The exterior is dominated by eighteenth-century 'Gothic' and by a fine screen wall of stone by James Wyatt. The Chapel, however, is a seventeenth-century adaptation of the Great Hall built by Bishop Pudsey in the twelfth century and is the most beautiful piece of architecture of that date in Durham County. There are four tall arcades upheld by composite columns of four shafts, two of brown limestone and two of the Frosterley Marble, a polished black limestone much used in the northern churches and abbeys. The arches of the arcades are also of a local marble. Bishop Bek, in the early fourteenth century, made some alterations, but Bishop Cosin soon after 1660 altered the use of the hall to a chapel and placed in it some very fine woodwork which still remains an exciting and lovely collection of the craftsmanship of its period.[7]

While the chief glories remaining from the monastic period are the work of masons and stonecarvers, there is a second artistic survival that derives from the schools of woodcarvers who adorned the churches of the monasteries and priories with their art. At the dissolution much of the finely carved woodwork of the screens and stalls was taken by the purchasers of the monastic sites, and in many cases was given to or used in one of the parish churches and so preserved at least as an example of the artistic wealth of the monasteries. Among the splendid carved wood of canopied stalls and screens of the Middle Ages some of the northern churches have examples which rank among the finest English work still existing, particularly a group which pre-date the Renaissance influence which was so widespread in the south. Many writers have seen among these northern examples the evidence of a group of carvers whose work has a 'family likeness' by which it can be recognized. Examples of such carving are preserved in Ripon Minster, Aysgarth, and Wensley churches within the area of which we are writing, and at Beverley Minster, Flamborough church, Durham Castle, Manchester Cathedral, and in stall ends in a few smaller churches which can be traced as being dispersed from Bridlington Priory.[8]

In Wensley Church the woodwork which first catches the attention is the beautifully carved parclose of the Scrope pew. This was originally the screen given to Easby Abbey by Henry, Lord Scrope, who died in 1533. At the dissolution it was saved from the abbey by John, Lord Scrope, who removed it to Wensley church where it was erected about the Bolton pew which had formerly been the chapel of the Blessed Virgin Mary, served by Easby Abbey. There is also in the choir at Wensley a complete set of stalls with carved bench ends; an inscription carved upon them reads HENRICUS RICHERDSON HUJUS ECCLIE RECTOR HOS FECIT SUPTUS DNI MCCCCCXXVII SOLI DEO HONOR ET GLORIA. It is clear that 1527 is the date of the stalls and that they are the work of a single artist and his assistant who made them for this church. The stall ends have the 'family likeness' in a characteristic feature at the front edge. Here there is near the base of the poppy-head finial a monster, a beast with wings, its hindquarters resting on the side of the ogee arch which carried the finial, but its forequarters set on an elaborate corniced platform carried by a sturdy square shaft. This column is set diagonally to the bench end and is detached, its foot resting on a small penthouse with tiled roof, through which the shaft passes to rest finally on a base which continues the base carving of the stall end panel. This detached column thus appears supporting the beast's platform, is then free, but is clasped by the carved penthouse roof, free again, then based firmly in the bottom mouldings.

The detached column with beast is the feature of two bench ends at Aysgarth church, which have been made into supports for a reading desk. They came from Jervaulx Abbey and are of splendid workmanship. One has within the large crocketed ogee arch a large letter W, with a leaf above it, and below it a hazel bush with clusters of nuts, rising from a tun or large barrel. All this constitutes the rebus of W. Hazlington, said to have been abbot of Jervaulx, 1475–1510. The monster supported by the shaft is a lion. On the other bench end the monster is an antelope with a collar and chain, the chain being held in the left hand of a small man, seated, and wearing a belted smock. The screen dates from about 1500 and is canopied to carry a rood loft. The beam has monsters carved on it, one an elephant with a howdah and a dragon with the edges of the wings folded over. Both these figures are also found in carvings at Ripon and Beverley. The tracery of the screen has within it the rebus of Hazlington, like that on the bench end. Many parts of the screen retained the paint which had made it a brilliant object, and it has been possible to restore most of this, so that one has a chance here to see the woodwork as it appeared when first made. At Hauxwell near Richmond there are bench ends with the detached shaft and with 'monsters' of a dragon and a pelican. From St Agatha's Abbey, Easby, the stalls, all of them canopied and with miserere carvings, were taken to St Mary's church, Richmond, where they are well cared for and preserved.

At Ripon Minster the canopied stalls with miserere seats are particularly fine and have much in common, both in design and detail, with those at Beverley and at Manchester. The elephant carving is seen at Aysgarth, Ripon, Manchester, and Beverley; the subjects of the miserere carvings at Ripon are taken from the 'Biblia Pauperum' and include Jonah thrown overboard, Jonah cast up by the whale, Samson with the gates of Gaza, and many other subjects some of which are repeated in Beverley or Richmond. Documents at Ripon include accounts for work done by William Carver, alias Bromflet, there and at Bridlington, and an indenture for 1518 survives which contracts for him to carry out carved work for the Minster. It soon becomes clear from the documentation that he and several of his family, with other carpenters whom he supervised, were at work on choir bench ends and other carved work, all of which belongs to this 'family likeness' group, of which examples have been given. This William Carver was a prominent citizen of Ripon, and the screen and stall carvings at Ripon, 1489–94, Aysgarth and Jervaulx about 1500, Manchester 1506, Bridlington 1519, Beverley 1520–4, and Easby and Wensley 1527, can all be confidently assumed to be the work of him and his group, who were all members of the Joiners' Guild of Ripon.

Ripon was not the only northern centre of woodcarving; Hexham Abbey had a wealth of fine carving, mainly fifteenth century, but by an aberration of taste which seems to have been common to several church 'restorers' in the nineteenth century much of this work was removed and some even sold in the town for 5s. a cart-load when the church was 'restored' in 1858. This restoration was described by one writer as 'one of the most foolish and disastrous that have ever disfigured the history of even English iconoclasm'. Fortunately much of the evil of this removal has been effaced by the return in this century of all the surviving work, which had been scattered about the building and stores, into its original positions. A unique feature is a beautiful *pulpitum*. In the monastic church the rood screen marked the east end of the lay part of the church and behind it the pulpitum, an elaborate screen with preaching place or gallery, faced into the choir and formed the west end of the monks' church. The Hexham example is perfect and is unique in being made wholly of wood. In some ways it resembles a rood screen with a small loft. It was painted, and much of the original colour remains not only on the carving but in a series of sixteen portraits which occupy niches along the front – these include bishops of Hexham and Lindisfarne including St Cuthbert, St Eata, and St John of Beverley. There is a doorway each side of the central passage through the screen, over which there are pictures of the Annunciation and the Salutation. The pulpit projects from the gallery of the screen and has portraits of St Oswald and St Ethelreda. An inscription on the front states that it was made by Thomas Smithson, Prior of this church (1491–1524), so bringing this into the same period as the Ripon group.

The choir has thirty-six stalls, many with misereres which belong to the first quarter of the fifteenth century. The canopies have been removed; there are also some fine bench ends. There are many portions of screens formerly made around small chantries and chapels, scattered at the 'restoration' but now brought back, and many of these share the unique wealth of Hexham's painted woodwork. Much of this painted carving is associated with the Leschman chantry chapel and includes another remarkable group of portraits, dated about 1464–76. They are of seven bishops of Hexham – St Wilfrid, John of Beverley, Alkmund, Fredbert, Cuthbert, Eata, and Acca. These form possibly the finest group of fifteenth-

29. *Appleby Castle and town. The village descends the hill spur in the bend of the river to the church at its foot. Centre of a great Honour, this was one of the richer feudal baronies. The close agricultural pattern is typical of the Vale of Eden.*

30a. *Friar Head near Winterburn, built* c. *1580–90. A fine Elizabethan smaller mansion. Now a farm.*

30b. *Burnsall Grammar School, 1605, now a C. of E. Primary School. The building was given to the village by Sir William Craven, along with other charitable gifts.*

31a. *Field limekiln, typical of many hundreds to be found in all parts of the dales. Fed largely by land clearance boulders and from a small quarry nearby, using fairly local coal.*

31b. *A twentieth-century limekiln. The industries in the dales are changing in relative importance, quarrying and lime burning being a close second to farming with tourism a rapidly increasing third.*

32. *Ingleborough – from the south-west – the limestone plateau with summit pyramid firmly based upon it.*

century painting now remaining in England. There are many other fragments of carving and painting in the church, making altogether a magnificent gallery of fifteenth-century art in wood and colour, all the more impressive in contrast with the rather severe aspect of the grim pele towers and castles which dominate the northern scene.[9]

One must, however, remember the strong traditions of Celtic art preserved in the Lindisfarne Gospels and the fine school of Anglo-Danish sculptured stone crosses of the Hexham and Ripon schools. These and the schools of carving and painting suggest that around Hexham and Ripon there was an artistic urge which reached unique expression in something of peculiarly local character at more than one period of history. The poverty of the people prevented this from becoming a vernacular art, but the monasteries of Hexham and Ripon enabled it to come to fruition in at least two periods.

Art has little chance to flourish where the terms of living are hard and most livelihood is not far above a subsistence level. It is not to be wondered at that, with a hard climate and a shortage of rich land, native artists have not arisen in the Pennines until these easier times of the twentieth century. None the less a few artists of national repute have found inspiration in the dales scenery, and their work must be mentioned. The name that will always spring to mind in this connection is, of course, J. M. W. Turner, and, coupled with it, that of Thomas Girtin, who may have been in part responsible for Turner's first introduction to the area. There was a close connection between a group of London artists and the north during the later decades of the eighteenth-century. James Moore[10] (1762–99) became a fine artist of antiquarian and architectural subjects, and compiled many sketch-books based upon tours in various parts of the country. He published two works, among others, of importance: *A List of the Abbies, Priories and other Religious Houses, Castles, etc., in England and Wales,* in 1786, and nine years later *Monastic Remains and Ancient Castles in England and Wales.* Moore's method was to fill his notebooks with sketches, then in London to employ young artists as draughtsmen to make finished drawings for engraving and publication. In this work, in 1792, he employed the young Thomas Girtin (1775–1802) under the supervision of another artist, Edward Dayes (1763–1804). In 1794 Girtin went with Moore on an extended sketching tour of the Midlands.

In 1795 Girtin left the employ of Moore and developed his friendship with Turner. Turner and Girtin are said to have met in the studio of Raphael Smith where Girtin had studied, and the close association was continued when both Girtin and Turner were employed by Smith, who was a foremost engraver in mezzo-tint, as his colourists. A very important part in the education of these two artists was played by the meetings at what was called 'Dr Monro's Academy'. Dr Monro, a famous mental disease specialist, was also a great art collector, but besides buying original finished pictures he got sketches and unfinished work and employed Turner and Girtin in the evenings to complete works from the sketches. Cozens was one of his mental patients and Monro had many of his sketches worked up into pictures, Girtin doing the drawing and Turner the colouring. The two young men met many people in the art world and handled many works of art at these sessions.

About 1796 Girtin set out on his own to travel in the north and sketch for himself some of the many scenes he had learned of from his copyist work with Moore, Dayes, and Monro, and on this tour he did much sketching around Bolton Abbey, Kirkstall, and Malham, before going on to Richmond, Greta Bridge, and Barnard Castle. On this tour he met Lascelles at Harewood House, and stayed there, making drawings of the house and castle and of Kirkstall Abbey. There are more than thirty fine water-colours of the dales between Wharfe and Tees. Girtin's work seems to have had an influence on Cotman and De Wint, who both visited these areas, and also on Constable. It is possible that it also influenced Turner, or at least introduced him to the dales country and its possibilities. Turner in the previous year had spent some time sketching in Wales, but in 1797 set out to visit the country which Girtin had explored.[11] After a few sketches in Derbyshire he came by way of Sheffield and Rotherham, Conisborough Castle, Pontefract, and Wakefield, to Kirkstall Abbey near Leeds, and then on to Knaresborough and Ripon.

The next part of the journey was to Richmond, Rokeby, Eggleston, and Barnard Castle and then by Durham to Northumberland. Returning from the north he went by way of the Lake District to Lancaster then by Settle and Skipton to Bolton Abbey, Harewood, and York. At Harewood he was following closely in Girtin's tracks, for there he met Edward Lascelles and was commissioned by him to make drawings of the Castle and House and also of Kirkstall Abbey. On this tour he made nearly 200 sketches and from them contributed nine pictures to the next year's Royal Academy, three of them from Yorkshire. Before Turner came again to the north, Edward Dayes made a tour and prepared his *Excursion through the Principal parts of Derbyshire and Yorkshire*, not published until just after his death, in 1805. Turner, Sandley, Benjamin West, and Dr Monro are among the subscribers to the volume. Dayes says that the 'great object of this pedestrian Excursion was to visit the North and West Ridings of Yorkshire'. He follows the usual route by Sheffield, Conisborough, Wakefield, Kirkstall, and Otley to Bolton, which delighted him. He went on to Skipton and Settle and back over the hills to Malham, where he is eloquent on the Cove and tremendously moved by the majesty of Gordale Scar. Some of the potholes near Horton are described, as well as his journey over the moors and down to Askrigg in Wensleydale. He then visited Bolton Castle, Middleham, Richmond, and Fountains Abbey before returning to London via York.

The fortunate circumstances which brought Turner for his extended work in the Pennines were the introductions to two people – Dr Whitaker of Holme near Todmorden, later Archdeacon of Craven, and Mr Walter Fawkes of Farnley Hall near Otley. Whitaker, a man of means, was about to publish his first book, the *History of the Parish of Whalley and the Honor of Clitheroe*, a work soon to become a classic of local history. For this he commissioned Turner to make drawings with which it could be illustrated. Turner was introduced to Whitaker by a Halifax bookseller, Thomas Edwards, a famous bookbinder and a good artist. Edwards was often employed by and became a friend of Walter Fawkes and introduced Turner to his attention. After the Whalley history, Whitaker embarked upon his *History of Craven*, and then the *History of Richmondshire*. The 'Richmondshire' was published in two folio volumes which were to be the first two of a seven-volume *General History of the County of York* which the advertising sheet said was to be illustrated with landscape drawings by Turner and architectural drawings by Buckler. A great tour, on which these drawings of Wensleydale, Swaledale, and Teesdale were collected, occupied part of the summer of 1816, but before this Turner's more important connection had been made. Following the introduction by Edwards, Turner in 1808 or 1809 was asked by Fawkes to make some paintings of the scenery around Farnley, and among those made were drawings of Bolton, Barden, Gordale, and Weathercote Cave, for which Fawkes paid £10 each. Until the death of Walter Fawkes in 1825 Turner spent part of each summer in Yorkshire, though after the death of his friend he paid it only one brief visit.

Many of the Richmondshire drawings were acquired by John Marshall, the founder of the linen manufactury in Leeds, who in 1807 had entertained Wordsworth and taken him to see Bolton Priory. While there Marshall by his conversation persuaded or inspired Wordsworth to write his poem on the 'White Doe of Rylstone'. Some time later it was suggested that Turner might illustrate an edition of the 'White Doe', but in the end it was Birkett Foster who made the illustrations.

Birkett Foster was born of a family originating in Sedbergh, though he himself was born in Newcastle. His grandfather, Robert Foster, a Quaker, had started the worsted mill at Hebblethwaite Hall, which has already been mentioned in an earlier chapter. In 1794 his son Myles Foster made a partnership with Joseph

Dover, also engaged in the worsted and knitting wool trade, and the firm of Dover and Sons later built Farfield Mill and the Rawthey Bank Mill at Sedbergh. The Foster family was connected by marriage with the family of Dawson Watson of Sedbergh, which has been described as an 'artistic native family of which Sedbergh can boast'. Dawson Watson was an amateur, but his two sons J. D. and T. J. Watson became well-known professional artists. Myles Foster moved to Newcastle and Birkett was born there. Later, as a young man, he went to London and settled in the south of England. Some of his work was done as book illustration, of which the 'White Doe' and some of the illustrations of Scott are the best known of the northern ones.

There is another northern-born artist the majority of whose life was spent in and around Newcastle and the Tyne valley – the great engraver Thomas Bewick.[12] He was born in 1753, son of John and Jane Bewick of Cherryburn, near Mickley, in the Tyne valley. After a time at the little school at Mickley he was sent to the school of the Rev. C. Gregson at Ovingham on Tyne. Here he is reputed to have made sketches on every available space in his books, and also to have practised every moment he could get with chalk on the gravestones and the flagstones of the church. Nothing could stop him drawing. He was apprenticed to a Newcastle bookseller, Ralph Beilby, and learned seal cutting there. He worked for a time with an engraver, Jameson, and among other work engraved sword blades for William and Nicholas Oley of Shotley Bridge, members of the famous colony of German sword-makers. Steel stamps, moulds, dies, engraving on silver, and making the plates for bills of exchange, local banknotes, etc., gave him a very wide experience. In 1776 he went to London, but next year returned to make his permanent home in Newcastle. There he produced that amazing wealth of woodcuts which soon established him among the great artists of the north. His woodcuts are an endless source of joy through the intimate little pictures of northern scenes along the streams and rivers and around the farms and cottages, bits of everyday life and incidents both gay and sad. There is a completely northern flavour about them, which no one else has achieved.

Many of his early woodcuts were produced as illustrations of books, but in 1785 he began to make woodcuts of animals in preparation for his *History of Quadrupeds*. This was completed in 1790 and soon passed through eight editions. In 1797 and 1804 the two volumes of his *History of Birds* appeared, having 448 of his delightful woodcuts as figures and tailpieces. These volumes soon became classics, and in the last years of his life he was collecting illustrations for a further volume on fishes. Many of his finest woodcuts and blocks can be seen in the Hancock Museum and in the Central Reference Library, Newcastle upon Tyne.

11

Literature and Music

There is little in the north Pennines which could rightly be called a native literary tradition. The hard climate, lack of leisure, and low standard of living has not encouraged literary pursuits except of the humblest kind. As with the artists, the principal connections are with writers who visited the area and found there the inspiration for scenes in their writing, though the material basis, besides the scenery, might be slender or legendary. A clear example of this would be Wordsworth's use of local scenes around Wharfedale, along with legends found in Whitaker's *History of Craven*, from which emerged his two poems, 'The White Doe of Rylstone' and 'The Force of Prayer'. In his *History* Whitaker gives this story:*'In the deep solitude of the woods betwixt Bolton and Barden, the Wharfe suddenly contracts itself to a rocky channel little more than four feet wide, and pours through the tremendous fissure with a rapidity proportioned to its confinement. This place was then, as it is yet, called the Strid, from a feat often exercised by persons of more agility than prudence, who stride from brink to brink, regardless of the destruction which awaits a faltering step. Such, according to tradition, was the fate of young Romille, who, inconsiderately bounding over the chasm with a greyhound in his leash, the animal hung back, and drew his unfortunate master into the torrent. The forester, who accompanied Romille, and beheld his fate, returned to the lady Aaliza, and, with despair in his countenance, enquired, "What is good for a bootless Bene?" To which the mother, apprehending that some great calamity had befallen her son, instantly replied, "Endless Sorrow".... This misfortune is said to have occasioned the translation of the priory from Embsay to Bolton, which was the nearest eligible site to the place where it happened.'

* 2nd ed. 1812, p. 368.

This is the story which Wordsworth wrote up as 'The Force of Prayer'. The story, however, cannot be assigned to the death of the boy William, of Egremont, for, as Whitaker noted, he was one of the persons who signed the deed of transfer of Bolton manor to Embsay Priory to enable the establishment of Bolton Priory, and he died some eight years after that transfer was completed. Wordsworth stayed at Bolton Priory with the Rector, the Rev. William Carr, a great romantic and a competent landscaper who laid out paths and 'view points' with named seats throughout the Bolton Priory woods and did much to make their beauty known and accessible to the public. Being very much charmed by the scenery of all this part of Wharfedale, Wordsworth expressed the desire to embody his feelings in a poem. Carr drew his attention to, and persuaded him to use, the legend of the Strid, and also a further legend of a white doe said to be connected with the family of Norton of Rylstone and with Bolton Priory. This story is also given in Whitaker. With the addition of incidents from the Rising in the North, 1569, in which the Nortons forfeited their estates and several were executed, Wordsworth found sufficient material for his long narrative poem 'The White Doe of Rylstone, or the Fate of the Nortons'.

There has been much discussion of the origin of the two poems as well as of the authenticity of their incidents. J. H. Dixon, a native of Craven and a careful and critical writer, says in 1853, 'we had these particulars from Mr Carr himself, during a luncheon at his hospitable house' – that is, the suggestions which produced the 'White Doe' – and he implies that the 'Force of Prayer' had been written a little earlier.[1] An alternative story, but by no means so well known, is that when J. M. W. Turner was making the sketches for his illustrations for Whitaker's *History of Richmondshire* some of his drawings were acquired by John Marshall, the flax-spinner of Leeds. In 1807 Marshall had met Wordsworth and taken him to see Bolton Priory and woods, where by his conversation he persuaded Wordsworth to write the 'White Doe of Rylstone' for which he suggested Turner as illustrator. Turner did not do this, but later an edition was prepared which was illustrated by Birkett Foster.

Whatever may be the truth of the inspiration of these poems, their effect has been to give an almost unshakeable popular belief in their legends, to the complete eclipse of the true stories as they are documented. Even now the founding of Bolton Priory is credited in a reputable publication as being a memorial to William of Egremont's death. The publications of the charters of the Honour of Skipton have proved the falsity of this story, and their editor writes: 'There is no reason, as assuredly there is no desire, to doubt the truth of the legend that the boy of Egremont was drowned in the Wharfe at the Strid of Bolton – a legend which has been enshrined in moving passages in 'The Force of Prayer' and 'The White Doe of Rylstone' by Wordsworth; but an examination of the charter evidence makes it impossible to believe the popular tradition that the foundation of Bolton Priory was due to his mother's sorrow at his death.'[2] Similar doubts have been cast by critics on the story of the white doe. Whitaker states, after discussing the grant of the forfeited Rylstone estates to the Cliffords in 1605, 'At this time a white doe, say the aged people of the neighbourhood, continued to make a weekly pilgrimage from Rylstone over the fells to Bolton, and was constantly found in the Abbey Churchyard, during Divine Service, after which she returned home, as regularly as the rest of the congregation.' 'At this time . . .' would be at least thirty years after the Nortons left Rylstone, and Whitaker shows his evaluation of this as a legend by going on at length to quote similar white beasts which occur in legend in many places both in this country and others, concluding, 'It is curious to observe in how many ways these picturesque animals have been employed by poetical and historical fiction.'

The Pennine dales have their legends, but not many can be traced beyond the rather romantic late-Victorian writers. Whitaker, however, is our authority not only for a legend but for the transcript of an early ballad or metrical romance belonging to the Rokeby district, between Tees and Swale. He quotes from a MS. copy in his *History of Craven*, but in the *History of Richmond* a few years later he has found a better copy in a history of the Rokeby family by Rafe Rokeby the Younger, Secretary to the Council of York, compiled in 1565. This gives a long story in verse of which Rafe says, 'In King Henry the Seventh his raigne one Rafe Rokeby Esq. was owner of Morton (Mortham), who by reporte lived well and honestly in his calling; and I guesse that this was he that deceived the Fryers of Richmond with his Fellon Sowe, of the which a jargon or songe was made. . . .' The sow was

> The griseliest beast that ever might be
> She was bredd in Rokeby wood
> There was few that thither yood
> That came on live away
>
> Ralph of Rokeby, with full good will
> The fryers of Richmond gave her till
> Full well to garr them fare:
> Fryer Middleton by his name,
> He was sent to fetch her hame
> That rued him since full sare.

The friar took two companions and found the sow lying under a tree.

> She was so grisely for to meete,
> She rave the earth up with her feete,
> The bark came from the tree:

They struck and pursued her until she fled into a kiln.

> The sowe was in the kilne hole downe,
> And they were on the bankes abone,
> For hurting of their feete;
> They were so assaulted with this sowe
> That among them was a stalworth stew,
> The kilne began to reeke.
> Durst no man nigh her with his hand,
> But put a rope down with a wand,
> And heltered her full meeke;
> They haled her forth against her will,
> While they came unto a hill,
> A little from the streete.

The sow broke loose, turned the tables and for some time chased and harried the three men sorely.

> They had no succour but their feete,
> Itte was the more pitye.
> The field it was both lost and wonne;
> The sowe went home, and that full soon,
> To Morton on the Greene.
> When Rafe of Rokeby saw the roape,
> He wist that there had been debate,
> Wherin the sowe had beene.

Friar Middleton returned to Richmond, glad, after half a day's battle to have escaped with his life. The Warden eventually sent two other men, a Spaniard ('a bastarde sonne of Spaine') and Gilbert Griffin. Again there was a weary and desperate fight but in the end Gilbert managed to kill the sow, tear it to pieces, and take it home in the panniers of his horse.

And kest her on a horse soe high,
In two panniers well made of tree,
And to Richmond anonne
He brought her; when they sawe her come,
They sang merrily Te Deum,
The fryers every one.
They thancked God, and Saint Francis,
That they had wonne the beast of price,
And never a man was slaine;

Freare Middleton, by his name,
He wold nedes bring the fatt sow hame,
That rued him sine full sare.

Finis.

Rafe Rokeby's final comment is 'Belike the bragging fryer never bidd the shame in all his life but once'. This is an early example of the common north-country saying about a grievous mistake, 'Thou'l nobut (only) rue but once, and that's for life.'

The 'Rookhope Ryde' has been mentioned* as a ballad made within three years to remember one of the great raids of the Border rievers in 1569. The rhyme is simple and has a very rustic flavour, but the story is thrilling.

Rookhope stands in a pleasant place
If the false thieves wad let it be,
But away they steal our goods apace
And ever an ill deeth may they dee.
And so is the men of Thirlwa' 'nd Willie-haver,
And all their companies thereabout
That is minded to do mischief
And at their stealing stands not out
But yet we will not slander them all,
For there is of them good enow,
It is a sore-consumed tree
That on it bears not one fresh bough.

This tolerance arises no doubt from the frequent honest trade which had been held with the Borderers from time to time, not all of whom were habitual thieves.

* See Chapter 5.

After some discussion of the circumstances among the Borderers leading to the raid, the occasion is given –

> For Weardale men is a journey ta'en
> They are so far outo'er yon fell
> That some of them's with the two earls
> And others fast in Bernard Castell.
> There we shall get gear enough
> For there is nane but women at hame.
>
> Then in at Rookhope Head they came
> They ran the forest but a mile,
> They gathered together in four hours
> Six hundred sheep within a while.

Many verses are now taken up with the speeding of the news to the bailiff, who though many men were away, called together a force.

> But when the bailiff was gathered
> And all his company
> They were numbered to nere a man
> But forty under fifty.
> The thieves were numbered a hundred men,
> I wat they were not of the worst
> That could be choosed out of Thirlwa' and Willie-haver,
> I trow they were the very first.
> But all that was in Rookhope Head
> And all that was in Neukton-cleugh
> Where Weardale men, o'ertook the thieves
> And there they gave them fighting eneugh.

Here there follows some account by name of those who were killed and the ballad tails off with no clear conclusion except –

> Thir limmer thieves, they have good hearts,
> They never think to be o'erthrown,
> Three banners against Weardale men they bare
> As if the world had been their own.
> Thir Weardale men, they have good hearts,
> They are as stiff as any tree
> For, if they'd every one been slain
> Never a foot, back man would flee.

186

The song concludes with a request for prayers for the singer who only aims to entertain.

The long unsettled Border Marches provided subjects for a large volume of ballad and tradition – the affrays with Border Wardens as well as with the local population sharing with the exploits of individual raiders as heroes of story and song. This wide field of tradition spread through the Border dales, over the Bewcastle Fells, the North Tyne and the Tyne valley, and a fringe of it reached into the northern dales, giving rise to such efforts as the 'Rookhope Ryde' and 'The Fray o' Hautwessel'. This latter was the story of a raid carried out by famous moss-troopers on the town of Haltwhistle in 1589, when part of the town was burned and some famous borderers were killed.[3] The ballad is not very long, but in its style it is typical of a large group, less sophisticated than the Rookhope story, which was composed by a schoolmaster. Among other verses this is characteristic –

> Then cam Wat Armstrong to the toun,
> Wi' some three hundred chiel or mair,
> And sweir that they wad bren it down;
> A' clad in Jack, wi' bow and spear,
> Harneist reet weel, I trow they were:
> But we were aye prepared at need,
> And dropt ere lang upon the rere
> Amangst them, like an angry gleed.

Wat Armstrong was killed and the others driven back. Watchers were set on a prominent point near the town by an order of 6 Edw vi 'The Township of Hautwesyl to keep a watch of the Crawcragge with 2 men in the day. Setters and searchers of the day watch and night watch of Hautwesyl John Rydly, Heughe Cranaw, and Nicholas Blenkinsop Bayliff of Hautwesyl'.

As the Border troubles were reduced, the rebellion of Lord Derwentwater in 1715 and the execution of Ratcliffe, Earl of Derwentwater, as a traitor, on Tower Hill, 24 February 1716, took their place as motifs of song and story. The residence of Derwentwater was at Dilston Tower on the Devilswater, less than four miles east of Hexham, and many songs remained in oral tradition in that area for many years.

On a more cheerful note a song still widely known and sung by so many as to have taken a proper place among our national folk music is 'The Lass of Richmond Hill'. This has frequently been misappropriated to Richmond Hill in the south but its origin at Richmond, Yorkshire, is fully documented. On the highest fringe of the town of Richmond there is a large old house called 'the Hill' or occasionally 'Richmond Hill'. The 'Lass' was Frances I'Anson and the song was written and given to her by Leonard McNally, who married her shortly after. Frances was descended from a family for at least seven generations connected with Leyburn in Wensleydale and on her mother's side with Richmond and Swaledale. Her mother was Martha, daughter of Ralph Hutchinson of the Hill House, Richmond, who in 1761 had married William I'Anson. William's father, grandfather, and great-grandfather were all called William and all were of Leyburn, as were earlier generations. Frances was born on 17 October 1766 at the Hill House, and McNally was right in addressing her in the now famous words,

> On Richmond Hill there lives a lass,
> More bright than May-day morning. . . .

Not far from Richmond, Stainmore has a few literary connections. Rokeby manor was sold by the Rokebys to Sir Thomas Robinson, who made it his family seat for more than a century. In 1742 it was sold again to the Earl of Carlisle and then later to John Sawrey Morritt, who was succeeded by his son John Bacon Sawrey Morritt. Morritt acted as host to a distinguished group of nineteenth-century figures. At the end of the eighteenth century Turner was a visitor, preparing in 1797 the drawings of the Junction of Tees and Greta and of Brignall Banks, both engraved later for Whitaker's *Richmondshire*. One senses that, particularly in Brignall Banks, Turner was deeply moved by the scene and romanticized it, but none the less presented much of its spirit. Girtin also painted here and at Greta Bridge, and saw something of Rokeby.

The best-known association with Rokeby is, of course, that with Sir Walter Scott, who stayed at Rokeby Park in 1802, 1812, 1815, 1826, and again in 1831, the repeated visits over nearly thirty years being enough evidence of his love for the place. It provided him with the title and subject matter for his *Rokeby*. Southey was guest at Rokeby in 1812 and 1829, and Dickens in 1832. Ruskin was a guest who, when writing later of Turner's work in the Alps, says of him, 'But Turner evidently felt that the claims upon his regard possessed by those places which first had opened to him the joy, and the labour, of his life, could never be superseded; no Alpine cloud could efface, no Italian sunbeam outshine, the memory of the pleasant dales and days of Rokeby and Bolton; and many a simple promontory, dim with southern olive, many a low cliff that stooped unnoticed over some alien wave, was recorded by him with a love, and delicate care, that were the shadows of old thoughts and long-lost delights, whose charm yet hung like morning mist above the chanting waves of Wharfe or Greta.'

Dickens used Greta Bridge and Bowes in his *Nicholas Nickleby*, where, after the long coach journey through the night, 'he (Nicholas) and Mr Squeers, and the little boys, and their united luggage, were all put down together at the *George and New Inn*, Greta Bridge'. From there they proceeded by cart to the infamous Dotheboys Hall at Bowes. It was not far away, at Barnard Castle, where Dickens was staying in 1838 at the King's Head while collecting material for *Nicholas Nickleby* and there met Master Thomas Humphreys, the clockmaker who had his shop at Amen Corner, near the church. From this encounter Dickens adopted the title for *Master Humphrey's Clock*.

Of native writers there are not many, but two deserve mention in the northern area: Bewick and Surtees. Bewick has already been mentioned as an artist, engraver, and woodcutter, but many of his finest woodcuts were made for the illustration of his own books on natural history, all of which soon attained the rank of classics. His first great work was *A General History of Quadrupeds*, published in 1790 and by 1824 in its eighth edition. Work was begun on a *History of Birds* and the first volume was published in 1797, with 117 woodcut figures and 91 tail pieces, though the second volume, with its 101 figures and 139 tail pieces, was not ready until 1804. These, along with the text, represent a tremendous achievement on Bewick's part when we remember that he continued a very active business in book illustrating, engraving, and woodcut for all sorts of commercial purposes. In 1818 he brought out an edition of the *Fables of Aesop and others*, with woodcuts by himself. After his retirement from business and up to his death he was employed from time to time in woodcuts for a volume on the history of fishes, but although many woodcuts were completed the text was never written.

Of very different character was Robert Smith Surtees, the famous sporting writer. In 1831 he published his first work other than articles in the *Old Sporting Magazine*, under the title *The Horseman's Manual*, a treatise mainly devoted to the law relating to horses. He became a friend of Rudolph Ackerman and with him started the *New Sporting Magazine*, which he edited until 1836. He soon branched out into sporting fiction, of which some of the well-known volumes are *Handley Cross, Mr Sponge's Tour*, etc., and the adventures of his character Mr Jorrocks. He married Elizabeth Jane daughter of Addison Fenwick of Pallion Hall, and became the squire of Hamsterley, living at Hamsterley Hall in Weardale. He died in 1864, but his books still remain sporting classics.

In the Durham dales there is an overspill area in which the Border Ballad type of song and story was part of the local tradition, and in a comparable way the Yorkshire dales share the fringe of the remarkable area of dialect writing which centres on the heavy industrial districts from Sheffield to Halifax. In all the northern parts of England, dialect, in all its variants, is still very much a living language, although the last half century has seen the growth first of a marked bilingualism and then of a rejection of dialect by women and girls. While dialect is still the language of men at work, on the farm or in the mine or workshop, the vast majority of women want their children, and try themselves, 'to talk better'. With them the rising standard of living means something approaching standard English, middle-class speech, and a dropping of dialect. Fortunately with a good proportion of men the dialect remains their native language and anything else becomes an acquired second language, less expressive and more restrained, for more formal occasions and purposes. This retained dialect is not that of the stage and the BBC but is a language rooted in Anglian, Danish, and Norse syntax and vocabulary, sounding rough to gentle ears, but forceful and adequate for every range of experience and emotion.

There is a large volume of dialect poetry and prose which is dear to the heart of the people in a way that 'literature' never is or can be. Dalesfolk who could 'mak nowt' (make nothing) of the standard poets, and would find them speaking of a foreign world, will treasure a tattered volume of Tom Twistleton or Tommy Blackah, or will spend years looking for any chance of getting their own copy. Copies are loaned only to the most trusted friends; great portions can be recited along with poems by Hartley and others, not usually on the concert platform but, as I have often heard them, in the shippon, the blacksmith's shop, the builder's yard, or wherever men are working or congregated together. Long miles of hard fell walking have been forgotten as dialect song and story were exchanged, or an hour's shelter from the heavy storm, spent under a wall or handy rock, has passed like a few minutes while exchanging dialect poems with shepherd or peat cutter or any other true-born dalesman.

Dialect writing is concerned with the events of everyday life around the farm and the countryside – courts, aristocracy, classical myth, society have no place – the flavour of the shippon and the mine, the rough life and the little events of the kitchen, experiences, humour, sympathies, and emotions of very ordinary people are the warp and woof of it. There are two forms in which most of this dialect writing is preserved – the small volume often printed very locally, in which a poet has collected his modest output, and the 'Almanac', a form almost unique to the north. The earliest almanac was *The Shevvild Chap's Annual*, 1836, followed by others, but John Hartley's *Halifax Original Clock Almanac*, 1867 (still appearing annually as *The Clock Almanac*), set the general pattern. Opening with a monthly calender and remarks, some humorous and some philosophical, it then becomes a collection of poems and prose stories, the stories in particular being humorous adventures of working folk. It circulates over much of Pennine Yorkshire, and many of its poems have been collected in volume form as *Yorkshire Lyrics* and its prose as *Yorkshire Puddin'*. Other almanacs appeared in Airedale and Nidderdale and two on Tyneside before the last quarter of the nineteenth century. At Hawes, Thomas Hiscock printed his *Wensleydale and Swaledale Almanack* from 1887 to 1917.

The dialect poetry is in recorded form at least as old as the seventeenth century, for John Ray, who visited these parts as a naturalist, got together in 1674 his *Collection of English Words*. . . . A Yorkshire dialect poem had appeared while Ray was collecting his 'words', 'A Yorkshire Dialogue in Yorkshire Dialect; between an Auld Wife, a Lass and a Butcher', 1673, printed at York by Stephen Bulkley. This soon had its imitators and its form was adopted by W. Carr for his *Horae Momenta Cravenae, or the Craven Dialect, exemplified in Two Dialogues between Farmer Giles and his neighbour Bridget – to which is annexed a copious glossary*, 1824. In a later edition the glossary was greatly expanded (2 volumes) and this became an important source for dialect vocabulary.

Between Border Ballads in the north and the dialect poetry of the southern dales there is still an abundant vernacular literature, mainly of the nineteenth century, and most dales cherish their own local poet, almost all being working men with only the addition of a rare schoolmaster – Blackah, a miner of Greenhow; Twistleton, blacksmith of Settle; Story, schoolmaster of Gargrave; Harland of Swaledale (*Reeth Bartle Fair*); Watson, miner, of Teesdale; Waller of upper Weardale, and so the list could be continued, all putting into verse their love of their dale and the sentiments of their own folk. The esteem in which their work is held is proof that it is really of the people.

The world of music in the Pennines reflects a pattern very similar to that which is presented by literature; there is no outstanding composer who was born in the area or made his mark there, but there is a widespread making of music through amateur choirs and bands. The dales folk are in fact very musical. For a century and a half the nonconformist chapels have had their choirs, and robust congregational singing has been an important part of their services. Choir practices week by week in adult choirs made up equally of men and women, anniversaries, 'services of song', and the regular presentation of Handel's *Messiah*, have brought music into a very important place in the life of the population.

By the trick of climate and environment and possibly of physical lineage, the Pennine folk, like the Welsh, are blessed with resonant, sweet voices which blend perfectly in harmony in part singing. Not much is known of the more strictly classical music of the concert hall, but the oratorios of Handel, Mendelssohn, and Haydn, and a wide range of anthems, part songs, and hymn tunes are the backbone of all groups, from two or three gathered round the fireside to the competing choirs at a dales festival. While the coming of sound radio and television has reduced the spontaneous singing in the homes, and chapel and church choirs have dwindled with the reduced congregations, there has been a growth in the number of choirs associated with Women's Institutes and in classes in choral singing and musical appreciation organized by the Local Educational Authority and the Workers' Educational Association, and joint concerts are from time to time provided by groups of such classes and choirs.

Not many composers have come from the dales, but one at least is widely remembered. William Jackson was born in Masham in 1816 and was almost self-taught in music. By 1845 he had composed an oratorio, *The Deliverance of Israel from Babylon*, which was given its first performance at the Leeds Musical Festival of that year, and was received with acclamation. This was followed by other oratorios, and after a few years Jackson moved to Bradford and was invited to become the first conductor of the Bradford Festival Choral Society. This choir, with the Bradford Old Choral, has contributed to the musical education of thousands of Yorkshire folk, and the combined choirs still make music. In the early years of this century, the 'Old Choral' and the 'Festival Choral', as they were known, gave concerts which were the highlights of each winter, and their singing of the *Messiah* was the subject of note-by-note analysis and comparisons for months. Chapels all over the dales augmented their choirs to give the *Messiah* and even the smallest choirs would give a service of 'selections'. Many folk, indeed, started the round of *Messiah* performances early in October, and before the end of winter would have heard it ten or fifteen times, taking note of promising soloists and all the fine shades of 'rendering' and interpretation. Such an apprenticeship meant that many thousands of dales folk of the older generations could take up the *Messiah* at any point, and without score could assist with exactitude in any of the choruses or solos with their appropriate part.

In remote places with few voices and resources the *Messiah* was still given. Long ago two uncles of my own grandmother, miners but musicians, arranged a complete score of the *Messiah* for their two instruments, clarinet and trombone, and for the two fiddles and the cornet of three fellow miners. This little group came into great demand in parts of Wensleydale and Swaledale for the accompaniment of the *Messiah*, either together, or on occasions, as once in the tiny Lunds Church in Mallerstang, with just the trombone and clarinet. It was a well-remembered performance and widely talked of during my grandmother's youth.

lying above the thin-bedded Yoredale strata of the lower part of the fall.

34. Littondale, looking south-east. Note the limestone terraced topography. Villages of Litton and Arncliffe.

36a. *Kisdon Falls – on the Swale, near Keld. The Pennine Way passes alongside them.*

36b (below). *From Ten End on the Pennine Way, looking across the head of Wensleydale to the Great Shunner Fell; Snaizeholmedale in the foreground.*

The great love of the music of the *Messiah* and the blending of the pure dales voices made impossible any sense of the comic or inappropriate in such accompaniment.

The flavour for a wider world of music for some singers was introduced in the second half of the nineteenth century by the possibility of getting by the newly opened railways to the Leeds Musical Festival or even to York, and so hearing larger and professional choirs. In Wensleydale the Hon. Lucien Orde-Powlett, of Lord Bolton's family, was a gifted organist (1855–1905), giving his services at Wensley and Leyburn. His interest in the dales singers was such that he organized Tournaments of Song, held annually in Wensleydale, Swaledale, and Eskdale, which did much to stimulate local choirs and musical societies. Masham had a musical Society before 1877, and had probably had one forty years earlier when Jackson was making music there.

There was everywhere a deep interest in hymn-singing, and a great number of tunes were written by local chapel organists and choirmasters, a few of which were of great merit and popularity. Some have reached the official hymn-books and many have been printed on postcards or as broadsheets, and the number of these deeply loved tunes, usually with a very local name such as 'Gunnerside', 'Rimmington', or other village or feature, speaks of the musical sense of the people.

When we speak today of brass bands and their music, our thoughts turn naturally to National Contests and to Colliery and Works bands with famous names. In the nineteenth century the brass band was a feature of village life in the Pennine dales, particularly in those areas dominated by mining. There was a strong tradition, still occasionally met with, that for a man who spent his working hours in the confined air and damp of the mine the exercise afforded to the lungs by playing a wind instrument was very beneficial. I remember my grandfather and other old men of mining stock, who, if I showed signs of a chesty cough, would say, as a matter of course and of habit, 'Thou wants to bloo the dust off thi' lungs.' Surely this saying arose from a memory of the dangers of silicosis and miners' pthisis.

Brass bands were well established by the early years of the nineteenth century, for there are items among the mining records of gifts or subscriptions towards the cost of instruments for bands in most of the mining areas. In the northern dales where the London Lead Company were the chief employers, bands were greatly encouraged, and the accounts of the Company include generous grants for further instruments for the Stanhope band in 1825, as well as, the same year, for instruments and uniforms for a band at Long Marton. In 1839 bands were begun at

Nent Head and at Middleton in Teesdale, to which, similarly, were made annual contributions of £10 with other occasional grants for special purposes. In 1835 the miners from a wide area sent a deputation to the Court of the Company to express the interest taken in the bands by people all over the area. Other bands were soon formed at Mickleton, Garrigill, Dufton, and Egglestone, and their progress is noted right to the end of the Company in 1905.

An early band in upper Weardale was the Peat Hill Band, which in 1840 was enlarged, changing its name to the Stanhope Saxhorn Band. The saxhorn was a family of brass wind instruments rather like the cornet, which were invented by a Mr Sax about 1840, so the Stanhope Band was evidently well up to date with the fashion. For some years many bands in the north of England distinguished themselves as saxhorn bands and developed a new tone by the use of a number of the saxhorn trumpet-like instruments, which in time in the dales became the accepted brass band tone. In the Allendales there were soon several saxhorn bands, at Allenheads, Carshield, and two at Allendale Town, and with the many bands in Weardale and all over the London Lead Company areas band parades and competitions became a regular feature of northern life.

In Swaledale and Wensleydale too, bands were formed, though not quite so early. Many of the villages in Swaledale, Keld, Muker, Gunnerside, Low Row, Reeth, and others had bands, and a common feature of these villages was the 'Bandroom'. This was often a small detached building, stores or stable on the ground floor and the first floor reached by outside stone stairs. 'Bandroom' was usually painted over the doorway and it was in this room that all practice took place, often with the villagers gathered outside to listen, criticize, and judge the progress. The bandroom at Muker held only sixteen persons at most, and the band with their instruments found even twelve a tight fit. It is told that on one occasion, when practising a test piece, the band got so near perfection that one listener outside rushed up the steps and shouted in at the door, 'Champion, lads, you'll never better that, come outside and listen for yourselves.'

Muker band had been formed in 1879, £45 having been subscribed for the cost of instruments, and they practised two or three nights a week, soon learning to play the National Anthem. On 8 May 1879 they gave their first public performance in the market square. The band soon became confident, touring Swaledale, Wensleydale, and Coverdale at Christmas-time, and on some occasions playing at Richmond in competition with older and larger bands. This travelling was mostly done on foot, and it was not unusual for the band, after playing in Wensleydale, to set off a little before midnight to walk 'over the tops' to Muker, sometimes as much as fifteen miles or even more. Later they became less hardy or more ambitious and hired horses and traps to cross over the tops to Askrigg for the start of their day's programme in Wensleydale. Muker Band was well known in Coverdale, and for many years they led the Foresters' Club Walk at Carelton in Coverdale as a matter of course. It is interesting and encouraging to note that in December 1965 this band had twenty members and a number of younger youths and men waiting for vacancies. There has been a great revival of interest during the last few years in brass band playing. A similar story to this could be told of many of the bands from all over the Pennines.

Even in the opening years of this century my rich childhood memories include that of being taken out of bed in the early hours of the morning, and stumbling along with a crowd of others, men, women, and children, to greet the local 'Silver Band' on its return from a Crystal Palace contest. As the bands progressed it was always their ambition to secure silver instruments for their better tone. When at last the awaited train had safely delivered the bandsmen and their instruments from this excursion into the foreign 'south', the whole crowd marched down to the river bridge to hear the band play its test piece, where we firmly believed the water, the woods, and the surrounding hills gave a resonance and setting far superior to anything the Crystal Palace or any other place could supply. For many years before about 1905 this was an annual occurrence, and a similar welcome was given to the 'Prize Choir' on its return from competitions and festivals. All our Pennine people would put themselves out, walking great distances and rising at unusual hours for the chance of hearing and greeting 'their' bands and choirs.

In Wensleydale a Brass Band Contest Committee organized contests at Hardraw Scar. This magnificent waterfall is at the head of a steep-sided gorge, and on the floor of this, alongside the rushing water, the cliffs acting as a sounding board, the bands competed for prizes. Unfortunately, in 1899, a cloudburst altered the fall and the course of the stream in a way to make the continuance of the contests impossible. In 1920 a new owner, Mr Edmund Blythe, found time to remake part of the area and the band contests were renewed until 1926. The original festivals of brass band music are now only remembered by the very old folk, but they are still a strong tradition in the dale and will now no doubt be established as one of the local legends.

There have been a number of 'characters' in the dales, some connected with musical matters, and some known over a wide area. Of them all, perhaps Neddy Dick of Keld has found the strangest place in the local traditions. He played the harmonium, but added rows of bells, collected from grandfather clocks, and arranged so that they could be played at the same time as the organ. The effect was something more than just a curiosity and Neddy Dick developed considerable musical skill.

Among old characters whose names are still well known there are two whose connections were with the early theatre. They are Samuel Butler and Tom Airey, who were respectively responsible for theatres in Richmond and Grassington. The Richmond story is connected with one Tryphosa Brockwell, born in Teesdale in 1729, who married a strolling player. After much experience, acting in barns and any odd place that could be found, she became more and more interested in the proper stage. However, after a second marriage, she took as her third husband Samuel Butler, a stay-maker of York, and with him established a northern circuit, visiting Ulverston and Kendal, Northallerton, Beverley, Whitby and Harrogate in turn. Having taken over the company in 1773, Butler in 1788 got permission to build a theatre in Richmond as a permanent centre. There people like Macready, Kemble, Kent, and others acted under his production. After his death in 1812 his son continued the theatre until 1830. The theatre was then turned to use as a warehouse with no real alteration, and was discovered in its original unchanged form. Refurbished, it opened again as Richmond's Theatre Royal in August 1943. It is a perfect and unique specimen of a Georgian theatre. Butler was an energetic manager and his company had a period of success during which he built more theatres: at Ripon in 1792, Harrogate in 1788, Northallerton in 1800, and Beverley four years later. After his death in 1812 the theatres were continued by his son.

Old Tom Airey was born in Grassington in 1771 and became the carrier between Grassington and much of the dale, and the market town of Skipton. In Skipton he frequently attended the small theatre there and became passionately attached to the drama. By 1807 he had managed to join the company acting there and was thus able to act with Edmund Kean, Harriet Mellon, later Duchess of St Albans, and other notable actors. His passion for the theatre grew and to satisfy it he started his own company in Grassington, acting at first in the attic of a public house, but soon, with help, moving to a large barn which was made into a comfortable theatre. The company also gave performances in the surrounding area, at Gargrave, Kettlewell, Arncliffe, and other spots in the dales. Tom died in 1842 but the name continued in the district – his son was carrier and postmaster and established a good coaching and posting business.

Such characters are no monopoly of Yorkshire – their counterparts were to be found all over the north of England. They were people who followed one particular interest passionately. They worked to earn a living so that they could live for their hobby. Some like Butler left their regular occupation and gave their whole time to their interest; others like Sam Stables kept on their ordinary job. He spent long nights and weekends in the dales fiddling at parties and weddings, collecting and preserving the folk music but meanwhile working for his bread as a gardener. He became widely known for his skill, and his quick and witty repartee, and his love for his fiddle soon made him a character known and sought out over a very wide area.

Nowadays many potential characters move away from the dales to develop their talents in the cities, and rarely come back to the dales; whether we are richer or poorer for this is a question for which I have not found the answer.

12

The Pennine Way

Many places and scenes have been mentioned under a variety of interests and by now some impression of the character of the Pennine Dales must have been gained. One great feature and a prime asset of this area remains to be described, and it is one which can draw together many of the strands of interest which we have already noticed – the Pennine Way. Over thirty years ago Tom Stephenson, a writer for the *Daily Herald*, being asked if there was in this country anything comparable with the Appalachian Trail of North America, suggested a walk of about 250 miles along the 'backbone' of England, the Pennines and the Cheviot. This walk would include some of the wildest and highest moorlands in the country, would cross all the northern dale heads, and would include many peaks over 2,000 ft O D. Such a tour would give a comprehensive view of our best mountain country, and short diversions could take the walker into the best of the dales or the Lake District or along the Roman Wall. Starting in the heart of Derbyshire at Edale, it would cross the whole length of West Yorkshire, Durham, and Northumberland, and touch on parts of Westmorland, Cumberland, and a corner of Lancashire.

There was an enthusiastic response to this idea and the newly formed Ramblers' Association, successor to the National Council of Ramblers' Federations, representing most of the outdoor organizations, took on the task, with Tom Stephenson as their secretary and prime mover, of exploring, planning, and promoting such a trail. The Ramblers' Association was before long a body of national standing, which contributed memoranda to the Government and distinguished members to Government committees such as the Scott Committee on Land Utilization in Rural areas, 1942, and the Hobhouse Committee on National

Parks and Access to the Countryside, 1947. The Hobhouse Committee in their deliberations on National Parks gave their blessing to the idea of the long-distance paths such as the Pennine Way, the Pilgrims' Way, and the South Downs Way. The Pennine Way by this time was well matured – Tom Stephenson had planned a practical route for its whole length – and this route was walked by a group including sympathetic M.P.s with Silkin and Hugh Dalton and other Labour M.P.s among them (Plate 16c). Thus the National Parks Act became law in 1949 and the Pennine Way was designated in 1951, but it was left to local authorities to establish the right of way over each section. Some authorities such as Manchester and Huddersfield, anxious about their water gathering grounds, stood firm in opposition and some landowners with grouse moors also refused their co-operation. However, by unflagging effort and protest, Tom Stephenson, supported by the Ramblers' Association and a growing body of public opinion as well as the efforts of the National Parks Commission, at last won the fight, and on 24 April 1965 the Pennine Way was officially declared open by the Minister of Land and Natural Resources.

The Pennine Way is not intended in any sense as an easy-going 'walk'. In parts it crosses wild country; it travels over the highest Pennine summits; it is for long distances exposed, rugged, and adventurous, and it calls for skill and practice in every degree of fell walking. It is an 'adventure trail' 250 miles long, and the efforts of well-meaning and timid people to make it less than this, to provide it with a continuous line of cairns and way marks, so that the user needs neither compass, map, nor 'mountain sense', must be resisted.[1]

The way starts in Edale in Derbyshire and soon enters the wild moorlands of Kinder and Bleaklow, which it crosses before leading to Blackstone Edge, thus providing some of the roughest walking to be had in this country. Trawden Forest, with remarkably few trees, leads on to the edge of the Brontë Moors near Haworth, then by quieter country into and through the Craven Lowlands to enter the area we are describing in this book, by Gargrave. From Gargrave, after a short journey over fields, it gets on to the bank of the river Aire, which is followed by riverside footpath right up to Malham village.

Just beyond the village on the road on the west the familiar Pennine Way sign-post points into the fields below Malham Cove, and here meets the first of the great limestone features of Craven. Turning into these fields, the opposite hillside is terraced with a wonderful display of Anglian lynchets,* and in the short distance to the foot of the Cove a few Iron Age field boundaries are crossed.

* See Chapter 4 and Plate 9.

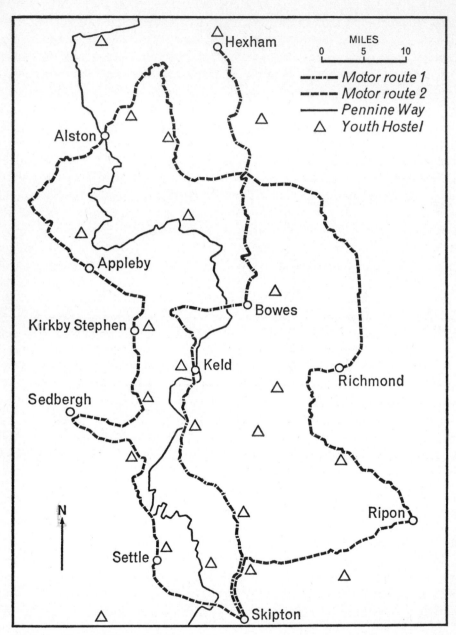

Map 8 *Pennine Way and motor routes*

The Cove is a huge curved precipice of white limestone, 240 ft high, with a slight overhang, its white face marked with dark browny-black vertical streaks of lichen, from the appearance of which and the questions of a friend Charles Kingsley is supposed to have got the idea and inspiration for his chimneysweep Tom hero of *The Water Babies* (Plates 5 and 6). Others besides Kingsley have found the Cove and the magnificent limestone gorge of Gordale, a mile to the east, inspiring. Turner, Girtin, Gray, Wordsworth and many others have commemorated this scenery in colour and in words. Gray, in 1769, found Gordale impressive. After describing his approach and entry to the gorge part, he says, 'it is the rock on the right under which we stand to see the fall, that forms the principal horror of the place'. He was terrified by the height of the crags, about 380 ft, and the fear of their collapse. Wordsworth, who wrote a sonnet to it, though from William Westall's painting and not from the place itself, calls it

> Gordale chasm, terrific as the lair
> Where the young lions crouch.

The Pennine Way climbs the steep screes to the west of the Cove and then crosses the magnificent clints of the limestone pavement which make its summit. Here the very regular jointing pattern of the limestone and all stages in its weathering out can be studied. The Cove forms the terminus of the Dry Valley, a fine grass-floored, precipitous-sided gorge ending at the lip of the Cove, and leading from below Malham Tarn. In its course there is a 'dry waterfall', 80 ft high, at Comb Scar. This was all a river valley during the later stages of the Ice Ages and for long after. As ice which had filled the joints in the limestone melted and as the large volume of silt washed in from the glacial debris gradually diminished, the water from the Tarn and from the uplands around found its way into the re-opened joints and the surface valley became dry. The stream was still at least intermittent in 1569 when a boundary dispute describes land as 'beinge betwixt the watter of Gordell on thone side and the watter of Malhme descendinge from Malhme Watter Terne into and down a gill called Watlows and so to Malhme Cove on thother side'. Writing in 1786 Hurtley says that, after occasional cloud-bursts, water from the Tarn reaches the Cove lip and makes a mangificent cascade.[2] It is known that twice in the early nineteenth century water reached the Cove, but in small quantity, and was blown away as spray before it reached to the base. Today there is a very pleasant path up the floor of the dry valley.

On the east side of the Cove the Way follows an ancient monastic track, Trougate, up to Malham Tarn. On the left side, one mile from the Cove and a couple of hundred yards from the track, is the Water Sinks, where the overflow water from the Tarn now disappears into the ground to reappear at Aire Head Springs, which were passed about a quarter of a mile before reaching Malham village. Soon the Way passes alongside the Tarn then goes behind Malham Tarn House, which was first a sheep farm of Fountains Abbey, then a farmhouse after the Dissolution, a hunting lodge of Lord Ribblesdale, and later a country mansion extended by Walter Morrison, a wealthy manufacturer. After other owners it is now the property of the National Trust and is used as the Malham Tarn Field Centre of the Council for Field Studies. More than 1,200 students a year can take part in courses of all kinds related to the magnificent surrounding country. Much of the ground round the Tarn is a Nature Reserve and bird sanctuary and is not open to the public.[3]

On leaving the Tarn House woods, having passed behind the house and through the extraordinary limestone cutting which was made to relieve unemployment, the path goes up a shallow limestone valley, north to Tennant Gill, and then climbs Fountains Fell by a track made in the late eighteenth century for the use of the colliery, which covers the summit with its numerous bell-pit shafts. Two coal seams in the base of the Millstone Grit (coals which occur at many places in the Dales) were worked here and the coal used for lead smelting and calamine roasting at the Smelt Mill on Malham Moor as well as for domestic sale. A small square building with a domed roof is a very early coke oven, the coke being made for experiments in zinc smelting, which were not however a success. Past the small tarns on the summit the descent on the west side is by a miners' track and a footpath past Rainscar farm to Dalehead. This is the meeting place of several drove ways* and the site of Ulfkill Cross, a boundary mark between the lands of Fountains and Salley Abbey, mentioned in the twelfth century.

From Fountains Fell, the next peak of Penyghent is seen to perfection, and indeed from almost any angle appears to many dales folk to be the most perfect of all our fells. Its colour is always a special feature, and its shape, either the blunt pyramid as seen from the south or the long crouching lion-like mass which is seen from the west, can never be forgotten or mistaken (Plate 20). There is no other rival to it except Ingleborough, and a surprising number of people put that in second place. Penyghent summit provides one of the finest viewpoints in Yorkshire, the view to the west dominated by the magnificent foreground of Ribblesdale with Ingleborough towering above its mighty foundation platform

* See Chapter 6.

of limestone scars and pavements (Plates 7, 13 and 32). In every direction there is a long view over the fells, away to the sea in Morecambe Bay, or north-west to the Lake District mountains and the Cross Fell country. It is a place on which to linger before seeking the old quarry track down the west side from the saddle between Penyghent summit and Plover Hill.

On the way down, two famous potholes are passed – Hunt Pot and Hull Pot – which remind us that Craven is a land singularly rich in potholes and caves.[4] From these a green lane is followed down to Horton in Ribblesdale. The route enjoys a few quiet miles above Horton, leaving the high fells and keeping along the valley side, having as its chief excitement the changing views of the surrounding fells. It passes across Birkwith Moor, near to Ling Gill, now a Nature Reserve. This is a deep limestone gorge preserved for its flora and for the wonderful water-worn forms of its limestone.[5] The track crosses the head of the gill by an ancient pack-horse bridge, sufficiently important in times past to carry an inscription: 'This bridge was repayred at the Charge of the whole West Rideing, anno 1765.'

After Ling Gill a length of the Roman road from Bainbridge to Ribchester climbs on to the slopes of Dodd Fell, and a path continues round the west side of the fell on to Ten End, with the remote Snaizeholmedale on our left (Plate 36a). Looking back from Dodd Fell there is a fine view of the 'Three Peaks' – Whernside (2,419), Ingleborough (2,373), and Penyghent (2,273) – and we think of the youthful energy that since 1892 has made the Three Peaks Walk the ambition of most of our fell walkers. The aim is to visit the summit cairns of all three peaks in a complete circuit in one day, the minimum possible distance in which this can be done being 20¼ miles, every yard of the way to be done on foot. For many years now there has been a growing rivalry to create a record time, and this has obscured the original happy idea of a fine fell walk. Times have now been recorded, varying from 7¾ hours by two men of over fifty, to 4 hours and 27 minutes by a cross-country runner. Most walkers of the Pennine Way, however, will be content to admire the grandeur of the Three Peaks and to envy the vigour of those who make the walk.[6]

Near Ribblehead the former drovers' inn and market of Gearstones is left on the west and the route followed by Dodd Fell to Hawes in Wensleydale. Hawes, on market day, is still a busy place, though the market is now less than it was in the later nineteenth century. Across the Ure, Hardraw Scar, a lovely waterfall, can be visited by a very short detour before the long ascent of Great Shunner Fell is begun by the green track leading north-west from Hardraw, formerly a very busy track serving the many pits of the colliery which flourished here. The fell is climbed by way of several beacons or cairns over Black Hill Moss and Jinglemea Crag, which lead on to the broad peaty summit (Plate 36b).

This summit stands at the centre of a fine ring of high fells and affords one of the best impressions of the mass and extent of the west Yorkshire moorlands. To the east Lovely Seat, or as it is known locally Lunnerset, is the highest point of Abbotside and Muker Common; to the west High Seat, Hugh Seat, and Sails are all over 2,000 ft but are not much more than prominent points on a moorland which is for miles and miles above 1,800 ft O D. The view to the north and north-east is equally one of almost unbroken high level moorland stretching from Nine Standards Rigg (2,170), to Rogan's Seat (2,203), across upper Swaledale. The Cross Fell range and the Lake District Hills provide more distant views.

The steep valley of Stockdale descends just north-east of the summit, and the green track on its north side, reached by keeping almost along the contour round the head of the valley, leads direct to the hamlet of Thwaite. A footpath across the stream goes around the south-east flank of the splendid hill of Kisdon, keeping a good height up the fell side, and turning into the impressive Kisdon gorge with Kisdon Falls at its head (Plate 36a). These and the Catrake Falls just behind Keld are two of the many fine waterfalls to be found in these parts. Keld is strangely attactive, a small cluster of houses and farms on the edge of the river gorge, the noise of Catrake Foss giving it a sense of always being alive. The Congregational chapel at Keld had an interesting personality connected with its history. It was founded in 1789 when an itinerant preacher Edward Stillman came to the district. He became the minister at Keld, and in 1818, wanting to enlarge the chapel, walked to London and back, begging £700 on the journey. He lived in poverty on an income seldom more than £15 a year, but ministered for forty-eight years. In the neighbouring hamlet of Thwaite, Cherry and Richard Kearton, naturalist explorers and pioneers of animal photography, were born in 1871 and 1862, Cherry living until 1940.

From Keld a way is taken up the side of East Gill, with its very charming waterfalls, and by moorland paths on the east of West Stonesdale to Tan Hill on Stainmore. This today is a well-advertised inn, claimed to be the highest in England, 1,732 ft above sea level, on the summit of a motor road from Swaledale, by Arkengarthdale, and over to Barras and Brough in the head of the Vale of Eden. Another motor road joins this one at Tan Hill, coming up from Swaledale by Keld and West Stonesdale. The inn is now not much more than a place of tourist curiosity, busy on the public holidays and at the weekend, but for more than two centuries, and particularly in the eighteenth and early nineteenth centuries, it was a place full of life and of vital importance to at least two sections of the public. Since the thirteenth century there have been collieries working the Tan Hill coal, a good seam in the base of the Millstone Grit, and serving much of the country round about, some of its coal being at times taken to Richmond castle, to the local smelt mills, and for a time even to Appleby. Colliers from the numerous pits which are scattered around found much of their diversion here. Drovers on their way between Scotland and parts of the dales and gypsies from the horse and pony fairs at Brough Hill Fair all knew this lonely inn, and many riotous and roisterous companies gathered here, when high-spirited arguments and even fights, tricks, and sporting games enlivened the meetings. There were some occasions when not so happy travellers were trapped by snow and were cut off from the world long enough for them to weary of their limited company. Nowadays the biggest events are the sheep sales, when farmers arrive from a wide countryside and the lively company of men, dogs, and sheep is backed by the exchange of news (Plate 39b).

From Tan Hill four miles of rough walking along the ridge of Sleightholme Moor and then by the beck brings us to Sleightholme on the great drove road that comes down Teesdale and into Arkengarthdale. The line of this road is followed north by God's Bridge, then across the Stainmore road and over Baldersdale and Lunedale. At Wythes Hill, however, the Pennine Way leaves this drove road, turns north-east to Middleton in Teesdale station, then north-west along the south bank of the Tees, past Holwick and on the crags which fringe the river below High Force. The High Force and its long gorge through the Whin Sill are river scenery of splendid character and grand scale and must be visited. Two miles beyond High Force the Way crosses the river by the bridge at Wat Garth, goes to the bridge over the Langdon Beck at New House, then returns to the north bank of the Tees under Widdybank Fell and the Falcon Clints, following this bank right up to the bridge at the head of Cauldron Snout. Here again there is a magnificent waterfall and rapids over the Whin Sill dolerite crags, just below which the Maize Beck joins the Tees from the west. Crossing the bridge we go to the drovers' ford at Birkdale, then west along the north bank of Maize Beck for two and a half miles to a ford, and then, in a further mile and a quarter, reach High Cup Nick. All this way from High Force to High Cup Nick we have been circuiting round the great mass of Mickle Fell (2,591), the highest mountain in Yorkshire, though from Cauldron Snout we have been in Westmorland and before that, north of the Tees, in Durham. Mickle Fell is largely a Nature Reserve in the care of the Nature Conservancy, and as the habitat of much of our rarer flora access to it is restricted, though bona fide naturalists wishing to go to the summit can get permission from the Nature Conservancy.

High Cup Nick is one of the outstanding geological scenes in the north, a deeply cut valley which has cut right through the Whin Sill, leaving the vertical cliffs of dolorite as a frieze around both sides and the head of this smooth, U-shaped, and deep valley. The Way continues along the edge of the western crags then on a long slant down the Cross Fell scarp to the attractive village of Dufton. This old village had a period of prosperity under the London Lead Company in the nineteenth century, when it was the residence of one of the District Agents and the administrative centre for the Westmorland properties of the company. After Dufton comes a long climb back on to the high fells up the Swindale Beck between Dufton and Knock Pikes. These sharp conical Hills are weathered out of the varied hard rocks of the mass of Lake District rocks which lie between the inner and outer Pennine Faults, with the Carboniferous rocks of the Pennines on the east and the New Red Sandstones of the Vale of Eden on the west.[7] There is a fine ridge walk over Knock Fell (2,604), and on to Great Dun Fell (2,780), where the weather and radio station makes a scientific colony in this greatly elevated and empty space of moorland. The walk continues over Little Dun Fell (2,761), on to the summit of Cross Fell (2,930). It is said by local tradition that the original name of Cross Fell was Fiend's Fell, but that when the area was first Christianized by St Augustine a cross set up on its summit caused the change of name. At present there is a Fiend's Fell about four miles north-west on the same ridge.

The summit is a gently sloping plain a mile long and half a mile wide, and was the scene of strange events in the 1830s, when great political meetings were held here, accompanied by sports and dancing and the music of brass bands. The wide views obtained from the summit have been described in Chapter 1. A descent is made at the north-west end, down to a mine track which is followed all the way into Garrigill. All mining geologists respect the name of Westgarth Forster, who in 1809 published his book *Section of Strata*, which became a classic of mining literature for the north.[8] He lived in Garrigill and his grave in the little churchyard was renovated in 1935 in his memory after a centenary memorial service in the church. At a tea in the village hall the tables were lavishly decorated with choice mineral specimens, the pride of the old mining families from all the area round about.

From Garrigill we go for three and a half miles along the riverside to Alston Bridge, then continue down the lovely South Tyne valley. Keeping down the west side of the river, we soon pass Whitley Castle, a splendid Roman fort with multiple ramparts. From Alston northward there is eleven miles of lovely river valley worth exploration, with woods, rocky river scenery, the fine railway viaduct at Lamley, and the beautifully placed Featherstone Castle. Diversions from the Pennine Way into the valley of the South Tyne will certainly prove popular. After crossing Blenkinsop and Thirlwall Commons the Roman Wall and its Vallum is reached, and the Pennine Way turns eastward along these for more than ten miles before turning north across the Northumberland moors and out of our area. The total length of this wonderful footpath within the area we are studying is 120 miles of adventurous walking and lovely country.

For the motorist there is a route which in some ways is the road equivalent of the Pennine Way (Map 8). It has of course many variants and is not a dedicated or defined 'way', but it is very popular. Leaving Skipton a route can be taken up Wharfedale, past Kilnsey, Kettlewell, and Buckden, then through Langstroth-dale, passing the quaint Hubberholme Church with a fine rood screen dated 1558. By the upper reaches of the Wharfe the pleasant pasture and the rocky bed of the river attract countless visitors at the weekend. Over Fleet Moss the motor road goes into the head of Duerleydale and along its east side, descending to Gayle, where it meets the Pennine Way, then past the cheese factory and into Hawes. Across the valley to Hardraw the Pennine Way has climbed the breast of Shunner Fell, but the motorway goes up to Simonstone and then by the Butter-tubs road to the pass between Shunner Fell and Lovely Seat, crossing the watershed at 1,726 ft. Descending the west side of Cliff Beck, the road goes among the potholes which have given their name, the Buttertubs, to the pass (Plate 38). These are deep solution pits in the limestone, spectacular and fascinating, on the side of a road which is itself a fine route along the edge of a deep gill, affording grand views down Swaledale. At Thwaite at the foot of the hill we again cross the Pennine Way, but turn north-west to Keld, then up West Stonesdale for Tan Hill. The motorist will be well advised to make a stop in Keld to see the Kisdon and Catrake falls. From Tan Hill, already described, the road goes north-west to Barras, then turns east to join the famous (or in snow, infamous) A66 over Stainmore. Rey Cross, the former boundary of Northumberland and Strathclyde, is passed at the summit of the climb on to Stainmore, then a mile farther east a house called Old Spital on the roadside is the monastic Spital on Stainmore, maintained for the hospitality of travellers by the nuns of Marrick Priory until the Dissolution, after which it became a coaching inn until the mid nineteenth century.[9] Continuing to the east we again cross the Pennine Way at God's Bridge and Pasture End, then quickly reach Bowes with its Roman Fort, Norman castle, and all the Dickens traditions of Dotheboys Hall and school-master Squeers.[10]

A moorland road north from Bowes could be followed through the quiet

Quaker village of Cotherstone, with its tradition of a good local cheese, then by Romaldkirk and across the Tees at Eggleston. This was one of the great smelting centres of the London Lead Company, where much important experimental work in metallurgy was carried out in the early nineteenth century. There are ruins of the smelt mills up Blackton Beck. Now we have put half the width of the Pennines to the west of the road, and two equally attractive alternatives lie before us. The motorist can turn north-west up Teesdale through Middleton in Teesdale, where the London Lead Company made their later headquarters and built a model village at Masterman Place,[11] and then along to High Force four and a half miles updale. The road then continues to Forest, one and a half miles away, after which it follows the biggest tributary of the Tees, Langdon Beck, up to and over Yad Moss, crossing the summit at 1,937 ft, into Cumberland, at the very head of the South Tyne. Keeping to the east side of the valley the road leads to Garrigill, then Alston, Slaggyford, and Featherstone, and so to Haltwhistle just south of the Roman Wall. At many points along this route there is ample reward for a stop or a diversion, and of course extensive forays can be made along the Roman Wall in both directions. The road through the Tyne valley is full of interest on the way to Newcastle. Equally good is the Irthing valley west to Carlisle.

From Bowes the motorist could take an alternative route by going forward to Barnard Castle, where time could profitably be spent in seeing the town itself, the castle and other old buildings, the bridge, and the fabulous Bowes Museum, just on the edge of the Tyne. The story of this Museum is almost as remarkable as the building. John Bowes of Streatlam Castle, son of an Earl of Strathmore, chose to live in Paris and there married a French actress, much his junior. She was a woman of some artistic talent, interested in painting. The couple spent six months each year abroad and became art collectors, accumulating a fine collection of furniture, silver, paintings, china, and art treasures, mainly French and Spanish. These would have been housed in Paris but for the troubled political state of the country, so to accommodate them Bowes had a palace in French style designed by Jules Pellechet (1829–1903), which was started in 1869, built solely to house the collections. His wife, who became Countess of Montalbo, died at Streatlam in 1874 before the completion of the building. Bowes died in 1885, leaving by will an endowment of £100,000, but as his affairs were very involved the Court of Chancery suspended the winding-up of the estate. It was not until 1897 that through the efforts of a local solicitor, J. Ingram Dawson, something was done to make the will effective and to appoint trustees of the Museum.[12] Since that time a collection of local material has been added, a process which is being rapidly extended. It is now one of the most interesting, and certainly the most unusual, of the museums in the north.

From Barnard Castle a route on the east of the district could be chosen by which to visit many of the castles already mentioned in Chapter 10: Streatlam and Raby, Bishop Auckland Palace, the castles of Brancepeth, Durham, and Newcastle. A fine moorland route could be taken by going updale to Eggleston then turning due north over Bollihope Common, climbing up the valley of the Egglehope Burn, traversing the fells at 1,678 ft, crossing the head of the Bollihope valley and then down to Stanhope in Weardale. The direct road crosses the Wear by a ford, but in any but fairly fine spells a diversion will have to be taken half a mile to the west to the main road bridge. There is little in Stanhope to attract the visitor, but immediately there is a stiff climb alongside the abandoned track of the Stanhope and Tyne railway* to the Weatherall Engine at 1,415 ft, then forward, still north, to Hisehope Head at 1,561 ft, on the summit of Muggleswick Common. Just before the summit there is a road fork to the west by which in five miles we reach Blanchland. Here the remains of Blanchland Priory form the parish church, and the cloisters are now the framework of part of the village. The gate-house and part of the monastic buildings are now dwelling houses, and all the village has a medieval aspect. From Blanchland a wild moorland road across Blanchland Moor crosses into Tynedale at Hexham, where the abbey as well as the market town are of great interest.

The forward road over Muggleswick Common goes down to Edmonbyers then on to Shotley Bridge in the Derwent valley, which can then be followed to Newcastle. By any of these routes described from Skipton, most of the dales and many high moorland watersheds will have been crossed. The road surfaces are excellent, the views very wide, and the villages attractive, and for those who cannot face the rigours of the Pennine Way these routes would offer a fine overall survey of the Pennine country.

In the routes so far described the south-west part of the area and the Vale of Eden have been neglected. These can quite well be visited by routes which in no way duplicate those already given. It might be convenient to start from Settle, which is on the main road west from Skipton to Kirkby Lonsdale. The road up Ribblesdale through Horton in Ribblesdale provides grand views of the Ingleborough and Penyghent mountain masses, and at Ribblehead enters into a wild upland moorland with views of Whernside and many other of the higher fells. Turning along the Hawes road through Gearstones for three and a half miles, a

---

* See Chapter 7.

road to the west is the road down Dentdale. This is a charming valley, with typical Norse scatter of isolated farms along the valley sides, and only one village, that of Dent. Here, in the middle of the village, along the cobbled narrow main street, is the granite memorial to Adam Sedgwick, the great geologist, who was born here of an old dales family. The lower part of Dentdale is beautiful, with varied woods and high colourful fells, from the point where the Dent Fault is crossed and the dale enters the slaty rocks. At the foot of the dale, after crossing the Rawthey, there is the little country town of Sedbergh, with its quaint street, its interesting church, and its public school. Behind it rise the Howgill Fells, one of the most beautiful of the Yorkshire hill masses (Plate 1). Turning north through the town and proceeding right up the Rawthey valley, the Howgills on the left and the dales fells on the right make this a wonderful road, and the river from point to point offers fine rocky scenery. This road can be followed to Kirkby Stephen, passing, near Kirkby, Wharton Hall, a good medieval mansion,* and the exciting river scenery of Stenkrith Park, near the old (lower) Kirkby Stephen station.

An alternative would be to turn, as one leaves Sedbergh, along the Garsdale road and travel the length of this dale to the Moorcock Inn at the foot of Mallerstang. Garsdale, Dentdale, and Sedbergh were the strongholds where Quakerism first took firm root in the mid seventeenth century. It was in Sedbergh churchyard that George Fox preached, then at Briggflats, a lovely old meeting-house just outside the town and worth a visit, and at Firbank Chapel, perched high on the fells to the west of the Lune, and collected from the farmers and yeomen of the area his first band of followers.

At the Moorcock a road turns up Mallerstang and travels the length of this narrow valley between Mallerstang Edge and Wild Boar Fell. It is a through valley and has always offered a gateway from the Vale of Eden, and of course, Scotland, down into the heart of the Yorkshire Dales, and has been a highway for the Scottish raiders from the eleventh century onwards. To give some measure of protection against these unwelcome visitors, the northern end of Mallerstang had Hartley, Lammerside, and Pendragon Castles, the ruins of the last two of which can be seen near the road. Wharton Hall and other houses were fortified and many refuges in the hills were used by the local population. At Outhgill, in Mallerstang, the great scientist Faraday was born, his father being blacksmith there.

Kirkby Stephen is a bustling market town full of interest, particularly on

* See Chapter 9.

market days. From here Brough Castle, a little over four miles to the north-east, is well worth a visit. It was sited near a Roman fort, became one of the Clifford Castles, and now, in the hands of the Office of Works, is well displayed and documented. The main road, A66, runs down the Vale of Eden, though a secondary road would cut out this busy road and Brough by going direct from Kirkby through Great Musgrave to join the A66 four miles short of Appleby. Here is a town which demands a lengthy stop. It is perched partly on a hill along-side the river Eden, with the Castle at the head of the hill with a long main street down the hill to the church at the bottom, and a market hall and court room near the middle (Plate 29). It is the county town of Westmorland and was the seat of the Cliffords, Veteriponts, Hothfields, and other families in that succession.

From Appleby to Penrith A66 is still followed, but Penrith and Brougham Castles should be seen as well as the impressive earthworks near Eamont Bridge.* Penrith can be by-passed by taking the Culgaith and Langwathby road just after Temple Sowerby and going into Langwathby, a village with a fine green. All the way from Kirkby Stephen the Vale of Eden has offered a lovely countryside, with the impressive accompaniment of the great Cross Fell scarp on the east and views of the Lake District fells on the west, as well as many very attractive villages. From Langwathby the road makes a great climb to a summit at over 1,900 ft on Hartside, where a stop must be made to admire the wonderful views of the Lake District mountains, the Solway Firth, and, on a clear day, the mountains of south-west Scotland. This Hartside road is notorious for the snow blockages which in winter close it for days at a time, yet it is one of the very busy and useful roads from Penrith to Hexham and Newcastle. From Hartside summit there is a long steady fall to Alston, and the Roman road, the Maiden Way, may be seen as a green road coming across the fells from the south and crossing the main road about two miles from the summit of Hartside. Alston, said to be the highest market town in England, at 1,000 ft above sea level, has a very steep main street and an interesting market cross.

Another moorland climb follows Alston on the Hexham road over into the Allendales, but this climbs only to 1,546 ft then runs down the west side of West Allendale. At Whitfield, just after the church, a crossroad can be followed to Allendale Town, but it would be rewarding to continue a further mile and a half along the Hexham road to see the junction of the East and West Allen and the magnificent river gorges above Staward Peel. After the Alpine-type road climb from the river bridge to High Staward a turn south-east takes one to Allendale

* See Chapter 3.

Town, the centre of the Beaumont lead mines, then up East Allendale to Allenheads and over Coalcleugh Moor at 1,936 ft and quickly down to Cowshill near the head of Weardale. Through St John's Chapel, Eastgate, Stanhope, and Frosterley to Wolsingham will give one time to admire the character of Weardale. East of Wolsingham one meets the Darlington road and, turning south on this, could follow it just through West Auckland to Royal Oak, where a road goes due south through Pierce Bridge, the Roman fort at the crossing of the Tees. This road, B6275, takes one direct to Scotch Corner on the A1. Then shortly a road turns west to Richmond, only four miles away.

Richmond is a town with many attractions; a fine castle and two interesting churches, a lively farmers' market, the Grey Friars, medieval streets such as Finkle Street, an old river bridge, and, not far downriver, Easby Abbey and church. The walks along the river bank are particularly fine and can be followed upstream for two miles. The road up Swaledale follows the river gorge for nearly four miles through fine wooded country, then turns over by Downham and Bellerby to Leyburn, one of the markets for Wensleydale. From Leyburn by Middleham with its great castle of the Nevilles, the road through Masham to Ripon gives a good idea of the richer farmlands of the eastern foothills of the Pennines. Ripon again is a busy market town with a fine minster though it is rather overshadowed by the beauties of Fountains Abbey two and a half miles to the west. After visiting the Abbey and Fountains Hall the road to Pateley Bridge is followed, which though it climbs only a little over 800 ft gives very fine views over the mid parts of Nidderdale, a valley we have not otherwise visited. Pateley Bridge is the old centre of the dale, with its market and its old flax and linen industries described in an earlier chapter. From Pateley there is a famous climb, though of little significance to modern cars, up Greenhow Bank on to Greenhow Hill, nearly a thousand feet in about two miles. Greenhow was a centre of lead-mining from Roman times and probably earlier, and now, with the mines closed, is a high moorland with a wide scatter of miners' cottages and intakes, with shaft heaps in every direction, and with ruined smelt mills and dressing plants in the valleys. At an ancient boundary, Craven Cross, we come into the West Riding part of the Yorkshire Dales National Park, and into Wharfedale, passing by Hebden to Grassington. Just before leaving the Greenhow Hill plateau the Stump Cross Caverns on the south of the road are very fine and well laid out for the passing visitor.

Grassington is the principal village of Upper Wharfedale, formerly a market centre but now the main calling place for motor coach tours and weekend visitors. A thriving little place (population about 1,200) with cafés and shops and fine surrounding country. From here Skipton is only nine miles. From Ripon Nidderdale could have been left out if the road to Skipton via Blubberhouses and Bolton Bridge had been taken, and Bolton Priory could have been visited half a mile from Bolton Bridge. This whole round would with its diversions be about 220 miles.

After these long-distance routes for ramblers and motorists we must return to the more modest walker and say a little of what the area holds for him. The coverage by the Youth Hostels Association hostels is as good as in any part of the country except perhaps the Lake District, and in the area we are describing there are twenty hostels, well spaced in the dales except for Weardale. They are all set in excellent walking country where both valley and fell walks are available in abundance. Over much of the Pennines *de facto* access – that is, permitted access to walkers – supplements the large areas of commons, and except for three specific areas – the Chatsworth Estates around Bolton Abbey and Barden in mid Wharfedale (excepting the pitiful few acres of agreed access), the large area of military training ground around Richmond, and the many thousands of acres of the Nature Reserves of Moorhouse and Mickle Fell in upper Teesdale – most of the uncultivated high ground can be used by the walker who will observe the Country Code and care for the countryside which he enjoys. In all the dales there are frequent stretches of riverside path and every village has its walks to local beauty spots, to castle, abbey, or historic building. There are few parts of the country where a person can have more confidence of finding interesting walks to suit whatever length or kind he fancies.

Conclusion

The Pennines between Airedale and Tynedale include at least ten main dales and far more minor dales, each with its own special character such that no person who really knows them could ever doubt in which dale he happened to be even on a quite cursory view. And yet all these dales have a remarkable unity. They are drawn together by the splendid moorland plateau into which they are cut, a group of 'tops' which offers some of the finest walking country in Britain but which at the same time has a number of mountain roads which enable the adventurous motorist to obtain wide views over them. Their most surprising feature is perhaps the unobtrusive wealth of beautiful detail. Each tributary stream seems to hide waterfalls and rocky gorges in its course, any one of which would rank anywhere as a beautiful scene in its own right. This detail appears to be almost inexhaustible, so that the visitor can explore in any part of the dales with the certainty of finding an ample reward.

The lower dales have a background of rich dairy farming life, with parks, halls, castles, abbeys, and villages in a charming setting. There is an abundance of historic and architecturally interesting building still preserved, and in areas like the Greta valley a strong literary tradition. In the upper dales the villages are smaller and more austere but no less interesting. Castles and abbeys are replaced by the earthworks of prehistoric man and by the Roman road and occasional camp, while the landscape of rock and fell is less overlain by hedges and trees and is seen in all its stark anatomy and severer beauty.

Life in the dales goes along at a good tempo, even if one is apt to look critically at the weather and make and exchange one's own slow-spoken and cautious forecast as the opening news on an encounter with a friend and neighbour. Sheep and cattle appear to be everywhere and take their full place as a topic of conversation. The weekly markets are great social as well as business events at which all the farmers and as many of their wives as can be sufficiently persuasive or forceful foregather to exchange news and conduct business. Lamb sales, 'shows', 'sports', and 'fairs' are now drawing bigger and bigger crowds from the towns, and their events, once eminently local, are now being shared with the more professional competitors.

Of course the real test of dales life is to look at it in winter. It is then that the Women's Institute programmes become crowded, and that Young Farmers' Clubs, Youth Clubs, and groups of many kinds find their events overlapping. Naturalist, Dramatic, Musical, and many other societies as well as University and Evening Institute extra-mural classes all claim their share of the limited number of evenings that a week can offer, and the question which visitors still ask – 'What do you find to do in winter?' – is seen in its fullest absurdity.

The beauty and interest of the dales country, with its well-established way of life and its vast reserves of little-altered wild life, have been recognized by the designation of the Yorkshire Dales National Park, the creation of the Teesdale and Moorhouse National Nature Reserves and of many other parts as Nature Reserves of more local character as areas of Special Scientific Interest. The creation of a Rural Development Board which includes within its boundary all the area described in this book, along with the Cheviots and land up to the Scottish Border, will re-create some of the life on the hill farms and check the decline of the last hundred years. This will enrich the life of the uplands and enable more young folk to find their life's occupation in this countryside, which many at present leave with regret.

This designation of special areas is not without its acute problems. Within many of the dales – in particular, Ribblesdale, Wharfedale, lower Wensleydale, Teesdale, and Weardale – there is a thriving and developing quarry industry on a very large scale of working. Economically this is a most valuable and natural development and brings much needed employment into the area. Can the Planning Authorities control this with all its attendant problems of dust and noise, and, most of all, with its great demand for heavy traffic along the country roads, so that its desirable progress does not injure the equally desirable natural beauty? This is not an insoluble problem but it is not one capable of rapid or easy solution. An acceptable compromise, if it is to endure, demands great skill and equally great understanding and forbearance on both sides.

The attraction of the area and the rapid increase in mobility of the population is bringing thousands of cars into the winding, narrow roads as well as along the main roads of all the dales. Quiet places are now becoming noisy and crowded at the weekends. Pressure is increasing for wider roads, which would only in-tensify and tempt more traffic. Noisy sports like motor and motor-cycle trials

215

(essentially races), water ski-ing and boating on some of the reservoirs, are being demanded more and more, and together with the ever-increasing number of caravans with applications for permanent commercial sites are threatening those very attractions which people come to enjoy. Are our demands going to destroy the very things we most admire? The basic problems arise from the deployment of increasing numbers of an urban population into remote rural areas. There must be a long transitional period, with an inevitable clash of outlook and habits, before the urban-minded adjust themselves to the life of the country. It is certain that all the powers of education, planning, and control must be focused on the preservation of the countryside from urbanization. To maintain both sanity and health this increasing urbanization must be balanced by areas of rural life and natural beauty. We can create 'new towns', and are doing so, but we cannot create new dales and mountains with their natural beauty and solitude. We must treasure those we have for the deeper aesthetic value they display, for the physical, mental, and spiritual refreshment they can afford to the town-weary majority. The rural farming community must be helped to live comfortably on the land, but not by its commercialization and destruction. The majority of those who farm in the dales have a deep-rooted love of them which would prefer to keep their beauty and quiet, but if farming is allowed to decline then they will be bound to seek profit by other means.

Tourism is an industry that will develop in the dales, but only if their characteristics can be maintained. By education the visitor must be taught not to destroy the thing he loves; he must be helped to understand and respect the life and routine of the farmer and to respect the land.

At the footpath survey tribunals held during the last few years too many landowners and farmers have secured the closure of short footpaths. The retention of many of these paths, cleared of obstructions and clearly marked, would tempt the person trying to escape from the noise and danger of traffic, would reduce the trespass on farmland, and would keep more gates safely closed. But this demands a responsive understanding between town and country that at present is all too rare. The Countryside Act, the training which children are getting through 'field study' activities, and the growing numbers of young folk in outdoor organizations give promise of improvement. The demand for patience and acceptance of some measure of control, however, cannot be avoided.

Some planners see in the near future the need to control the volume of traffic into and through the National Parks and other areas of increasing tourist attraction. The new motorways are bringing populations of fifteen to twenty millions within an hour's run of the dales and the Lake District. Are these lovely areas to

37. Eggleston Abbey on the banks of the Tees. A Premonstratensian foundation with much land in the dales.

39a. *The Buttertubs Pass – between Wensleydale and Swaledale. The 'Buttertubs'
potholes are on each side of the road near the railing. Looking to the head of
Swaledale.*

The Buttertubs – a pothole showing fluting of the limestone by water solution.

39b. *Sheep Sales at Tan Hill, said to be the highest Inn in England,
at 1,732 feet above sea level.*

18. Enclosure swelling of 1702. Long tongues extending from large pastures come down to a stream to give cattle drinking places.

be opened to more and ever more cars, without limit, until they become one vast car park with crowded, jammed traffic on every road on to which a car can force its way? Or are we as a nation going to accept a measure of planning and control as the price of keeping our greatest treasures? This choice has not yet been put to trial nor explained to the nation with sufficient force and clarity; it is still left too much to the voice of a rather quiet minority. It is a choice that cannot be avoided if we are to keep for the enjoyment of future generations such areas, and there are many, as the dales which this book has tried to describe.

Bibliographical notes

CHAPTER I

1   WROOT H. E., 'The Pennines in History', *Naturalist* (Feb. 1930), pp. 45–60.
2   HOUGHTON F. W. and FOSTER W. H., *The Story of the Settle–Carlisle Line* (Norman Arch Publications, Bradford, 1948).
3   THOMPSON W., *Sedbergh, Garsdale and Dent* (Jackson, Leeds, 1892).
4   The best general view of this area is obtained on the $\frac{1}{4}$-inch-to-1-mile Ordnance Survey map, 5th Ser, sheet 9, which includes the whole. The area is contained on the 1-inch-to-1-mile Ordnance Survey map, 7th Ser. sheets 76, 77, 78, 83, 84, 85, 89, 90, 91.
5   The name Craven has long been the subject of speculation, but at last with the completion of A. H. Smith's *The Place-names of the West Riding of Yorkshire*, part 6, English Place Name Society, vol XXXV, (Cambridge, 1961), we have an authoritative statement. The name was that of a Domesday wapentake, also of an archdeaconry and a general regional name. It is assumed to be of Celtic origin and may be connected with Welsh *craf*, 'garlic'. Whitaker and others associated it with 'crag', a rocky area.
6   HOSKINS W. G. and STAMP D., *The Common Lands of England & Wales* (Collins, London, 1963).

CHAPTER 2

1   EASTWOOD T., *British Regional Geology. Northern England* (H.M. Geological Survey, London, 1946).
    WRAY D., *British Regional Geology. The Pennines and adjacent areas* (H.M. Geological Survey, London, 1936).
2   RAISTRICK A. and ILLINGWORTH J. L., *The Face of North West Yorkshire* (Dalesman Co, Clapham, 1949 and 1965).
    STAMP D., *Britain's Structure and Scenery* (Collins, London, 1946).

3 TROTTER F. M. and HILLINGWORTH S. E., 'The Alston Block', *Geological Magazine* (1925), pp. 433–48.

4 HUDSON R. G. S., 'On the rhythmic succession in the Yoredale Series in Wensley-dale', *Proc. Yorks. Geol. Soc.*, 20 (1924) pp. 125–36. This is a subject of con-tinuing research and many papers will be found in the subsequent volumes of the Geological Society journal.

5 TOPLEY W. and LEBOUR G. A., 'On the intrusive character of the Whin Sill of Northumberland', *Quart. Journ. Geol. Soc.*, 33 (1877), pp. 406 ff. This is the basic paper and has been followed by many more. But all of them cover special aspects or localities, and there is no general account.

6 DUNHAM K. C., 'Geology of the Northern Pennine Ore Field', vol. I, 'Tyne to Stainmore', *Mems. Geological Survey of Great Britain* (London, 1948). This, besides the account of mining, has an excellent summary of the geology of the area.

7 RAISTRICK A., 'The Glaciation of Northumberland and Durham', *Proc. Geol. Assoc*, 42 (1931), pp. 281–91.

DWERRYHOUSE A. R. 'Glaciation of Tees, Wear and Tyne valleys', *Quart. Journ. Geol. Soc.*, 58 (1902), pp. 572–608.

Papers on various dales areas Swaledale, Wensleydale, Wharfedale, Settle district, and W. Yorkshire generally by Raistrick, will be found in the *Proceedings of the Yorkshire Geological Society.*

8 PEARSALL W. H., *Mountains and Moorlands* (Collins, London, 1950).

LEWIS F. J., 'The geographical distribution, of vegetation in the basins of the Eden, Tees, Wear, and Tyne', *Geog. Journ.*, 23 (1904), pp. 313–31.

SMITH W. G. and RANKIN W. M., 'Geographical distribution of vegetation in Yorkshire, pt. II. Harrogate and Skipton District', *Geog. Journ.*, 22 (1903), pp. 149–78, with map.

9 RAISTRICK A. and BLACKBURN K. B., 'Late-glacial and post-glacial periods in the North Pennines', *Trans. Northern Naturalists' Union*, I (1931, 1932), 3 pts., pp. 16–28, 29–36, 79–103.

10 MANLEY G., 'The Climate of the Northern Pennines', *Quart. Journ. Roy. Met. Soc.*, 62 (1936), pp. 103–13.

MANLEY G., 'The occurrence of snow-cover in Great Britain', ibid., 65 (1939), pp. 2–27.

CHAPTER 3

1 RAISTRICK A., *Prehistoric Yorkshire* (Dalesman Co., Clapham, 1965), a very general and popular account applicable to the whole area of this book.

Victoria County Histories for Yorkshire, Durham, Cumberland, and Westmorland have sections on prehistory.

2 CLARK T. G. D., *The Mesolithic Age in Britain* (Cambridge, 1932).

3 The Craven Museum, Skipton, has, besides the Elbolton Cave collection, a very good collection of the archaeology and mineralogy of Craven. The biggest collection of cave animal remains is in the private collection of the Pig Yard Museum, Settle, where there is also a fine collection of Romano-British material from the caves.

4 BENNETT W., 'Giants Graves, Penyghent', *Yorks. Arch. Journ.*, 33 (1937), pp. 318–20.

5 ATKINSON R. J. C., *Excavations at Dorchester, Oxon.* (London, 1951). This discusses the meaning and character of this type of monument, and Yorkshire examples are described in Thomas N., 'The Thornborough Circles, near Ripon, N.R.', *Yorks. Arch. Journ.*, 38 (1955), pp. 425–45.

6 RAISTRICK A., 'Bronze Age settlement of the North of England', *Archaeol. Aeliana*, 4th Ser., 8 (1931), pp. 149–65, with maps.
'Bronze Age in West Yorkshire', *Yorks. Arch. Journ.*, 29 (1929), pp. 354–65.
FOX C., *Personality of Britain* (Cardiff, 1932).

7 RAISTRICK A. and HOLMES P. F., 'Archaeology of Malham Moor', *Field Studies*, 1 (Field Studies Council, London, 1962), pp. 73–100.

8 GREENWELL W., 'Antiquities of the Bronze Age found in Heathery Burn Cave, Durham', *Archaeologia*, 54 (1894), pp. 88–114.

9 PEDLEY R., 'The Brigantes in Britain', *Trans. Arch. & Archaeological Soc. of Durham*, 8 (1937), pp. 1–16.

10 RAISTRICK A., 'Prehistoric cultivations at Grassington, W. Yorkshire', *Yorks. Arch. Journ.*, 33 (1937), pp. 166–74, with plan.

11 WHEELER M., *The Stanwick Fortifications*, Soc. Ant. London (1954).

12 RAISTRICK A., 'Lead Mining and smelting in W. Yorkshire', *Trans. Newcomen Soc.*, 7 (1926–7), pp. 81–96.
RAISTRICK A. and JENNINGS B., *History of Lead Mining in the Pennines*, Longmans Green (London, 1965).

13 RAISTRICK A., 'Roman remains and roads in W. Yorkshire', *Yorks. Arch. Journ.* 31 (1933), pp. 214–23.
MARGERY I. D., *Roman Roads in Britain*, 2 (London, 1958).

14 WRIGHT R. P., 'A Roman shrine to Silvanus on Scargill Moor, near Bowes', *Yorks. Arch. Journ.*, 36 (1946), pp. 383–7.

CHAPTER 4

1 STENTON F. M., *Anglo-Saxon England* (Oxford, 1950), p. 80.

2 CRAWFORD O. G. S., 'Arthur and his battles', *Antiquity*, No. 35 (1935), pp. 277–91.

3 MOORMAN F. W., *Plays of the Ridings. Potter Thompson* (London, 1920–) pp. 43–72.

4 SMITH A. H., 'Place-names of the West Riding of Yorkshire (pt. 8. Intro.), *English Place Names Society*, vol. 36 (Cambridge, 1962).

5 DEANSLEY M., *The Pre-Conquest Church in England* (London, 1962).
   CHADWICK N. K., *Studies in the early British Church* (Cambridge, 1958).

6 RAISTRICK A., 'The Norseman's legacy to the North Country', *Northern Review*, 3 (1948), pp. 141–6.

7 ADDLESHAW G. W. D., *The beginning of the Parish system*, St. Anthony's Hall publications No. 3 (York, 1953).

8 COLLINGWOOD W. G., *Northumbrian Crosses of the pre-Norman age* (London, 1927).

9 DARBY, *Domesday Geography of the North of England* (Cambridge, 1962).

CHAPTER 5

1 RAISTRICK A. and CHAPMAN S. E., 'Lynchet Groups of Upper Wharfedale, Yorkshire', *Antiquity*, 3 (1929), pp. 165–81.

2 PEAKE H., *The English Village. The origin and decay of its community* (London, 1922).

3 EKWALL E., *Scandinavian and Celts in the North-West of England* (Lund, 1918).

4 Durham was made a county Palatine under the Bishop about 1080–2. 'Pope Gregory by his bull directed to the king commanded an establishment of the See of Durham, with all its possessions by royal charter, and that the bishop should therein enjoy, within his territories, all similar royal liberties and dignities as the king held by his crown in other parts of his realm' (Hutchinson W., *History of the County Palatine of Durham*, 1 (1785), p. 133).

5 *Bolden Book*, Surtees Soc., 25 (1852).

6 CLAY C. T., 'The Honour of Skipton , *Early Yorkshire Charters*, 7 (1947), *Extra Ser. 5. Yorks. Record Ser.*

7 RAISTRICK A. and JENNINGS B., *History of Lead Mining in the Pennines* (London 1965), Chap. 5.

8 KNOWLES D., *The Monastic Order in England* (Cambridge, 1940).
   The Religious Orders in England (Cambridge, 1950).

9 PURVIS J. S., 'Monastic Chancery Proceedings (Yorkshire), *Yorks. Record Series*, 88 (1934).

10 RIDPATH G., *The Border History of England and Scotland* (1848).

11 BATES C. J., 'The Border Holds of Northumberland', *Arch. Aeliana*, new ser., 14 (1891).

CHAPTER 6

1 *The returns for the West Riding of the county of York of the Poll Tax laid in the second year of the reign of King Richard the Second (AD 1379)*, Yorks. Archaeol. Soc. (Leeds, 1882).

The Poll Tax MSS for many areas have been printed from time to time, if not they are to be found in the Public Record Office.

2 MCCUTCHEON K. L., 'Yorkshire Markets and Fairs to the end of the eighteenth century', *Thoresby Soc.*, 39 (Leeds, 1940), pp. 1–186.

3 RAISTRICK A., *Green Tracks on the Pennines*, (Clapham, 1962).

4 CRUMP W. B., 'Saltways of the Cheshire Wiches', *Trans. Lancs. & Cheshire Ant. Soc.*, 54 (1940), pp. 84–142.

5 HALDANE A. R. B., *The Drove Roads of Scotland* (London, 1952).

6 HURTLEY T., *A Concise account of some Natural Curiosities in the environs of Malham, in Craven, Yorkshire* (London, 1786).

7 RAISTRICK A., 'Story of the Limekiln', *Dalesman*, 22 (1960), pp. 545–54.

8 SMAILES A., 'The Lead Dales of the Northern Pennines,' *Geography*, 21 (1936), pp. 120–9.

9 P.R.O. C 33/125, C 33/126 (1613).

10 YOUNG A., *A Six Months Tour through the North of England*, (London 1770), Vol. 2, pp. 212–16.

CHAPTER 7

1 RAISTRICK A. and JENNINGS B., *History of Lead Mining in the Pennines* (London, 1965), Chap. 9; and for a detailed local account of the Grassington Moor Mines, *Trans. Newcomen Soc.* 29, (1955), pp. 170–93.

2 HARTLEY H. and INGLEBY J., *The Old Hand-knitters of the Dales* (Clapham, 1951).

3 Members of the Society of Friends from Settle, Sedbergh, and Kendal supplied yarn and taught some of the navvies knitting, in an attempt to alleviate the hardship and boredom of their construction camps.

4 RAISTRICK A., 'Water Power in the Dales', *Dalesman*, 22 (1960–1), pp. 703–8, 867–70; and 23 (1961), pp. 99–103.

5 RAISTRICK A. and JENNINGS B., *History of Lead Mining in the Pennines* (London, 1965), Chaps. 7, 9, and 10.

6 BAILEY J., *General View of the Agriculture of the County of Durham* (London, 1810), Chap. 6, pp. 86–99.

7 RAISTRICK A., 'The story of Dent Marble', *Dalesman*, 13 (1952), pp. 442–5.

8 In 1965 planning permission was given for the reopening of one of the 'marble' quarries on Coums Fell, Dentdale, the stone to be used for making fireplaces.

9 ALLEN J. C., *The North Eastern Railway* (London, 1964), gives the best account of this railway and of the Hownes Gill Inclines.

10 RENNIE, BROUN, and SHIRREFF, *General View of Agriculture of the West Riding of Yorkshire* (London, 1794), p. 107.

11 GRAHAM J. J., *Weardale Past and Present* (Gateshead, 1939), Chap. 11.

12 RAISTRICK A., *Two Centuries of Industrial Welfare* (London, 1938).

13 GRAHAM J. J., op. cit. pp., 125–7.

14 GEORGE BIRKBECK, founder of the Mechanics Institutes, born at Settle in 1776, was brother of the Birkbecks mentioned as being concerned in the worsted business at Skipton and in the dales.

15 RAISTRICK A. and JENNINGS B., *History of Lead Mining in the Pennines* (London, 1965), Chap. 12.

CHAPTER 8

1 See the advertising pages in many of the cheap 'tourist guides' which were published in the latter years of the nineteenth century.

2 For a wider study of this problem see *Rural Transport*, a report made to the Dartington Trustees by St John Thomas (Dawlish, 1960).

3 *Motor Vehicles in National Parks*, Ramblers Association, 1963.

4 CALVERT T. C., *The Story of Wensleydale Cheese*, Dalesman booklets (Clapham, 1946).

5 Annual Reports of the Forestry Commission. H.M.S.O. *National Forest Parks*, Booklet No. 6, Forestry Commission (H.M.S.O., 1961).

6 Youth Hostels Association, *A Short History of the Y.H.A.*, 1965.

7 *Pattern of Power*, issued by the Central Electricity Generating Board, 1963, gives much information about overhead lines and their problems.

CHAPTER 9

1 See Chap. 3: WALTON J., *Homesteads of the Yorkshire Dales* (Clapham, 1947).

2 RAISTRICK A. and HOLMES P. F., 'Archaeology of Malham Moor', *Field Studies*, (1962), p. 90, and Figs, 11, 12.

3 Remains of Anglian houses are very rare and most of the available evidence by illustrations is reasonable 'restoration'.

4 The 'long' house seems to lie always in the uplands, commonly above or around 1,000 ft O D. At Hubbercove in Wharfedale, SD 67644 (a name not now appearing on the map, being replaced by Heights), eight long houses form a small hamlet, but apart from these most of the many long houses are found in isolation.

5 RAISTRICK A., 'Dolly of Kimpergill', *Dalesman*, 14 (1952) pp. 377–9.

6 WALTON J., 'Cruck-Framed buildings in Yorkshire', *Yorks, Arch. Journ.*, 37 (1948), pp. 49–66; and 'The Development of the Cruck Framework'; *Antiquity*, 22 (1948), pp. 179–89.
    ADDY S. O., *The Evolution of the English House* (1905).

7 Yorks. Arch. Soc. MSS collections, DD 121/31.

8 FORD T. F., 'Some buildings of the seventeenth century in the parish of Halifax', *Thoresby Soc. Misc.*, 28 (Leeds, 1928).

SANDERSON G., *Architectural Features of the Settle District* (Bradford, 1911).

9 Royal Commission on Historical Monuments, *Westmorland*.

10 WALTON J., *Homesteads of the Yorkshire Dales* (Clapham, 1947), p. 26 and Fig. 7.

11 TURNER H., *Some Accounts of Domestic Architecture in England*, 2 (1853) pp 231–4 with plans and elevations.

CHAPTER 10

1 PEERS C. R., *Richmond Castle*, H.M. Office of Works, Guide (1926).

2 TURNER H., *Some Account of Domestic Architecture in England*, 2 (1853), pp. 332–4, with plans and elevation.

3 ibid, pp. 227–31.

JACKSON G., *Bolton Castle* (Clapham, 1946).

SALZMAN L. F., *Building in England down to 1540* (Oxford, 1952), App. B, pp. 30, 454–6. Mason's contract for building part of the castle.

4 PEVSNER N., *The Buildings of England, Co. Durham* (1953), p. 142.

5 MORRIS J. E., *Northumberland* (1916), pp. 134–7.

6 RICHARDSON W., *The Monastic Ruins of Yorkshire*, 2 vol. (York, 1843).

7 PEVSNER N., *The Buildings of England. Co. Durham* (1953), pp. 52–6.

8 PURVIS J. S., 'The Ripon Carvers', *Yorks. Arch. Journ*, 29 (1928), pp. 157–201.

9 MORRIS J. E., *Northumberland* (1916), pp. 196–201.

10 MOORE J., *A list of Abbies, Priories and other Religious Houses, etc. in England and Wales* (1786).

Monastic Remains and Ancient Castles in England and Wales (1792).

11 WROOT H. E., 'Turner in Yorkshire, his wanderings and sketches', *Thoresby Soc. Misc.* (1936), pp. 221–42.

12 BEWICK T., *A Memoir of Thomas Bewick written by himself* (1887).

CHAPTER 11

1 DIXON T. H., *Chronicles and Stories of the Craven Dales* (1881), Chap. V.

2 CLAY C. T., 'Early Yorkshire Charters', vol. VII, 'The Honour of Skipton', *Yorks. Arch. Soc. Record Series. Extra Series*, V (Wakefield, 1947), p. 14.

3 RICHARDSON M. A., *The Local Historian's Table Book. Legendary Division*, 1 (Newcastle on Tyne, 1842), pp. 306–12.

CHAPTER 12

1 *The Pennine Way*, Ramblers' Association (1963), with map.

The Pennine Way, Youth Hostels Association (1964), with map.

The Pennine Way, National Parks Commission (1965), with map and leaflet.

2 HURTLET T., *A Concise Account of some Natural Curiosities in the Vicinity of Malham in Craven, Yorkshire* (1786), pp. 55–6.

3 RAISTRICK A. and OLIVER L. G., 'Malham Tarn House,' *Field Studies*, 1, No. 5, pp. 89–115.

4 MITCHELL A., *Yorkshire Caves and Potholes*, 1, North Ribblesdale (Skipton, n.d.).
   THORNBER N., *Pennine Underground* (Clapham, 1947).

5 Permits are needed by visitors to the Nature Reserves, Ling Gill and Colt Park. These are issued by the Nature Conservancy, 19 Belgrave Square, London, S.W.1.

6 THORNBER N., *The Three Peaks* (Clapham, 1949).
   The Three Peaks Walk, Youth Hostels Association, (1963), with map.

7 VERSEY H. C., *Geology of the Appleby District* (Appleby, 1941).

8 FORSTER W., *A Treatise on a Section of the Strata from Newcastle on Tyne to the mountain of Cross Fell in Cumberland*, 3rd. ed., revised by W. Nall, with a memoir (Newcastle, 1883).

9 WALKER G., *The Costume of Yorkshire in 1814*, ed. by Edward Hailstone (Leeds, 1885), Plate 20, The Moor Guide. He was attached to the Spital Inn, which succeeded the 'Hospital of Rere Cross' or the Spital of Stainmore, granted to Marrick Priory in 1171.

10 RAMSDEN D. M., *Teesdale* (1947), pp. 149–54.

11 RAISTRICK A., *Two Centuries of Industrial Welfare* (1938).

12 DAWSON J. I., *Reminiscences of a rascally lawyer* (Kendal, 1949), Chap. IV, for an account of the origin and revival of the Trust for Bowes Museum.

Index

Acca, Bishop of Hexham, 81
Addingham, 83, 120
Adult Education, 141, 215
Aidan, 75
Aire (river), 26, 29, 202
Aire Gap, 16, 34, 57, 74
Airedale, 49, 70, 86, 94, 120, 128, 148, 154
Airey, Tom, 196
Ais Gill, 21
Aldborough, 61, 63
Allendales, 24, 29, 91, 92, 99, 104, 161, 194, 211
Alston, 15, 104, 109, 122, 139, 208, 211
Alston Block (diag. 1), 23, 29, 36, 40, 42
Alston Moor, 32, 43, 91, 92, 97, 129
Alum Pot, 28
Angles, 71, 72, 73, 74, 75, 86
Anglian place names (map 5), 72, 74
Anglian village, 86, 87, 149
Anglo–Danish crosses, 81, 82, 177
Appleby, 23, 144, 205, 211
Appletreewick, 102, 162
Arco Wood, 36
arctic plants, 48, 50
Arkengarthdale, 92, 93, 105, 113, 125, 142, 204, 205
Arncliffe, 58, 107, 113, 121, 196

Arthur, (king), 70, 71, 160
Ashgill Force, 37
Askrigg, 26, 29, 37, 84, 94, 105, 113, 120, 195
Askrigg Block (diag. 2), 26, 27, 49
assarts, 93
Auckland, 81, 103, 126
Augill Beck, 40
Augustinian canons, 93
Aycliffe, 89
Aysgarth, 56
Aysgarth church, 174, 175
Aysgarth Falls, 31, 42, 120
Azilian people, 53

'badgers', 109
Bain (river), 45
Bainbridge, 67, 84, 88, 105, 113, 203
Balder (river), 25
Balderdale, 25, 26
bandroom, 194
Barbondale, 26, 35
Barbon fault, 40
Barden Fell, 49, 143
Barnard Castle (town), 103, 108, 113, 120, 126, 208, 209
Barwick in Elmet, 70

227

Batty Moss, 21
Baugh Fell, 23, 49
Bede, 80
Benedict Biscop, 75, 80
Bernicia, 72
Bewick, Thomas, 180, 189
bilberry, 47
Binchester, 61, 65
birds of the moorlands, 50
Birkbeck of Settle, 120
Birkett Foster, 179, 182
Bishop Auckland palace, 103, 126, 173, 209
Black Death, 101
Blanchland (village), 113, 209
Bolden Book, 89
Bollihope, 67
Border raiders, 185, 186, 187
Bordley stone circle, 57
Boss Moor fair, 112
boulder clay, 44, 45
Bowes, 25, 65, 109, 113, 189, 207, 208
Bowes Museum, 208
Bradley grange, 95
brass bands, 193, 194, 195
Brigantes, 60, 62, 63, 64
Brigantia, 63, 64, 67, 71
Brimham grange, 95
'broggers', 109, 118, 119
Bronze Age, 48, 56, 57, 58, 65
bronze workers, 65
Brough Hill fair, 113, 205
Brough under Stainmore, 26, 40, 65, 113, 139, 148, 204, 211
Brougham, 65
Buckden, 84, 113, 133, 207
Buckden Pike, 44
burial mounds, 55
Burnsall, 82, 130
Butler, Samuel, 196
Bywell Tower, 172

Calder (river), 70

Caratacus, 63
Carboniferous system, 34, 35, 36, 37, 40
Carlisle, 23, 110, 114
Carperby, 57, 87, 104
Cartimandua, 63
Castles (map 7), 38, 39, 164
    Appleby, 99, 166, 167, 211
    Augill, 99, 167
    Aydon, 99
    Bamborough, 43, 72
    Barnard, 31, 99, 166, 167
    Beaufront, 99
    Bellister, 99
    Blenkinsop, 99
    Bolton, 31, 170, 171
    Bowes, 99, 207
    Brancepeth, 99, 167, 170, 209
    Brough, 99, 166, 167, 211
    Brougham, 99, 166, 167, 211
    Burton in Lonsdale, 165
    Bywell, 99
    Cotherstone, 99
    Dacre, 99
    Dunstanburgh, 53
    Featherstone, 31, 99, 167, 170, 207
    Halton, 99
    Hartley, 99, 210
    Howgill, 157
    Kirkoswald, 99
    Lammerside, 99, 210
    Langley, 99, 170
    Middleham, 31, 165, 167
    Pendragon, 71, 99, 160, 210
    Penrith, 99, 211
    Prudhoe, 99, 104, 167
    Raby, 31, 99, 167, 209
    Ravensworth, 99, 170
    Richmond, 31, 71, 99, 166
    Ripley, 167
    Scargill, 99
    Sedbergh, 165
    Skipton, 101, 167
    Staindrop, 167
    Streatlam, 99, 167, 170, 209

Castles – *contd*
    Thirlwall, 99
    Witton, 99
    York, 99
Castle Carrock, 40
Catterick, 61, 63, 65, 75
Cauldron Snout, 31, 35, 43, 205
Cautley Spout, 31
Caves (map 4)
    Attermire, 53
    Calf Hole, 53
    Clapham, 28
    Elbolton, 54
    Heathery Burn, 58
    Kinsey, 53
    Stump Cross, 28, 212
    Victoria, 52
    White Scar, 28
cave remains, 50, 52
Celtic culture, 60, 70, 77, 177
Celtic fields, 70
Celtic place names, 70, 79
Celtic towns, 61, 79
Chapeldale, 28
'characters', 195, 196, 197
cheese making, 95, 140, 141
choirs, 128, 191, 192, 193, 195
Christianity, 59, 75
Cistercian Order, 93, 94
Cleveland ores (iron), 124
climate, 48, 49, 52
clints, 46
Clitheroe, battle of, 97
Clough (river), 29
Cnut, 82, 167
Coal Measures, 40, 74
coal workings, 114, 202, 203, 205
commons, 30, 122
Congregationalists, 128
Conistone, 87, 107
Consett & Derwent Iron Company, 124
Corbridge, 65, 104, 161, 172
Cotherstone Moor, 25, 113
Cotman, John Sell, 178

cotton grass, 47
cotton spinning mills, 120, 121
Council for Preservation of Rural England, 51
Coverdale flags, 37
Cowshill, 93, 125, 212
Cow shoes, 112
Cracoe, 151
Craven, 16, 26, 35, 63, 74, 91, 94, 97, 107, 108, 111, 112, 113, 121, 182, 183, 199, 203
Craven Faults, 28, 40, 42, 45
Craven Museum (Skipton), 54, 57, 60
Cretaceous system, 43
Croglin Water, 25
Cronkley Scar, 29, 31
Cross Fell, 15, 23, 40, 44, 45, 49, 65, 206
cruck building, 151, 152, 153, 155
Crummackdale, 35
Cumberland, 77

Daddry Shields, 93
dairy farming, 126, 137
dalesman character, 32, 190
Danish conquest, 75, 76, 82
Danish place names (map 5), 76
Dayes, Edward, 177, 178
De Wint, 178
Deepdale Beck, 25
Deira, 72, 75
Dent, 21, 29, 88, 119, 120, 123, 130
Dentdale, 21, 23, 29, 88, 114, 123, 126, 136, 210
Dent fault, 40
Dent Lordship, 91
Dent marble, 123, 124
Derwent (river), 24, 25, 47
Devil's Water (river), 24, 29
Devonian system, 36
Dewbottoms, 58
dialects, 79, 80, 190, 191
dialect glossaries, 191
dialect poetry, 190, 191

INDEX

Dickens, Charles, 188, 189, 207
Domesday Survey, 83, 84
dragonesque brooches, 65
Driving Road, 114
drove roads, 104, 109, 111, 112, 113, 114, 205
'drovers', 106, 109, 110, 111, 112, 126, 137, 203, 205
drumlins, 45
Dublin–York kingdom, 77
Dun Fell, 49
Durham, 76, 83, 89, 92, 124
Durham dales, 79, 98, 109, 122, 159, 189
Durham, Palatine Bishopric, 84, 88, 89

East Allen (river), 24
Eastgate, 67, 89, 212
East Gill, 29
Ebchester, 65
Eggleston, 57, 113
Elmet, 70, 72
enclosures, 30, 110, 121, 122
Escomb church, 80, 149, 172
Ewe Close, 61

fairs, 104, 105, 106, 107, 111, 112, 113, 205, 208
Falcon Clints, 27, 205
farming pattern, 49, 88, 109, 121, 126, 135, 137
faults (diag. 3), 28, 40, 42, 45, 206, 209
Fawcett, 64
Fawkes, Walter, 179
Fellon Sow of Rokeby, 183, 184, 185
feudal service, 89, 90, 91
field churches, 81
Finghall, 82
flags, 36, 37
flax industry, 122, 125
Flintergill, 29
footpaths, 216

forestry, 31, 142
Forestry Commission, 142
forests, 48, 82, 84, 88, 94
    Arkengarthdale, 105, 142
    Barden, 84
    Elmet, 70
    Hamsterley, 142
    Knaresborough, 104
    Langstrothdale Chase, 84, 105
    Litton, 94, 105
    Lune, 25, 26
    Mewith, 84, 91
    Skipton, 84
    Slaley, 142
    Stainmore, 25
    Stanhope, 89
    Teesdale, 105
    Weardale, 89, 105, 125
    Wensley, 84, 95, 105, 157
Fountains Fell, 26, 94, 202
Fountains Hall, 163, 212
Fremington, 64
Friars Head, 162, 163
Frosterley marble, 124, 139

Gaping Gill, 28
Gargrave, 67, 70, 98, 196, 199
Garrigill, 37, 127, 206, 208
Garsdale, 23, 29, 88, 94, 99, 114, 123, 136, 210
Gayle, 120
Gearstones, 11, 94, 111, 114, 203, 209, 210
Gelt (river), 25
Giant's Grave, 55
Giggleswick Scar, 28
Gilling, 82
Gilsland, 112, 113
Girtin, Thomas, 173, 177, 178, 188, 201
glacial climates, 48
glacial lakes, 45, 95
Gordale Scar, 28, 31, 179, 201
grammar schools, 129, 130

Grassington, 28, 43, 56, 61, 64, 83, 87, 112, 121, 125, 133, 134, 212
Grassington Moor, 57, 115
Great Close fair, 111, 112
Great Limestone, 138
Great Scar Limestone, 26, 36, 42, 46, 138
Great Whernside, 23, 26
Greenber Edge, 61
Greenhow Hill, 28, 49, 115, 116, 139, 212
Greenhow Hill mines, 43, 64, 95, 125, 212
Gregory Hill Fort, 64
Greta (river), 25, 31, 142, 158, 188
grikes, 46
Grinton, 64
Grisedale, 88

Halfdan, 76
'hall', 154
Halton Gill, 55
Haltwhistle, 49, 187, 208
Handel's Messiah, 191, 192, 193
Hardraw band contest, 195
Hardraw Scar, 31, 37, 203
Hardraw flags, 37
Hauxwell, 82, 175
Hawes, 105, 119, 120, 126, 203, 207
Hayshaw Bank, 64
Healaugh, 84
heather moors, 26, 47, 50
Helwith Bridge, 21, 36
henge monuments, 55, 56
Hexham, 40, 75, 81, 104, 113, 134, 176, 177, 209, 211
Hexhamshire, 91, 94, 97
Hexham carvings, 81, 176
High Cup Nick, 43, 205, 206
High Force, 31, 35, 43, 205, 206
hill farms, 137
hill forts, 60, 63, 64
Hipswell Hall, 158

Holwick, 43, 205
Hopper, Christopher, 128
Horton flags, 36
Horton in Ribblesdale, 35, 95, 139, 203, 209
Howgill Fells, 23, 26, 35, 120, 136, 210
Hunderthwaite, 97
Hurst mines, Swaledale, 64

Ice Age, 44, 201
Ilkley, 61, 65, 67
Independents, 127, 128
Industrial Revolution, 118
Ingham, Benjamin, 128
Inghamites, 128
Ingleborough, 21, 23, 26, 40, 44, 63, 67, 202
Ingleton, 35, 37, 40, 139
Ingleton Glens, 31, 35
intake (diag. 5) 114, 115, 116, 117, 122
inter-glacials, 52
Ireshopeburn, 93, 125, 127
Iron Age, 58, 61
iron making, 95, 124, 125
Isur-Brigantium, 64, 67

James the Deacon, 75
juniper, 48
Jutes, 71

Kearton, Cherry and Richard, 204
Keld, 31, 204, 207
Kendal, 118, 119, 136
Kendal–Lancaster canal, 136
Kettlewell, 64, 69, 87, 105, 107, 121, 196, 207
Killington Hall, 157
Kilnsey Crag, 28, 31, 207
Kilnsey grange, 94, 95

Kingsdale Beck, 35
Kingsley, Charles, 201
Kirkby Lonsdale, 26, 40, 86
Kirkby Malham, 81
Kirkby Malzeard, 91, 108, 113
Kirkby Ravensworth, 130, 157
Kirkby Stephen, 23, 86, 113, 119, 139,.
    154, 155, 210
Kirkby Thore, 65, 157
Kirkhaugh, 57
Kisdon, 28, 31, 204, 207
knitting, 118, 119

labour, 121
Lake District, 23, 44, 57, 63, 78, 107,
    120, 130, 204, 211
Lanchester, 65, 67, 104
Langdale axes, 54
language of the Celts, 79
Lass of Richmond Hill, 187, 188
La Tene culture, 60
Lea Green, Grassington, 61, 67, 150
lead mining, 64, 89, 91, 94, 95, 116, 125,
    129, 151, 202
Leck Fells, 23
Leeds, 70
Leyburn, 75, 105, 126, 139, 193, 212
libraries, 129
lime, 114, 117, 124, 138, 139, 140
limekilns, 95, 114, 124, 138, 139
limestone pavements, 46
Lindisfarne, 75, 76
Linton, 83, 120, 122, 125, 130
Linton Mires, 48
Litton, 94, 97
London Lead Company, 116, 127, 129,
    193, 194, 206, 208
'long house', 152, 154, 162
Low Row, 121
Lune (river N.R. Yorks), 25
Lune (river W.R. Yorks), 35
Lunedale, 25, 26, 113
lynchets, 85, 86, 87, 199

Macaulay, 31
Malham, 26, 40, 57, 121, 199
Malham Cove, 26, 28, 31, 199, 201
Malham Moor, 42, 46, 57, 58, 61, 88,
    94, 107, 113, 114, 148, 202
Malham Moor fair, 107, 111, 112
Malham Tarn, 35, 45, 48, 51, 201
Malham Tarn Field Centre, 202
Mallerstang, 23, 29, 71, 99, 155, 160,
    210
marble, 89, 90, 123, 124
markets, 102, 103, 104, 105, 107, 112,
    114, 126, 131, 135
    Alston, 104
    Appleby, 114
    Askrigg, 105
    Auckland, 103, 126
    Barnard Castle, 103, 114, 126
    Carlisle, 114
    Carperby, 104
    Darlington, 114
    East Witton, 105
    Grinton, 105
    Hawes, 105, 126
    Hexham, 104, 113
    Kettlewell, 105
    Leyburn, 105
    Masham, 105, 112
    Middleham, 104
    Middleton in Teesdale, 105
    Northallerton, 114
    Penrith, 114
    Richmond, 103, 126
    Ripon, 104, 112, 126
    Settle, 107
    Skipton, 102, 103, 112, 114, 122
    Stanhope, 105
    Wensley, 104, 105
    York, 114
market roads (map 6), 104, 106, 108
Markinfield Hall, 159
Marshall, John, 179, 182
Masham, 105, 106, 108, 112, 113, 192
    193, 212

Mechanics Institutes, 129, 141
Mesolithic, 48, 53, 54
Mesozoic period, 43
Metcalfe of Nappa, 157
Methodism, 127
Mickle Fell, 25, 205, 213
Mickleton Moor, 25
Middle House, Malham, 58
Middle Limestone, 37
Middleham, 67, 70, 104, 165, 212
Middleton in Teesdale, 26, 43, 49, 109, 194, 205, 208
Middleton Fells, 23
Middleton Hall (diag. 7b), 156, 157
mills, 95, 96, 97, 118, 120, 121, 122, 123, 125
Mill Gill Force, 37
Millstone Grit, 23, 37, 40, 42, 46, 74, 114, 202
mine laws, 92
mineral fields (diag. 3), 43, 92, 125
mineral veins (diag. 3), 41, 43, 92
mining depression, 122, 125, 138
monasteries (map 7), 38, 75, 80
    Blanchland Priory, 31, 94, 173, 209
    Bolton Priory, 31, 93, 101, 103, 140, 173, 182, 213
    Bridlington Priory, 94, 95
    Byland Abbey, 94, 95
    Coverham Abbey, 31, 94, 173
    Durham Cathedral, 76, 81, 124
    Easby Abbey, 31, 94, 173, 174, 175, 212
    Egglestone Abbey, 31, 94, 173
    Embsay Priory, 93, 103
    Fountains Abbey, 31, 94, 95, 97, 140, 162, 172, 173, 202, 212
    Furness Abbey, 94, 97, 162
    Hexham Abbey, 75, 80, 94, 149, 172, 176
    Jervaulx Abbey, 31, 94, 95, 105, 140, 173, 175
    Lindisfarne Abbey, 75, 76
    Marrick Priory, 207

    Rievaulx Abbey, 94
    Ripon Minster, 75, 149, 172, 174, 175, 176
    Salley Abbey, 94, 97, 202
    Wearmouth monastery, 80
    York Minster, 80
monastic estates, 93, 94, 95, 97
monastic granges, 94, 95
monastic mills, 95, 96, 97
monastic wood carving, 174
Monk's road, 58
Moore, James, 177
Moorhouse Reserve, Teesdale, 49, 215
moorland, 26, 46, 47, 50
Mortham Tower, 99, 158, 161
motor cars, 135, 137, 207, 215
motte and bailey, 164, 165, 166
Muker Band, 194, 195

Nappa Hall, 157, 161
National Parks, 31, 143, 144, 145, 199, 216
Nature Conservancy, 51, 205
Nature Reserves, 49, 51, 202, 203, 205, 213, 215
Neddy Dick of Keld, 195
Neolithic, 48, 54, 55, 58
Newbiggin Hall, 157
Nidd (river), 26, 29, 120
Nidderdale, 28, 40, 49, 78, 91, 92, 93, 94, 95, 96, 104, 108, 120, 122, 125, 126, 143, 212
Nine Standards Rigg, 26, 204
Norse houses, 149, 150
Norse place names, 77, 78
Norse settlement, 77, 87, 91, 94
Norse stock, 32
Northallerton, 114, 196
Northumberland, 43, 110, 159
Northumbria, 72, 75, 82
North Lancashire, 77
North Tyne (river), 99, 104, 187

INDEX

Old Durham, 67, 70
Ormside Hall, 157
Ovington Tower, 172

Pack horses, 106, 118, 119, 123
Parkergill Force, 37
Pateley Bridge, 28, 40, 64, 126, 143, 144,
   212
Paulinus, 75
peat, 46, 47, 48
Peat Hill Band, 194
pele towers, 99, 159, 160, 161
Pencil Mill, Teesdale, 35
Pennine Chain, 16, 42
Pennine faults, 40, 41
Pennine Way, 31, 198–206
Penrith, 56, 114, 211
Penyghent, 21, 26, 40, 44, 202, 203, 209.
Phillips, John, 36
Pictish raids, 67, 70
Pierce Bridge, 65, 104, 212
Pleistocene period, 44, 52
Poll Tax of 1379, 101
population, 101, 125, 133, 134, 139
pot holes, 28, 203
Potter Thompson, 71
pre-Cambrian, 35, 36
Premonstratensian order, 94
Presbyterians, 127, 128

Quakers, 127, 210
quarry industry, 215
   lime, 124, 125, 138, 139
   marble, 123, 124, 139
   roadstone, 138, 139
   slates, 35, 139

Railways, 21, 23, 124, 131, 132, 133, 209
rainfall, 46, 49
Ramblers' Association, 198, 199
Ramsgill, 96, 107

Ravenstonedale, 23, 61, 119, 154
Rawthey valley, 23, 29, 35, 37, 88, 136,
   165, 210
Reeth, 83
reservoirs, 25, 26, 123, 143, 144
rhythmic deposition, 36
Ribble (river), 26, 29
Ribblehead, 21, 45, 49, 94, 203, 209
Ribblesdale, 21, 23, 28, 35, 36, 37, 42, 61,
   74, 84, 107, 136, 139, 202, 203, 209,
   215
Richmond, 31, 96, 99, 119, 126, 130,
   134, 165, 187, 188, 194, 196, 205, 212
Richmond Honour, 84, 90
Ripon, 75, 102, 104, 108, 126, 134, 172,
   196, 212
Ripon carvers, 175, 176
Ripon school of crosses, 82, 177
Risehill, 21, 49
Roman
   altars, 66
   conquest, 62, 63, 64, 65
   forts, 65, 66, 67, 206, 212
   lead mines, 64
   pottery, 67
   roads, 26, 64, 65, 103, 104, 203, 211
   signal stations, 67
   villas, 67, 70
   Wall, 43, 67, 207, 208
Romano–British settlements, 61, 67, 148
roofing slate, 36, 37, 151, 152, 153
Rookhope Ride, 98, 185, 186, 187
Rural Development Board, 215
rural depopulation, 121, 122, 125, 134,
   139
rural electrification, 145
rural transport, 133, 134, 135
Ruskin, John, 188

Salt roads, 109
Saxhorn bands, 194
Saxon pirates, 67, 70, 71
Scargill Moor, 66

Scotch cattle, 110, 111, 112, 117, 126
Scots raids, 96, 97, 98, 99, 101, 155,
    159, 170, 185, 186, 210
Scott, Sir Walter, 112, 188
Scrope family, 171
Sedbergh, 29, 88, 91, 94, 119, 121, 127,
    128, 130, 136, 140, 165, 179, 180,
    210
Semer Water, 45, 59, 60
Settle, 21, 40, 86, 95, 107, 108, 120, 121,
    126, 136, 209
sheep dipping, 30
sheep farms, 94, 95
Sherburn in Elmet, 70
Shunner Fell, 203, 207
Silurian rocks, 36, 45
Silvanus, 66, 67
Silver band, 195
silver mines, 92
Site of Special Scientific Interest –
    S.S.S.I., 51, 215
Skipton, 16, 45, 91, 102, 103, 108, 112,
    114, 120, 126, 133, 134, 136, 142, 207
Skyrethorns, 53
Slates, 35, 37, 152, 153
Smelthouses, 95
Sneep, 31, 71
soils, 46
Southerscales, 67, 94
South Tyne, 24, 29, 37, 47, 57, 65, 77,
    88, 91, 99, 206, 207, 208
Spennithorne, 82
spinning gallery, 120
spinning industry, 118, 119, 120, 121
spoon fibulae, 65
St John's Chapel, 93, 212
staff-rood, 81
Stagshaw Bank fair, 112, 113
Stainforth, 35, 55, 84
Stainmore, 25, 26, 29, 40, 49, 57, 63,
    67, 70, 74, 77, 78, 94, 99, 153, 188, 207
Stainmore syncline, 42
Stanhope blast furnaces, 125
Stanhope Park, 67, 89

Stanwick, 60, 63, 64, 82
Starbotton, 84
Startforth, 103
Staward Pele, 31, 99, 161, 211
Stephenson, Tom, 198, 199
stocking knitting, 119, 120
stone circles, 56, 57
Strathclyde, 70
Strid, 181, 182
Stubblick Dyke (diag. 3), 40, 42
Studfold, 95
Surtees, Robert Smith, 189
Swaledale, 26, 29, 32, 42, 61, 64, 78, 81,
    82, 84, 92, 94, 95, 96, 105, 115, 119,
    120, 121, 125, 128, 192, 194, 207, 212
Swinnergill, 29
Swinsty Hall, 154, 155
Synod of Whitby, 75, 80

Ta Dyke, 64, 64
Tan Hill, 26, 204, 205, 207
Tees (river), 25, 29, 31, 43, 158, 205,
    208
Teesdale, 29, 35, 43, 86, 92, 95, 99, 109,
    115, 127, 128, 139, 144, 153, 205, 208,
    213, 215
terminal moraines, 45
Tertiary period, 43
textile mills, 118, 119, 120, 121, 123, 125,
    180
theatre, 196
Thornton Force, 31, 35
Thornton Tower, 99
Three Peaks Walk, 203
Threshfield, 83
Toft Hill, 60, 63
tourists, 130, 131, 216
Tow Law blast furnaces, 125
tower houses, 159, 170
Turner, J. M. W., 173, 177, 178, 179,
    182, 188, 201
Tyne valley, 25, 40, 49, 91, 99, 103, 160,
    161, 172, 187, 208, 209

235

INDEX

Uldale, 23
Ulfkill Cross, 202
unconformity, 35, 36
Ure (river), 26, 31, 45, 143
Uther Pendragon, 71

Vale of Eden, 24, 45, 57, 63, 65, 74, 97, 99, 113, 154, 206, 209, 210, 211
Vale of York, 83
Venutius, 63

Walburn Hall, 161
Walker, George, 119
Warcop Fell, 29
Washburn (river), 120, 122, 143
water power, 118, 121, 122, 123
Wear (river), 24, 25
Weardale, 29, 43, 67, 74, 81, 88, 92, 93, 94, 97, 98, 109, 114, 122, 125, 127, 128, 144, 194, 212, 215
Weardale Iron Company, 125
Wearhead, 93
Well, 70
Wenning (river), 26, 35, 37, 74
Wensley, 82, 104, 174, 193
Wensley church, 82, 174, 175
Wensleydale, 26, 29, 37, 42, 47, 49, 56, 59, 78, 84, 86, 87, 94, 99, 105, 114, 128, 139, 140, 165, 170, 192, 193, 194, 195, 203, 215
Wesley, John, 127, 128
Westgarth Forster, 206
Westgate, 89
Westmorland, 49, 61, 120, 154, 155

West Witton, 82
Wharfe (river), 26, 29, 181, 182, 207
Wharfedale, 37, 42, 47, 49, 54, 56, 63, 64, 78, 82, 84, 86, 91, 93, 120, 139, 154, 173, 181, 182, 212, 215
Wharton Hall (diag. 7a), 155, 156, 210
Wharton, Phillip Lord, 128
wheelhead crosses, 82
Whernside, 23, 26, 203, 209
Whin Sill, 42, 43, 139, 205, 206
Whitaker, T. Dunham, 179, 181, 182, 183, 188
Whitley Castle, 65, 206
Wild Boar Fell, 23, 40, 210
Wilfred of York, 75, 80
Willimotswick, 161
Winterburn Chapel, 128
Wolsingham, 74, 81, 89, 98, 109, 130
Womens' Institutes, 141
Woodhall, 61
wool, 118, 119
woollen yarns, 119, 121, 123
Wordsworth, William, 181, 182, 183, 201
Workers' Educational Association, 141
Wycliffe on Tees, 82

Yeoman clothier, 154
yeoman farmer, 154
Yoredale Series, 29, 36, 37, 46, 114
York, 61, 63, 75, 80
York Minster, 75, 80
Yorkshire Dales National Park, 31, 144, 212, 215
Young Farmers' Clubs, 141, 215
Youth Hostels Association, 144, 213